Under the editorship of

DAYTON D. McKEAN

University of Colorado

OTHER TITLES IN THE SERIES

The Government of Republican Italy
JOHN CLARKE ADAMS and PAOLO BARILE

British Parliamentary Democracy
SYDNEY D. BAILEY

The Federal Government of Switzerland
GEORGE A. CODDING, JR.

Government and Politics in Israel
OSCAR KRAINES

The Indian Political System
NORMAN D. PALMER

Contemporary Government of Germany
ELMER PLISCHKE

Norwegian Democracy
JAMES A. STORING

In Preparation

The Second Republic of Austria
H. PIERRE SECHER

Contemporary

Government

of Japan

THEODORE McNELLY
UNIVERSITY OF MARYLAND

HOUGHTON MIFFLIN COMPANY · BOSTON

To

My Mother

CONTENTS

FIGURES AND TABLES   viii

PREFACE   ix

A NOTE ON BIBLIOGRAPHY   x

GLOSSARY: *Political Parties and Labor Unions*   xi

1. Japanese Government Before 1945   1

2. The American Occupation and the New Constitution   25

3. The Throne and Popular Sovereignty   48

4. The Cabinet   73

5. The Diet   97

6. Political Parties and Pressure Groups   114

7. Local Government and the Judicial System   154

8. Foreign Relations and National Defense   171

9. Democracy in Japan: An Assessment   207

THE CONSTITUTION OF JAPAN   211

INDEX   221

FIGURES

1. The Separation of Powers and Checks
   and Balances   69

2. The Organization of the Executive Branch   77

3. The Evolution of Political Parties   115

4. The Prefectures of Japan   155–156

5. The Japanese Empire and Its Partition   172–173

TABLES

1. Japan's "Line of Emperors Unbroken
   for Ages Eternal"   70

2. Japanese Cabinets   95

3. House of Representatives Election Results   150

4. House of Councillors Election Results   151

5. Results of July 1, 1962, House of
   Councillors Election   152

PREFACE

This volume is designed to introduce the student and the general reader to the institutions of Japanese government as they function today in their historical and social setting. Recent events have pointed up the need for a better understanding between the United States and Japan. The Japanese, who have been closely associated with Americans in the course of military occupation, alliance, and trade since the Pacific War, have continuously shown a keen interest in American politics. American concern with Japan, however, has for various reasons been sporadic, and the author hopes that his modest effort may help to bridge the gap in understanding between the countries.

I have followed the Japanese practice of putting the family name before the given name of individuals. The Hepburn system of romanizing the Japanese language has been followed, except that Japanese words which have been adopted into the English language according to Webster's *Unabridged Dictionary* are given with the usual English spelling, without long marks. I have made it a rule to avoid Japanese words and to use standard English translations for all Japanese terms, as indicated in Kenkyusha's *New Japanese-English Dictionary*. The official Japanese term is supplied where appropriate.

The author is grateful to the General Research Board of the University of Maryland for a grant which made it possible to devote the summer of 1961 to research concerning the Japanese executive branch.

For many helpful suggestions in the preparation of this book, the author wishes to acknowledge his indebtedness to Professor Dayton D. McKean of the University of Colorado, editorial adviser to Houghton Mifflin Company, Mr. Richard N. Clark of the Houghton Mifflin Company, Professor Elmer Plischke, Professor David Farquhar, and Dr. Harold Larson of the University of Maryland, Mr. Key Kobayashi, and Dr. Hattie K. Colton. Many thanks are also due to Miss Yoshi Takahashi of the University of Maryland Far East Division, and Mr. Andrew Kuroda of the Library of Congress, who assisted in gathering research material, and the author's wife, Myra, who typed the entire manuscript and assisted with the preparation of charts.

Of course, the author assumes full responsibility for errors of fact and interpretation.

THEODORE McNELLY

College Park, Maryland
January, 1963

A Note on Bibliography

In the footnotes and at the end of each chapter, the author has listed further readings in English. These lists are far from exhaustive, and for further suggestions, the reader is referred to Hugh Borton, Serge Elisséeff, William W. Lockwood, and John C. Pelzel, comp., *A Selected List of Books and Articles on Japan in English, French and German* (Cambridge: Harvard University Press, 1954), the *Bibliography of Asian Studies* annually issued by the *Journal of Asian Studies*, and, for material in Japanese, to Robert E. Ward, *A Guide to Japanese Reference and Research Materials in the Field of Political Science* (Ann Arbor: University of Michigan Press, 1961). Other Japanese materials are listed in Oka Yoshitake, ed., *Gendai Nihon no Seiji Katei* (Tokyo: Iwanami, 1958), and Robert A. Scalapino and Junnosuke Masumi, *Parties and Politics in Contemporary Japan* (Berkeley and Los Angeles: University of California Press, 1962).

In following contemporary affairs, the student may wish to consult *Pacific Affairs, Asian Survey* (formerly *Far Eastern Survey*), *The Japan Quarterly, Contemporary Japan, Orient/West, Transactions of the Asiatic Society of Japan*, the *Japan Report*, and *The American Universities Field Staff Reports*. Four daily newspapers in English are published in Tokyo. They are the *Asahi Evening News, The Mainichi*, and the *Yomiuri*, which are primarily adaptations for foreigners of the famous Japanese dailies of the same name, and *The Japan Times*. These English publications, especially the last-named, are less critical of American policies than are Japanese-language newspapers and magazines. For ready reference on current affairs, the author has found the *Asahi Nenkan* (yearbook), the *Asahi Jānaru* (weekly), and the *Shimbun Gappō* (monthly compilation of leading newspaper articles), all in Japanese, of considerable help.

The following books of a general nature on Japanese politics will be found of value in addition to those elsewhere cited:

Burks, Ardath W. *The Government of Japan.* New York: Thomas Y. Crowell Company, 1961.

Ike, Nobutaka. *Japanese Politics: An Introductory Survey.* New York: Alfred A. Knopf, Inc., 1957.

Maki, John M. *Government and Politics in Japan: The Road to Democracy.* New York: Frederick A. Praeger, 1962.

Quigley, Harold S., and John E. Turner. *The New Japan: Government and Politics.* Minneapolis: University of Minnesota Press, 1956.

Yanaga, Chitoshi. *Japanese People and Politics.* (New York: John Wiley and Sons, 1956.

GLOSSARY

Political Parties and Labor Unions

Jiyū-minshu-tō	Liberal-Democratic Party
Kaishin-tō	Progressive (or Reform) Party
Kensei-tō*	Constitutional Party
Kokumin-kyōdō-tō	People's Cooperative Party
Kokumin-minshu-tō	People's Democratic Party
Kyōsan-tō	Communist Party
Minsei-tō*	Democratic Party (in 1920's)
Minshu-jiyū-tō	Democratic-Liberal Party
Minshu-shakai-tō	Democratic-Socialist Party
Nikkyōso	Japan Teachers Union
Rōnō-tō	Labor-Farmer Party
Ryokufū-kai	Green Breeze Society
Saha	Left Wing
Sambetsu*	Congress of Industrial Unions
Seiyū-kai*	Political Friends Society
Shakai-tō	Socialist Party (often translated **Social-Democratic** Party)
Shimpo-tō	Progressive Party
Sōdōmei*	Japanese Federation of Labor
Sōhyō*	General Council of Japanese Labor Unions
Sōkagakkai*	Value-Creating Society
Teisei-tō	Imperial Party
Uha	Right Wing
Zengakuren*	All-Japan Federation of Students' Self Governing Associations
Zenrō*	Japan Trade Union Congress

*Usually not translated

1

Japanese Government Before 1945

The Land of Wa and the Kingdom of Yamato

Five thousand years ago, the Japanese Islands were inhabited by a rude people who made pottery such as archeologists are now unearthing in the western suburbs of Tokyo. Although archeological remains are plentiful, there are many conflicting theories concerning the origins of the prehistoric cultures and races of Japan. It appears that during the late paleolithic or mesolithic era waves of migration and cultural currents began to reach the Japanese archipelago from the coast of Asia. Once in Japan, migrant tribes could not move further eastward, and, as a consequence, various ethnic groups and cultures piled up and subsequently blended in Japan to produce the homogeneous ethnic, linguistic, and cultural pattern of the country.

The later invaders had the advantage of bronze or iron tools and weapons, which they had learned to make during the course of their migrations along the northern marches of the Chinese Empire. Some of the chieftains, as early as the first century A.D., sent missions to the Han court, where the eastern barbarians were known as Wa, or "dwarfs." Frequently the tribal leaders were women, and when the land became unified, it had several famous queens. The Wa rulers often sought to have their titles confirmed by the Chinese court.

By the fifth century, the Wa kingdom of Yamato had attained dominance in the Japanese islands and the Korean peninsula. Around 478, the Yamato ruler (Yūryaku) obtained from the Chinese Emperor the impressive title of "King of Wa and Generalissimo Who Maintains Peace in the East Commanding with Battle-Ax All Military Affairs in the Six Countries of Wa [Japan], Silla, Imna, Kala, Chin-han, and

1

Mok-han [five Korean states]."[1] Yamato managed to maintain a foothold in Korea until the victory of Silla over her fellow Korean kingdoms in 562.

The Yamato people were the ancestors of the Japanese of today. Although the Japanese race began as a mixture of North Asian, Chinese, Korean, Ainu, and, probably, Southeast Asian elements, by historic times (i.e., by the fifth century) "the greater part of Japan was inhabited by a racially homogeneous people unified by a common language and culture."[2]

The primitive Yamato society was a confederation of clans (uji), usually subdivided into branches, and hereditary guilds, which were normally attached to the clans as workers. Sometimes the guilds developed into independent clans, each with its own chieftain and ancestral deity. There were three classes of clans: (1) the Imperial Clan of the Emperor, which claimed descent from the Sun Goddess; (2) the Divine Clans, whose ancestors were gods associated with the Sun Goddess; and (3) Stranger Clans, of Korean and Chinese descent.

During the sixth century one of Yamato's Korean allies sent, by way of tribute to the Japanese monarch, the "Three Treasures" of Buddhism (Buddha, the Law, and the Priesthood) in the form of statues of the Lord Buddha, Scriptures, and several priests. A bitter controversy ensued in the court, as the clan of liturgists, who practiced ritual in honor of the indigenous deities, struggled to maintain their influence against the powerful military clan (Soga) which espoused Buddhism. By the end of the century, Buddhism, with its rich doctrine and ritual, and its potentialities for political exploitation, had captured the allegiance of the erstwhile pagan rulers.

In 604, the Regent Prince Shōtoku, a devout student of Buddhist literature, composed in Chinese his famous "Seventeen-Article Constitution." Shōtoku's Constitution was not an organic law of the kind with which we are today accustomed, but was, save for pious references to Buddhism, a collection of Confucian exhortations. Great emphasis was placed on the need for harmony, for the subordination of inferiors to superiors, and for diligence and honesty in the administration of state affairs. The court was determined to weaken the power of local chieftains and to end the feuding in the capital, which in 592 had culminated in the murder of the Emperor Sushun. Confucian pre-

[1] Ryusaku Tsunoda, William Theodore de Bary, and Donald Keene, comp., *Sources of the Japanese Tradition* (New York: Columbia University Press, 1958), p. 11.

[2] Edwin O. Reischauer and John K. Fairbank, *East Asia: The Great Tradition* (Boston: Houghton Mifflin, 1960), p. 462.

cept provided the ideology for the establishment of a centralized monarchy after the Chinese model. Thus Article Twelve of Shōtoku's charter enjoined:

> Let not the provincial authorities or the Kuni no Miyakko [local nobles] levy exaction on the people. In a country there are not two lords; the people have not two masters. The sovereign is the master of the people of the whole country. The officials to whom he gives charge are all his vassals. How can they, as well as the Government, presume to levy taxes on the people?[3]

In 603, Shōtoku, in emulation of the Sui monarchy in China, established a system of "cap-ranks," which would enhance the prestige of the imperial court. There were twelve ranks from top to bottom. Each rank was indicated by a silken hat of a different color, and the moral principles referred to were those of Confucian teaching, although in a somewhat unconventional order: greater virtue, lesser virtue, greater benevolence, lesser benevolence, greater propriety, lesser propriety, greater faith, lesser faith, greater justice, lesser justice, greater knowledge, and lesser knowledge. Occasionally thereafter, the system of court ranks underwent revision, and the edifying designations early gave way to ordinal numerals. While originally the ranks were intended to be hereditary, the merit system made some headway. The selection of officials on the basis of written examinations had begun in China during the Sui dynasty (589–618 A.D.).

As Chinese learning and the rising prestige of the Chinese (Sui) Empire made themselves felt in the island kingdom, the Wa ruler adopted the same title as that of the Chinese Emperor. Thus in 607, the Japanese suzerain sent a message to his Chinese counterpart: "The Son of Heaven in the land where the sun rises addresses a letter to the Son of Heaven in the land where the sun sets." The Sui Emperor was displeased with the discourteous tone of this missive from the eastern barbarians and directed that it should not again be brought to his attention.[4] The Japanese soon tired of being called Wa and referred to their country as "the land of the rising sun," in Chinese, Jih-pen (whence Japan); in Japanese, Nippon.

When the T'ang Empire of China replaced Japan as the arbiter among Korean kingdoms, it seemed more urgent, both for external and internal reasons, to strengthen the central authority in Japan. The principles of Shōtoku's Constitution were put into effect only piecemeal

[3] The text of Shōtoku's Constitution may be found in Tsunoda, pp. 49–53.

[4] Tsunoda, p. 12.

until 645, when a palace revolution resulted in the overthrow of the Soga clan by the Fujiwara and in the inauguration of the "Great Reform" (Taika).

Monarchy after the Chinese Fashion, 645–1192

The Edict of Reform[5] of 646 may be summarized as follows:

1. All hereditary guilds are abolished. Various local magnates are deprived of the manors and serfs which they have appropriated to themselves.

2. Governors are appointed to the home provinces and to the "outer" provinces. Communications are to be improved and made safer. The home provinces are to be divided into rural districts, composed of townships, each district to be under the authority of a district governor.

3. Registers of the population are to be drawn up, and land is to be redistributed according to the principle of "mouth-share-field" (i.e., each household is allotted land in proportion to the number of people in the household). The rate of the tax in the form of rice on the land is established.

4. The old taxes and forced labor are abolished, and a system of commuted taxes in kind (e.g., silk) is set up. Contributions are to be made, in a fixed ratio to the number of houses, of post horses, weapons, coolies, and good-looking waiting women for the court. In some cases, these contributions could be replaced with rice.

The primary purpose of the edicts seems to have been the redistribution of economic power in favor of the central government.[6] The centralizers frequently cited the Chinese doctrine, "Under the heavens there is no land which is not the king's land. Among holders of land there is none who is not the king's vassal," a principle neatly summarized by the Chinese motto: *kōdo, kōmin* — "public land, public people."

The number of provinces increased as more land was wrested from the Ainu and boundaries were changed. By the beginning of the ninth century, there were sixty-six provinces comprising 592 districts. The provincial governors appointed the district governors for life from among local clan chieftains and gentry, and the district governorships gradually became hereditary. Although the provincial and local governors performed civil, military, judicial, and religious duties

---

[5] An English translation of the reform edict is given in Tsunoda, pp. 74–76.

[6] George B. Sansom, *Japan: A Short Cultural History*, rev. ed. (New York: D. Appleton-Century, 1943), p. 97.

— they supervised Shinto shrines — their principal function seems to have been that of collecting and forwarding taxes to the capital, and, in the process, enriching themselves.

The Taihō Code of 702 set up a central administrative structure in imitation of that of the T'ang monarchy in China. Directly under the Emperor were the Department of Religion (Jingi-kan) and the Great Council of State (Dajō-kan). The former was an ecclesiastical commission which controlled affairs pertaining to the national cult, Shinto. There was no corresponding institution in the T'ang system, the Jingi-kan being a peculiarly Japanese institution. Although Buddhism seemed to eclipse the native "Way of the Gods," the cult of the Sun Goddess, the ancestress of the Emperor, was maintained to bolster the Emperor's claim to rule by divine right. The Emperor was in the custom of referring to himself as "manifest god." The Confucian idea that the mandate of heaven may be withdrawn from a wicked ruler and that the people might overthrow him was not adopted by the Japanese, where the hereditary principle prevailed over the merit system.

The Council of State was presided over by the Chancellor (Dajō-Daijin) and included the Minister of the Left (Sadaijin), the Minister of the Right (Udaijin), and other high officials. The Chancellor served as a kind of moral preceptor to the Emperor, and often this post was vacant. The Minister of the Left (or the Minister of the Right acting in his place) served as the chief administrative officer, and his functions roughly corresponded with those of a modern prime minister. Under the Council were the eight boards or ministries: Ministry of Central Affairs, Ministry of Ceremonies, Ministry of Civil Affairs, Ministry of Popular Affairs, Ministry of War, Ministry of Justice, Ministry of the Treasury, and Ministry of the Imperial Household.[7] These ministries, excepting Central Affairs and Imperial Household corresponded roughly to the six ministries of the T'ang administration. The names of these offices were for the most part self-explanatory. The Ministry of Central Affairs was concerned with transmitting the Emperor's decrees to the authorities concerned and memorials to the Emperor. The Ministry of Ceremonies determined promotion and degradation of officials. Civil Affairs was concerned with noblemen, ecclesiastics, and aliens; Popular Affairs with land, people, taxes, and forced labor. There was finally an Office of Censorship, which corrected evil customs and punished the misbehavior of officials.[8]

The transplantation of Chinese institutions to Japanese soil neces-

[7] Respectively, Nakatsukasashō, Shikibushō, Jibushō, Minbushō, Hyōbushō, Gyōbushō, Ōkurashō, and Kunaishō.

[8] Fujii Shin-ichi, *Tenno Seiji* (Tokyo: Yūhikaku, 1944), pp. 155–156.

sarily entailed dilution and compromise. The Japanese court could not afford to antagonize the clan chieftains and local gentry whose privileges would be wiped out by the principle of imperial centralization. Therefore, from the very beginning of the reform movement, although the clan nobles were replaced by imperial governors, the imperial governors and high ranking court officials were as a rule drawn from the traditional aristocracy. Notwithstanding pious professions to the contrary, the reforms were largely paper reforms.

The custom of the Yamato court was to maintain no fixed residence but to move from one place to another, partly because of Shinto taboos against death which required a change of palace after the death of an Emperor. However, missions to the T'ang court returned with dazzling descriptions of the Chinese capital, and plans were elaborated for the construction of a permanent Japanese capital, which was finally erected in 710 at Nara, near the present city of Kyoto. The capital was laid out with straight streets at right angles to one another, after the Chinese prototype. It also included a university where sons of the nobility could study the teachings of Confucius.

There seems to have been no real effort to spread Confucianism among the population or, for that matter, to replace the hereditary privilege with the more democratic merit system of the Chinese Confucianists. As Buddhism came more and more to enthrall the court, the capital included splendid temples of the faith in Chinese style, some of which are still standing. The indigenous Shinto deities seem to have been almost completely forgotten or else assimilated with the Hindu pantheon. Emperor Kōtoku (645–655) "despised the Way of the [Japanese] Gods."[9] Emperor Shōmu (724–749) was disturbed lest the construction of a great idol representing the Buddhist Vairocana, the Great Illuminator, might offend the Japanese Sun Goddess, but was reassured in a dream that the Buddhist deity and the Japanese deity were the same.[10]

During the consolidation of the Yamato kingdom, the court had carried on a number of drives to eliminate fraudulent claims to noble titles by the provincial gentry. Ordeal by boiling water was employed to ferret out falsification of genealogies. At the same time, the Imperial Clan reiterated its claim to descent from the Sun Goddess. In 712 the court published the *Kojiki* [*Record of Ancient Matters*] in Japanese, written with Chinese characters, and in 720 the *Nihongi* [*Record of Japan*], in Chinese. These were compilations of orally transmitted legends concerning the Age of the Gods and the founding

[9] Sansom, p. 93.
[10] *Ibid.*, p. 132.

of Japan by Jimmu Tennō, the first Emperor of the Yamato dynasty. The native Japanese religion was a compound of primitive nature worship, animism, and shamanism, and seems to have been brought by the Japanese from northern Asia at the time of their migrations. In the sixth century, with the coming of Buddhism, a name had been devised for the local faith: the "Way of the Gods," (Shinto).

According to the old histories, the divine couple Izanagi and Izanami, standing on the floating bridge of heaven, thrust a jewelled spear into the primeval brine, and when they pulled it out, the first of the Japanese islands congealed. Later, Amaterasu, the Sun Goddess, gave a mandate to her Heavenly Grandchild, Ninigi-no-Mikoto: "The Country of Goodly Grain with the promise of one thousand five hundred mellow autumns to come is the land where Our descendants shall become Sovereigns. You, Our Descendant, come and govern it. Come! The prosperity of the Imperial Throne shall be coeval with heaven and earth."[11] Amaterasu gave her grandchild some seeds, so that he, his descendants, and their subjects might eat rice grown from them. Ninigi-no-Mikoto took with him on his descent to the divine land the Three Sacred Treasures: the sacred jewels, the sacred mirror, and the sacred sword. The jewels and mirror had been used by the gods to entice the Sun Goddess from a cave which she had entered after being much displeased with the rowdy conduct of her brother, Susanoo. The sword had been obtained by Susanoo from the tail of a monster eight-headed serpent, whom he had managed to decapitate after getting it drunk on rice wine. These Three Sacred Treasures are even today in the possession of the Japanese Imperial Family, and have throughout the ages served as the Imperial Regalia as evidence of the legitimacy of the claim to the throne. It appears that the compilation of the Shinto scriptures by the court was primarily intended to increase the prestige of the imperial clan and the Yamato state by asserting the supernatural creation of the country and the divine origin of the dynasty.

In 769, during the reign of the Empress Shōtoku, a political crisis occurred when the sovereign proposed to abdicate in favor of her favorite, the Buddhist monk Dōkyō. A member of the nobility, however, reported the words of an oracle that:

> Since the founding of the Empire, there has always been a clear distinction between Sovereign and subject. No subject has ever been made Sovereign in the past. The successor to the Throne shall by all means be one of the Imperial family.[12]

[11] Fujii, p. 8.
[12] *Ibid.*, p. 176.

Although bloody succession disputes among imperial princes and princesses were the rule rather than the exception during the Nara epoch as before, the principle of legitimacy was maintained even against the apparent efforts of some of the clergy to establish a theocracy. For reasons which are not clear but which no doubt relate to the overweening pretensions of the Buddhist Church in Nara, the capital was transferred to Heian (Kyoto) in 795.

In 894, as the power of the T'ang dynasty waned, the sending of missions to the Chinese court was halted, and the influence of China on Japanese institutions declined. Native traditions of clan privilege and local autonomy reasserted themselves. The Fujiwara clan which had engineered the Taika reform became increasingly powerful in the capital. Although the positions of Grand Councillor, Chancellor, Minister of the Left and Minister of the Right continued in existence, the Fujiwara family set up more powerful posts in the court which they managed to monopolize.

The Fujiwara saw to it that Emperors abdicated very soon after reaching their majority, so that a Fujiwara Regent (Sesshō) would be the effective ruler on behalf of a child Emperor. When the monarch became of age, the Regent would become Civil Dictator (Kampaku), a title first assumed by Fujiwara Mototsune, who had served as regent during the reign of Yōzei (877–884). The Emperor was required to marry a Fujiwara lady, so that his offspring were quite as much the descendants of the Fujiwara as they were of the Sun Goddess. When the youthful monarch abdicated, a Fujiwara Regent would again rule. Regents, Civil Dictators, and Empresses all had to be chosen from among the Five Regent Families of the Fujiwara clan. Thus, nearly every Emperor had a Fujiwara mother, a Fujiwara grandfather, a Fujiwara uncle, a Fujiwara Regent, and a Fujiwara wife. With the exception that child Emperors later went out of fashion, the Fujiwara monopoly of high position in the court continued until the Restoration of 1867. This great family firmly established the principle of diarchy, or dual government, that the Emperor ruled in name only and that someone else exercised actual authority. In the sense that he reigns but does not rule, the Emperor has, with rare exceptions, been a "constitutional monarch" for 1300 years.

The Fujiwara ascendancy in itself was not the only factor to subvert the principle of imperial rule. The spread of the tax-exempt manors and the rise of a military nobility in the provinces also helped to destroy the power of the monarch. Notwithstanding the Taika principle of "public land, public people," from the very beginning the lands of the church and of certain officials were exempt from taxation. Shinto shrines had "god fields" and Buddhist temples had "temple fields" for which they did not have to pay taxes. To encourage the reclamation of additional land, Emperors would make it temporarily and then permanently exempt from taxes. Provincial and court officials were granted tax-free manors as compensation for their services — lands which became hereditary. Often imperial order would confer "gift lands" to court favorites. The profits from the cultivation of these lands by serfs, or occasionally by slaves, went to the temple or noble to whom they were assigned, and the Emperor received no share. As more and more areas became exempt, the burden of taxation on the non-exempt small-holders became greater. These subjects would often find it to their advantage to commend their lands to exempt neighbors, thus evading their obligations to the Son of Heaven. Often minor nobles would commend their lands, including land commended to themselves, to greater nobles. Thus, hierarchical structures of vassals — commendors and commendees — came into being. The Fujiwara princes of the court and the Tōdaiji (temple) were among the greatest immune landholders of the country and thousands of the Emperor's subjects looked to them for protection from the imperial taxgatherer.

Late in the eleventh century, to check the Fujiwara, Emperors began to take a direct part in the administration of the state. For example, Go-Sanjō (1069–1072) made notable efforts to check the increase of tax-free manors. Government by ex-emperors became a rule — a system known as Cloister Government (Insei), because often the former monarch would take the tonsure to become a Buddhist Pontiff (Hō-ō). The retired Emperor Shirakawa, for example, carried on much of the actual government during the reigns of his successors Horikawa, Toba, and Sutoku. However, most of the imperial edicts had to do with the manorial system, and were normally disregarded by the increasing powerful and independent territorial magnates.

As the court grew more effete and received less and less revenue it became incapable of enforcing its will and protecting its subjects in the provinces. Country gentry found it expedient to maintain bands of armed men and later small armies for protection. With increasing frequency the court commissioned one or another of the provincial nobles to punish recalcitrant vassals. In the eleventh and twelfth centuries the court had to call on the military barons to protect the capital itself from armies of Buddhist priests, whose religious processions were actually expeditions to extort additional privileges from the Fujiwara regents and the Emperor. In addition to certain of the Fujiwara, the greatest of the military barons were members of the Taira and Minamoto clans, descendants of imperial princes who had been sent to the provinces to seek their fortunes. In the latter half of the twelfth century, they were engaged in great civil wars with one another to determine the fate of entire provinces. By 1190, Taira Kiyomori was in control of most of the country and replaced the Fujiwara as Chancellor. But the Minamoto made a comeback in the sea battle of Dannoura in 1185, and in 1192, Minamoto Yoritomo was formally recognized as the feudal overlord of all of Japan.

In concluding the discussion of the fate of Chinese institutions on Japanese soil, we note that (1) the Confucian merit system did not displace the Japanese traditions of hereditary privilege and divine right, (2) the system of individual small-holders paying taxes to the imperial court gave way to a hierarchical feudal structure, (3) dual government (diarchy) in which the Emperor ruled only in name while clan leaders ruled in fact became an established principle, and (4) the central administration was, for all practical purposes, gradually superseded by military feudal barons.

Feudalism, 1192–1868

In 1192, the cloistered ex-Emperor conferred upon Minamoto Yoritomo the title of Barbarian-Subduing Generalissimo (Sei-i Tai Shōgun). This title had first been granted to Ōtomo Otomaro, a general in the wars against the Ainu on Japan's northern frontier, in 794. The Shogunate now became hereditary in the Minamoto clan. Although Emperors, ex-Emperors, and Fujiwara continued to perform ceremonies in Kyoto, the ruler of Japan for the next 675 years was the Shogun, a military dictator, who maintained his own feudal capital removed from the influence of the imperial court. Minamoto Yoritomo founded his capital in Kamakura, in eastern Japan, some 300 miles from Kyoto. His administrative structure was called the Bakufu (literally "tent government," meaning military government).

The chief organs of the Kamakura administration were three: (1) the Samurai Council (Samurai-dokoro), an administrative and judicial body concerned with the affairs of the military class, such as rewards and punishment, promotion and demotion, allocation of military duties, and criminal matters, (2) the Administrative Office (Man-dokoro) concerned with the administration of the domains of the Minamoto, and (3) a High Court (Monjū-sho), the final court for appeals of suits concerning rights of feudal tenure. The law applied was the precedents and feudal contracts which had developed during the last half of the Heian era, more frequently than the Chinese-inspired codes of Nara and early Heian periods. Throughout the country, newly established provincial constables and local stewards enforced the Shogun's authority.

After the extinction of Yoritomo's line with the death of the third Shogun, the government of the Bakufu was taken over by a line of Regents (Shikken) of the Hōjō clan (1226–1333), who governed on behalf of child Shoguns appointed from the court nobility in Kyoto. The Regency in 1232 issued the famous Formulary of Jōei, a compilation of feudal law based upon precedent.

The great accomplishment of the Hōjō Regents was the repulse of two attempted invasions of the land by the Mongols of Kubilai Khan, in 1274 and 1281. The Japanese defense was aided by the prayers of the people to the Buddhist and Shinto deities and by the "Wind of the Gods" (kamikaze), which on both occasions destroyed the enemy invasion fleets. The result of this experience was a conviction, inbred in succeeding generations, that the divine land of Japan enjoyed the special protection of the deities. Unfortunately for the Hōjō, the heroic defense effort had not resulted in the conquest of territories which could be distributed to samurai heroes who were hungry for rewards. The discontent of the military class hastened the overthrow of the Hōjō regime, and in 1333 the Regent Hōjō Takatoki and two hundred of his followers committed hara-kiri rather than surrender to the troops of Emperor Go-Daigo.

Fief-hungry barons found an opportunity for satisfying their ambitions in a succession war between competing claimants to the imperial throne. The war between the Northern and Southern Courts brought about the establishment of a new line of Shoguns — the Ashikaga. The Ashikaga set up their feudal capital in Muromachi, outside of Kyoto. However, the Ashikaga period (1338–1573) was one of unremitting civil war among feudal lords for more fiefs, and the power of the Ashikaga scarcely went beyond their own immediate domains. Jesuit missionaries who entered Japan in the latter part of the sixteenth century referred to the great feudal barons as "kings," since each seemed quite free from any control by either the court of the Emperor or the court of the Shogun.

The Ashikaga have been excoriated by patriotic historians because two of them declared themselves subject to the Ming dynasty of China. The motive seems to have been primarily commercial, since the "tribute" missions involved were primarily trading missions, and the Shoguns wished to smooth over difficulties with the Chinese court concerning Japanese pirate raids. Notwithstanding the political chaos, the period was one of rich achievement in the arts of painting, sculpture, and drama. The period of the "Country at War" was brought to an end by the great unifiers, Oda Nobunaga and Toyotomi Hideyoshi. This last was an adventurer of low birth who succeeded in gaining so much power that he acquired the rank of Kampaku (Civil Dictator), which normally was held only by the Fujiwara. He sent two great invading expeditions to Korea, with the declared intent to conquer China, but his death in 1598 brought an end to these efforts.

Tokugawa Ieyasu, a member of the council of regents set up to rule Japan until Hideyoshi's heir came of age, overthrew the fledgling dynasty. Following the decisive battle of Sekigahara, he became virtual master of all of Japan and, as a member of the Minamoto clan, was able to secure the title of Shogun in 1603. Ieyasu, like his illustrious ancestor Minamoto Yoritomo, was an administrator of the first order as well as a great general and established a regime which, under fifteen successive Tokugawa Shoguns, ensured unprecedented peace and political stability for Japan.

The policies of the Tokugawa which accomplished its great success were stringent control over the feudal barons and the Emperor, the isolation of Japan from the outside world, and the suppression of Christianity. In 1638, a revolt of peasants in Shimabara under the leadership of Christian samurai was put down with great severity. The support given the rebels by the Portuguese underlined the importance of suppressing an alien religion which could be used by domestic agitators and European states to subvert the regime and conquer Japan, just as the Spanish had taken over the Philippines a few decades before. The Catholic movement which had been flourishing in Kyushu was ruthlessly extirpated, and the Catholic states of Spain and Portugal were forbidden from sending missionaries or traders to Japan. Only the Dutch, who swore not to proselytize, and the Chinese, were allowed to trade in Japan. A limit was placed on the size of Japanese ships, so that no subject of the Shogun could carry on foreign trade.

Those barons who had recognized Ieyasu as their overlord before the battle of Sekigahara were designated "vassal lords" (fudai daimyō), while those who had not deferred to Ieyasu before the crucial battle were designated "outside lords" (tozama daimyō). The new Shogun redistributed the fiefs (han) in the land in such a way as to isolate the outside lords from one another. The outside lords were not permitted to serve as Elders (Rōjū) or Junior Elders (Wakadoshiyori), who advised the Shogun on the administration of the country. The new regime maintained a highly effective spy system to report any suspicious plotting or intrigue. The daimyo were not permitted to have contacts with the Emperor. The barons, as a rule, were required to spend every other year with their families at Edo (present Tokyo), the Shogun's capital, and every other year at their fiefs, leaving their families as hostages in Edo. The cost of maintaining sumptuous residences both in Edo and in one's domain, of processions to and from

Edo, and of salaries (paid in rice) to samurai retainers was ultimately ruinous to the feudal lords.

The trouble with the Tokugawa system of maintaining internal peace was that it worked all too well. The long period of domestic stability favored the expansion of the money economy at the expense of the rice economy and the rise of the commercial classes at the expense of the agrarian feudal classes. As the merchants in Edo and Osaka grew richer the daimyo and samurai grew poorer. Early in the regime, the Tokugawa dynasts had a huge surplus of gold hoarded in their treasury, but by 1868, when faced with civil war, the Shogun owed more than he owned.

The feudal regime was seriously weakened even before Perry arrived in Japan. Not only was its economic basis being subverted, but its ideology was undermined. The Bakufu had sponsored the conservative Chu Hsi school of Confucianism, which emphasized obedience and loyalty, but the Wang Yang-ming school, which emphasized intuition and action, became increasingly influential and was a potential encouragement to rebellion. Much more important, however, was the school of national studies (kokugaku). As philologists such as Motoori Norinaga (1730–1801) revived the study of the native literature, impoverished samurai learned that Japan, far from being ruled by the divine Emperor as decreed by the Sun Goddess, was actually being ruled by a usurper in the form of the Shogun. The Shinto revival provided the ideological basis for revolt. Ironically, the Mito branch of the Tokugawa clan subsidized a principal school of nationalist historiography which exalted the imperial family. A serious succession dispute in the middle of the nineteenth century further weakened the prestige of the Bakufu.

In 1853 Commodore Matthew Calbraith Perry left a message to be delivered to the Emperor calling for the opening of Japan and said that he would return the following year for a reply. The Shogun was faced with a dilemma. As Barbarian-Subduing-Generalissimo his duty to reject Perry's demands was clear, but he did not possess the military strength to repel the American barbarian. He circularized the daimyo to ask for their opinions as to what should be done and to get their support. Although a third of the daimyo recommended the rejection of the American demand, the Shogun felt that his forces were too weak to refuse Perry a treaty. Later, when the American consul, Townsend Harris, was attempting to negotiate a commercial treaty, the enemies of the Shogun rallied around the Emperor and popularized the slogan "Revere the Emperor; Expel the Barbarian."

In 1867, beset with difficulties on all sides, the Shogun Tokugawa Yoshinobu declared the Bakufu at an end. He assumed that he would be named a leading councillor in the "restored" imperial regime. When the western clansmen excluded him, he and his followers resorted to war but were quickly defeated.

The Meiji Restoration and Rule by Clan Oligarchs, 1868–1918

The men who had engineered the "Restoration" of the Emperor Meiji were samurai from the southern and western fiefs, or clans (han), of Chōshū, Satsuma, Tosa, and Hizen. Members of these clans were destined to monopolize effective political authority in Japan until the close of World War I. In 1868, on the suggestion of the western clansmen, the sixteen-year-old Emperor Mutsuhito (posthumously known as Meiji) issued the famous "Five-Article Charter Oath," which was intended to calm the apprehensions of rival factions and to outline the policies of the new regime:

1. Deliberative assemblies shall be widely established and all matters decided by public discussion.
2. All classes, high and low, shall unite in vigorously carrying out the administration of affairs of state.
3. The common people, no less than the civil and military officials, shall each be allowed to pursue his own calling so that there may be no discontent.
4. Evil customs of the past shall be broken off and everything based upon the just laws of Nature.
5. Knowledge shall be sought throughout the world so as to strengthen the foundations of imperial rule.[13]

To dramatize the transfer of political authority from the Shogun to the Emperor, the imperial capital was moved from Kyoto, where it had been located since 794, to Edo, the capital of the former Tokugawa Shoguns. Edo was renamed Tokyo, "Eastern Capital," and the Shogun's palace was taken over by the Emperor.

A "Constitution" was also promulgated in 1868 providing for a resuscitation of the Chinese-inspired institutions of the pre-feudal epoch. In 1871 and 1872, the daimyo transmitted their registers of land and of people to the Emperor to formalize the end of feudalism and the restoration of imperial rule. The fiefs of the *ancien régime* were replaced by prefectures (ken) administered by governors appointed by the Emperor, and the daimyo were granted liberal pensions. The samurai, also pensioned off, were deprived of their privileges, including the right to wear two swords.

[13] Tsunoda, pp. 643–644.

The many sweeping changes from feudalism to bureaucratic monarchy were subjects of bitter disputes. The government determined to concentrate on internal economic and political reform rather than engage in military adventures on the Asiatic continent, as was strongly urged by some leaders. This pacific policy alienated samurai who wished to cover themselves with glory in a war with Korea. When the government commuted the samurai pensions to niggardly lump sum payments, the warriors became rebellious. In 1877, discontented samurai in Satsuma rallied around Saigō Takamori, a restoration leader then out of power, and rebelled. The Emperor's newly organized conscript troops, trained by western methods and equipped with modern weapons, put down the uprising, and the new regime survived its first great test.

When the clan leaders Itagaki Taisuke of Tosa and Ōkuma Shigenobu of Hizen were forced out of the councils of the new regime, which fell increasingly under the domination of samurai from Chōshū and Satsuma, they demanded the establishment of a representative parliament and organized political parties. The authorities met the demands of the opposition with nominal concessions and police repression. In 1881, the government promised that a constitution providing for an elective parliament would be established in 1890. The Liberal Party (Jiyūtō), formed by Itagaki in 1881, called for a constitution based on the principle of popular sovereignty. Ōkuma's Progressive Party (Kaishintō), inaugurated in 1882, advocated a more conservative English form of parliamentarism. The government organized the Imperial Party (Teiseitō) in 1882 and charged the opposition parties with disloyalty to the Emperor. These early parties were formed primarily to support the ambitions of oligarchic leaders. From the beginning they were shot through with opportunism and personal factionalism. Devotion to political principle was notably absent from their make-up. Political parties in Japan did not and still do not represent grass roots movements. The present-day Liberal-Democratic Party is the direct lineal descendant of the political parties of Ōkuma and Itagaki.

Itō Hirobumi, a Chōshū leader, was entrusted with the formulation of a basic law and, following a world tour to study foreign constitutions, returned with a conviction that a constitution similar to that of autocratic Prussia would best suit Japan. Aided by a German advisor, Hermann Roessler, he and his close associates, working in deepest secrecy, produced a constitution which obtained the approval of the Privy Council, of which Itō was President. On Foundation Day (February 11), 1889, Emperor Meiji promulgated the Constitution of the Empire of Japan (Dai Nippon Teikoku Kempō) and the Imperial House Law (Kōshitsu Tempan), together with implementing ordinances. Itō hailed the new Constitution as the "Emperor's gift to the Japanese people" and published his own *Commentaries on the Constitution of Japan,* an article-by-article interpretation of the new basic law.

The 1889 Constitution was a splendid manifesto of the Shinto revival. Article I provided, "The Empire of Japan shall be reigned over and governed by a line of Emperors unbroken for ages eternal." "The Emperor," Article III stated, "is sacred and inviolable." Itō staunchly opposed the principle that the Cabinet should be answerable to the Diet. To make the Ministers of the Emperor responsible to the parliament would, he held, deny the principle that the Emperor rules. Lest the power of the purse be used by the Diet to control the executive, Itō's Constitution provided that when the Diet failed to enact the budget, the Government would carry out the budget of the preceding year.

The upper chamber of the Imperial Diet (Teikoku Gikai) consisted of a House of Peers (Kizoku-in) made up of peers, representative peers, representatives of the highest taxpayers, and imperial appointees. The peerage had been created in 1884 by Itō to rally former daimyo, court nobility, leading samurai, and wealthy merchants to the support of the new regime. The members of the lower chamber, the House of Representatives (Shūgiin), were elected by a relatively small electorate which met minimum taxpaying requirements. Japanese subjects enjoyed liberty of speech, press, and assembly "within the limits of law." The Constitution could be amended only upon proposal of the Emperor and with the approval of two-thirds of the members present in each House. The Imperial House Law, which regulated the succession to the throne, could not be modified by the Diet.

The Privy Council (Sūmitsuin), established by an Imperial Ordinance in 1888,[14] was made up of a President, Vice President, and twenty-five Councillors, all appointed by the Emperor on the advice of the Cabinet. The Constitution provided that they would "deliberate upon important matters of state when they have been consulted by the Emperor." The Council functions were made more explicit by an Imperial Ordinance of 1890[15] which empowered it to advise the Emperor concerning the Imperial House Law, the interpretation of the Constitution, the proclamation of martial law and imperial ordinances,

[14] Imperial Ordinance of April 28, 1888, on the organization of the Privy Council, W. W. McLaren, ed., "Japanese Government Documents," *Transactions of the Asiatic Society of Japan,* XLII, Part I (May, 1914), pp. 127–132.

[15] Tatsuji Takeuchi, *War and Diplomacy in the Japanese Empire* (Garden City: Doubleday Doran, 1935), pp. 33–34.

international treaties and agreements, the organization of the Privy Council, and any other matters submitted to its deliberation. Cabinet Ministers were entitled to participate in the meetings of the Privy Council and to vote. Decisions were by majority vote. The Privy Council was not permitted to receive petitions, representations, or other communications from the Diet, or from any Government office, or from private subjects of the Emperors, and could have official connection only with the Cabinet and Ministers of State. Itō regarded the Privy Council as "the highest body of the Emperor's constitutional advisors" and "the palladium of the Constitution."[16]

A principal characteristic of the Meiji Constitution was the irresponsibility of the executive. Normally, the most that the Diet could do was oppose, but the obstructionism of the Diet was weakened by the need to support the government during the Sino-Japanese War (1894–1895) and the Russo-Japanese War (1904–1905).

Although the agitation of such leaders as Ōkuma and Itagaki had forced the government's hand in issuing a constitution, another important factor was the popular demand to bring an end to the "unequal treaties." The Harris Treaty had served as the model for other treaties with the Western Powers, which all insisted upon extraterritoriality (exemption from Japanese jurisdiction) for their subjects in Japan. Not only was extraterritoriality an affront to Japanese sovereignty and national pride, but the treaty-established tariff resulted in flooding Japan with cheap Western manufactures, seriously depressing Japanese handicraft industries and making it impossible to protect and stimulate the industrialization of the country. By establishing a legal structure along Western lines, Japanese statesmen hoped to negate arguments that extraterritoriality was made necessary by the unjust and arbitrary features of oriental law. The enactment of the Imperial Constitution, the keystone of the new legal structure, paved the way for the adoption of law codes and a judicial system inspired by European models. By 1899, the last of the unequal treaties had been removed.[17]

Since the coming of Perry, the dominant factor governing Japanese political development has been foreign relations. Japan's leaders were keenly conscious of the European conquest of India and the Philippines and of Western imperialism in China. The success of Japan in warding off the Westerners contrasted with the fate of China after the Opium War (1839–1842). The failure of the Manchu Empire to

[16] Itō Hirobumi. *Commentaries on the Constitution of Japan,* trans. Itō Miyoji (Tokyo: Insetsu Kyoku, 1889), pp. 98–99.

[17] Chitoshi Yanaga, *Japan Since Perry* (New York: McGraw-Hill, 1949), p. 197.

achieve the political reforms necessary to save China from Western imperialism seems to have been largely due to the vested interest of the Confucian bureaucrats and Manchu dynasts in preventing basic change. In Japan, on the other hand, the samurai who had for centuries effectively administered the country, showed enthusiasm for rather than aversion to reform. No doubt the economic deterioration of the feudal system in Japan goes far to explain the willingness of the traditional leadership in that country to sponsor the fundamental political changes necessary to the preservation of the nation's independence.

Government by the clan oligarchs (hambatsu) meant that both by constitutional and by extraconstitutional means the samurai clansmen who had brought about the Meiji restoration were the effective rulers of Japan and prevented the political parties from establishing an executive responsible to the majority in the national legislature. The men who advised the Emperor on the choice of Prime Minister were an extraconstitutional group known as the genro, or elder statesmen.[18] With a single exception, the genro were drawn from the Chōshū and Satsuma clans. The original genro were Yamagata Aritomo (Chōshū), Inoue Kaoru (Chōshū), Ōyama Iwao (Satsuma), Matsukata Masayoshi (Satsuma), and Itō Hirobumi (Chōshū). Later comers were Katsura Tarō (Chōshū) and Saionji Kimmochi (a court noble). The elder statesmen saw to it that the premiership alternated between the samurai aristocracy of the Chōshū and Satsuma clans. Thus we find that between 1885 and 1918, every Prime Minister was drawn either from one or the other of the two western clans except for Ōkuma Shigenobu (of Hizen), who was premier in 1898 and 1914–1916, and Saionji Kimmochi (court noble), premier in 1906–1908 and 1911–1912. Following the death of General Yamagata in 1922 and of Matsukata in 1924, only one member of the genro remained: Saionji (d. 1940). The jūshin (senior statesmen), i.e., former Prime Ministers, took the place of the genro in the 1930's and early forties. They and the Lord Keeper of the Privy Seal (Nai-daijin) advised the Emperor on the appointment of premiers and on other important questions.

Relations between the Cabinet and Diet were normally poor. The Diet represented predominantly agrarian interests that balked at appropriating the substantial funds which the government demanded for expanding the armed services and establishing model industrial enterprises. Often the Cabinet would meet the recalcitrance of the lower house with a prorogation (suspension of the session) or a dissolution, and frequently the Cabinet itself would resign immediately following

[18] The genro should not be confused with the Genrō-in, a kind of senate created in 1875, which continued in existence until the enforcement of the Meiji Constitution.

a dissolution. The lives of Cabinets and of Houses of Representatives usually did not exceed two and a half years. Nevertheless, the First Sino-Japanese War and the Russo-Japanese War meant that the Cabinet could bring great pressure to bear on the Diet to cooperate in times of national emergency.

World War I provided the Japanese with an opportunity to expel Germany from her naval leasehold, railroad concessions, and other interests in Shantung province in China. At the same time, Japan was also able to exact important economic privileges from China, especially in South Manchuria and Inner Mongolia. As British industry was occupied with supplying the Allied war machine in Europe, Japan took over extensive British markets in Asia. However, inflation drove up the price of rice in Japan, and in 1918, riots in which peasants seized rice stores broke out throughout the country. The situation was of greater gravity than the genro could cope with. The Terauchi Cabinet fell, and Hara Takashi, the leader of the Seiyūkai party, became the first commoner to serve as Prime Minister of Japan. A Cabinet made up predominantly of members of the majority party was established. The power of the clan oligarchs appeared to be broken.

"Normal Constitutional Government," 1918–1932

Japan was not immune to the world-wide enthusiasm for democracy which had been kindled by the Allied victory in World War I and Wilsonian idealism. Liberal intellectuals and businessmen hoped that the accession of Hara, a party politician, would inaugurate a period of responsible cabinet government after the British model. They coined the expression "normal constitutional government" (kensei no jōdo) to designate the parliamentary-cabinet system which they wished to see established in Japan. The Cabinets from 1918 to 1922 and from 1924 to 1932 were headed by leaders of the majority party or majority coalitions in the Diet. On May 5, 1925, a universal manhood suffrage law was passed which gave the right to vote to all male citizens over twenty-five years of age, increasing the electorate from three to thirteen million. A week later, however, the "Peace Preservation Law" was brought into effect which "provided ten years imprisonment for those convicted of joining societies or parties advocating alteration of the Constitution, of the existing form of government, or of the system of private ownership of property."[19] The party Cabinets were no more tolerant of socialism and the labor movement than the oligarchic Cabinets had been.

[19] Hugh Borton, *Japan's Modern Century* (New York: Ronald, 1955), p. 310.

The rise of Chinese nationalism, which threatened Japanese interests in the Asiatic continent, and the world depression created problems apparently too great to be resolved in the framework of Japan's nascent parliamentarism. Japan had extensive economic and strategic interests in Manchuria which appeared to be imperiled by the anti-imperialist drive of Chiang Kai-shek's Nationalists. In 1928, Japanese troops in Shantung province clashed with Chinese Nationalist forces, and the Japanese military engineered the murder of an erstwhile friend of Japan, Marshal Chang Tso-lin, the warlord of Manchuria, who seemed to be inclining towards the Nationalist camp. A Chinese boycott of Japanese goods forced a Japanese retreat and the resignation of the Seiyūkai Cabinet of Baron Tanaka Giichi, which had favored a "positive" policy towards China.

The succeeding Minseitō Government of Hamaguchi Osachi won an absolute majority in the election of 1930. Hamaguchi made himself unpopular by practicing financial retrenchment and outraged the Navy in accepting an inferior naval ratio for Japan at the London Disarmament Conference. The Prime Minister was shot in November, 1930, by an ultranationalist and died the following year.

On September 18, 1931, a minor bomb explosion on the Japanese-operated South Manchurian Railway was used as a pretext by the Japanese Army in the Kwantung leasehold to seize the whole of Manchuria. The Kwantung Army acted on its own initiative without consulting either Premier Wakatsuki or Foreign Minister Shidehara.

The last of the party governments was that of Wakatsuki's successor, Inukai Tsuyoshi, whose Seiyūkai won an overwhelming majority in the 1932 elections for the House of Representatives. However, ultranationalists tried to overthrow the government on May 15, 1932, and assassinated the Prime Minister. Although party members participated in the succeeding Cabinet headed by Admiral Saitō Makato and subsequent governments, the executive branch ceased to be responsible to parliament and was dominated by the military and bureaucracy until the end of World War II.

Military Dominance, 1932–1945

The Manchurian Incident and the assassination of Inukai had brought an end to party government and began a new period of "transcendental" Cabinets. "Dual Government," in which the military was able to act independently of the civil branch, became the rule.

The constitutional basis for the autonomy of the military was the "independence" of the military prerogative of the Emperor in the Meiji Constitution. Articles 11 and 12, which provided that the "Emperor has the supreme command of the Army and Navy" and "determines the organization and peace standing of the Army and Navy" were interpreted by the services to mean that supreme command and the service ministries had a right equal to that of the Prime Minister to direct access to the Emperor. Since the Emperor, as a constitutional monarch, was expected to follow the counsel of his advisers, the right of direct access was very important.

An Imperial Ordinance of 1898 required that the Minister of War and the Minister of the Navy must be a general or a lieutenant-general or an admiral or vice-admiral respectively on the active list. The Army or Navy would not permit its officers to serve in a Cabinet unless it approved the composition and policies of the Cabinet. Since Cabinets had to have service ministers, the Prime Minister had no choice but to meet at least part way the demands of the Army and Navy. The services could cause the resignation or prevent the formation of Cabinets unacceptable to them. In 1912, the Saionji Cabinet, which enjoyed the support of a majority in the lower house, refused a demand by the Army for two additional divisions. The War Minister, on orders from his military superiors, resigned in protest. Because of the Army's attitude no successor was made available, and the Saionji Cabinet fell.

After the assassination of Prime Minister Inukai in 1932, Cabinets largely dominated by the military became the rule. An attempted coup d'etat on February 26, 1936, by young army officers resulted in the assassination of a number of members of the Okada Cabinet. Although the ringleaders were forced to surrender to loyalist forces and were summarily executed, the effect of the incident was further to strengthen the control of the Army over the state. After the Army had forced the resignation of the Hirota Cabinet in January, 1937, the "moderate" General Ugaki Kazushige was granted the mandate (taimei) of the Emperor to form a Cabinet. The Army, however, found him unacceptable and refused to participate so that on February 29, he was forced to admit his failure to form a government. Public interest in the matter was great, and it was suggested that Ugaki request the Emperor to command the Army to recommend a War Minister. Such a step "would have been constitutional though not politic."[20] General Hayashi Senjūrō, the Army's choice, became the new Premier.

In the elections of April, 1937, the Minseitō and Seiyūkai made common cause against militarism and fascism and won three-fourths of the seats in parliament. Nevertheless, they were not represented in the first Cabinet of Prince Konoye Fumimaro, of the Fujiwara nobility, who was made Prime Minister in order to achieve unity among the financial, industrial, military, and naval elements who ruled Japan.

[20] Yanaga, pp. 529–530.

The Japanese Army had failed to establish a puppet government for all of North China, as it had hoped, and Chinese resistance stiffened with the formation of a "United Front" of Nationalists and Communists under Chiang Kai-shek. The clash between Japanese and Chinese troops at Marco Polo Bridge, near Peking on July 7, 1937, rapidly developed into a full-scale, though undeclared, war. In November, the Imperial Headquarters was established to coordinate and centralize all Japanese military efforts in China. It would have direct access to the Emperor. The Diet in 1938 enacted a National Mobilization Law conferring sweeping powers on the Cabinet.

In June, 1940, Prince Konoye resigned the presidency of the Privy Council to devote his full energies to the establishment of a unified political structure. In July and August, the political parties voted themselves out of existence, and on October 12, Konoye, Prime Minister for a second time, announced the inauguration of the Imperial Rule Assistance Association (IRAA, Taisei Yokusan Kai), of which he was President. It appears that Konoye regarded the IRAA as a device for controlling the Army and terminating the war in China and that he did not originally intend the new organization to become a totalitarian political party, but the IRAA, with prefectural and local branches and affiliate organizations, was a tool of the government. It became increasingly totalitarian under the domination of bureaucrats and the military, and was used by Prime Minister Tōjō Hideki, during World War II, to indoctrinate the population with war propaganda and Shinto ideology and to control the Diet. In the House of Representatives election of 1942, 381 of the 466 successful candidates were nominees of the Tōjō Government. They organized the Imperial Rule Assistance Political Society (IRAPS, Taisei Yokusan Seijikai), "a political party to assist in the accomplishment of the Great East Asia War."[21]

The Political Heritage

The political heritage of Japan before 1945 embodied the following traditions: (1) aristocratic, rather than democratic, government, (2) emphasis on loyalty and discipline rather than individual self-expression, (3) militarism, (4) a confusing dispersion of political authority among feudal and monarchical institutions, (5) pride in a long history of national independence under a uniquely ancient dynasty, (6) indebtedness to traditional China and the Western world for political ideologies and institutions, and (7) strong family, clan, and local

[21] Supreme Commander for the Allied Powers, Government Section, *Political Reorientation of Japan: September 1945 to September 1948,* 2 vols. (Washington: Government Printing Office, n.d. [1949?]), I, 19.

loyalties. The following traditions were *weak or absent* in Japan's po-litical heritage: (1) belief in the right of revolution, conspicuous in the Chinese and Western liberal traditions, (2) the cult of material well-being, common in the West, (3) monarchical absolutism (except in theory), (4) subjection to alien rule, (5) political and economic individ-ualism, (6) the ideal of limited government (that "that government is best which governs least"), and (6) strong representative institutions.

It is the thesis of the author that the Japanese are not inscrutable and that their political institutions are not wholly unique as some conservative Japanese scholars and some Western experts would have us believe. The view that Japanese politics are what they are because the people are "orientals" does not, it seems to me, add much to our understanding. Japanese feudalism was not greatly different from European feudalism, and the establishment of a centralized state and the industrialization of Japan occurred at about the same time as simi-lar developments in Germany and Italy. In terms of ideological con-flict, social relations, technical development, and governmental insti-tutions, Japanese politics resemble those of Italy more than they do of any Asian state. The superficially exotic features of Japan which are the special subject of touristic propaganda should not blind the student to the fact that for over one hundred years Japan has been an active participant in Western civilization and has reached approxi-mately the same level of scientific and industrial development and political sophistication as the more advanced nations of Europe.

SUGGESTED READINGS

Beckmann, George M. *The Making of the Meiji Constitution: The Oligarchs and the Constitutional Development of Japan, 1868–1891.* Lawrence: University of Kansas Press, 1957.

Benedict, Ruth. *The Chrysanthemum and the Sword: Patterns of Japanese Culture.* Boston: Houghton Mifflin Company, 1946. On social ethics.

Borton, Hugh. *Japan's Modern Century.* New York: The Ronald Press Company, 1955. Emphasizes international relations and the de-velopment of political institutions.

Brown, Delmer M. *Nationalism in Japan: An Introductory Historical Analysis.* Berkeley and Los Angeles: University of California Press, 1955. A good introduction.

Fujii, Shinichi. *The Essentials of Japanese Constitutional Law.* Tokyo: Yūhikaku, 1940. A presentation of the conservative point of view.

Holtom, D. C. *National Faith of Japan: A Study in Modern Shinto.* London: Kegan Paul, 1938. On church-state relations.

Ike, Nobutaka. *The Beginnings of Political Democracy in Japan.* Baltimore: The Johns Hopkins University Press, 1950. On the democratic movement from 1868 to 1889.

Itō, Hirobumi. *Commentaries on the Constitution of the Empire of Japan,* translated by Itō Miyoji. Tokyo: Insetsu Kyoku, 1889. An authoritative interpretation of the Meiji Constitution by its principal author.

McLaren, Walter Wallace. *A Political History of Japan during the Meiji Era: 1867–1912.* London: George Allen and Unwin, 1916. Thorough.

Nitobe, Inazo. *Bushido: The Soul of Japan,* 16th ed. Tokyo: Teibi Publishing Co., 1909. Idealizes traditional ethics.

Norman, E. Herbert. *Japan's Emergence as a Modern State: Political and Economic Problems of the Meiji Period.* New York: Institute of Pacific Relations, 1940. A scholarly analysis by the late Canadian ambassador to Egypt.

Quigley, Harold S. *Japanese Government and Politics.* New York: D. Appleton-Century, 1932. Long the standard work in English.

Reischauer, Edwin O., and John K. Fairbank. *East Asia: The Great Tradition,* Vol. I. Boston: Houghton Mifflin Company, 1960. A well-balanced history.

Reischauer, Robert Karl. *Japan: Government — Politics.* New York: The Ronald Press Company, 1939. Succinct.

Sansom, George Bailey. *A History of Japan to 1334.* Stanford: Stanford University Press, 1958.

Sansom, George Bailey. *A History of Japan: 1334–1615.* Stanford: Stanford University Press, 1961.

Sansom, George Bailey. *Japan: A Short Cultural History,* rev. ed. New York: Appleton-Century, 1944. Political institutions are viewed as they develop in their social and economic context.

Takeuchi, Tatsuji. *War and Diplomacy in the Japanese Empire.* Garden City: Doubleday, Doran, 1935. Scholarly.

Tiedemann, Arthur. *Modern Japan: A Brief History,* 2nd ed. Princeton: D. Van Nostrand Company, 1962. Includes key documents.

Tsunoda, Ryusaku, William Theodore de Bary, and Donald Keene, comps. *Sources of the Japanese Tradition.* New York: Columbia University Press, 1958. Contains key documents for the study of political history.

Yanaga, Chitoshi. *Japan Since Perry.* New York: McGraw-Hill Book Co., 1949. Almost encyclopedic, this book is good for reference.

2

The American Occupation and the New Constitution

The Potsdam Proclamation and the Occupation of Japan

In the five years following World War II, the United States was able to pursue its policies in Japan with remarkably little direct interference from the other victorious Allies. While the United States experienced and still experiences countless frustrations in its German policies because of Soviet opposition, the Americans managed to do pretty much as they pleased in Japan.

The inability of the Soviet Union to participate effectively in the Allied Occupation of Japan stemmed largely from her lateness in entering the war against that nation. On July 26, 1945, in Potsdam, Germany, President Truman and Prime Minister Churchill, with Chiang Kai-shek's concurrence, issued a declaration which stated the terms for a Japanese surrender. The Potsdam Declaration (or Proclamation) was drafted principally by the United States.[1] Since the Soviet

This chapter is based in part on the author's "The Japanese Constitution: Child of the Cold War," in *Political Science Quarterly*, LXIV, No. 2 (June, 1959), 176–195. For a bibliography of Japanese and English materials on the Constitution see *Gaisei*, Summer, 1957.

[1] The Potsdam Declaration was based on a paper originally prepared by two U.S. State Department officials, Dr. George H. Blakeslee and Dr. Hugh Borton, a full year before the Potsdam Conference. F. C. Jones, Hugh Borton and B. R. Pearn, *Survey of International Affairs, 1939–1946: The Far East, 1942–1946* (London: Oxford University Press, 1955), p. 311n. For additional information on the history of the Potsdam Declaration see Herbert Feis, *Japan Subdued: The Atomic Bomb and the End of the War in*

Union was not at war with Japan when the Potsdam Declaration was issued, Russia had no voice in the forming of this historic document, which outlined Allied postwar policy for Japan. Fourteen days later, when Russia entered the war against Japan, she announced her support of the Potsdam principles. The issuance by the Western Allies of the Potsdam Proclamation independently of the Soviet Union foreshadowed the predominantly American character of the Occupation and ultimately a separate Western peace with Japan.

On August 11, 1945, shortly before Japan's final offer to surrender, the Soviet Foreign Minister suggested that there be two Allied supreme commanders in Japan: Marshal Vasilevski and General MacArthur. United States Ambassador Harriman protested that while the United States had been at war with Japan for over three and a half years, the Soviet Union had fought Japan only two days, and it was unthinkable that any but an American should be supreme commander in Japan.[2] Stalin later concurred with President Truman in the appointment of MacArthur as Supreme Commander, and on September 2, Allied and Japanese representatives signed the Instrument of Surrender aboard the *U.S.S. Missouri* in Tokyo Bay.

It was the United States that drew up General Order Number 1 which partitioned the Japanese Empire among the Allied Powers for accepting the surrender of Japanese forces.[3] Premier Stalin had asked that the U.S.S.R. be permitted to occupy southern Sakhalin and northern Hokkaido in addition to the areas already assigned to the Soviet Union. Truman agreed to the Soviet occupation of southern Sakhalin, but not of northern Hokkaido, thus preventing the Russian occupation of any part of the home islands of Japan. Truman had recently experienced Russian stubbornness concerning Germany, Poland, and the Balkans at the Potsdam Conference and was determined that he would "not allow the Russians any part in the control of Japan."[4]

The United States planned to have the deciding voice in the Occupation of Japan while the other Allies would be permitted only to air their views in the Far Eastern Advisory Commission. The Soviet

---

the Pacific (Princeton: Princeton University Press, 1961), pp. 15–27, and Department of State, *Foreign Relations of the United States, the Conference of Berlin (The Potsdam Conference) 1945* (2 vols.) (Washington: Government Printing Office, 1960), I, 884–903; II, 1265–1298.

[2] Feis, pp. 124–125.

[3] Text in Supreme Commander for the Allied Powers, Government Section, *Political Reorientation of Japan: September 1945 to September 1948*, 2 vols. (Washington: Government Printing Office, n.d. [1949?]), II, 423–436. These volumes will subsequently be cited as *Political Reorientation*.

[4] Harry S. Truman, *Memoirs.* Volume I: *Year of Decision* (Garden City: Doubleday, 1955), pp. 439–446.

Union, however, refused to participate in this Advisory Commission because of its purely consultative character. The Russians also declined an invitation to send Soviet occupation forces to Japan to serve under an American general. Japan was not divided into occupation zones to be administered by the different victorious Powers, as were Germany, Austria, and Korea. Instead, the Japanese homeland was occupied by American and British Commonwealth forces under the supreme command of a single American general. The nonparticipation of Russia and the overwhelming predominance of the United States in Japan were thus established from the beginning. The autocratic temperament of General Douglas MacArthur, Supreme Commander for the Allied Powers (SCAP), was to preserve and enhance the American predominance.

For four months, following the surrender ceremony, the victorious Powers were unable to agree on the organization of Allied control machinery for Japan. Thus General MacArthur was able to interpret and apply American interpretations of the Potsdam Declaration[5] largely as he saw fit.

General MacArthur served concurrently as Supreme Commander for the Allied Powers and as Commander-in-Chief, United States Army Forces, Pacific Area Command (C-in-C, AFPAC). In 1947, AFPAC became Far East Command (FEC). MacArthur had two Headquarters, one for SCAP and one for AFPAC. Each of the Headquarters had its own Chief of Staff and Assistant Chief of Staff. As of November, 1949, the following "SCAP Sections" existed: (1) Government Section, (2) Public Health and Welfare Section, (3) Office of the Civil Property Custodian, (4) Economic and Scientific Section, (5) Natural Resources Section, (6) Civil Transportation Section, (7) Statistics and Reports Section, (8) Adjutant General's Section, (9) Civil Information and Education Section, (10) Civil Intelligence Section, (11) Legal Section, (12) Civil Communications Section, and (13) Office of General Procurement Agent.[6] These Sections, staffed almost exclusively by American military and civilian personnel, issued directives to the Japanese Government for the enforcement of the Potsdam Declaration.

Because Japan had surrendered before the homeland was invaded,

[5] "U.S. Initial Post-Surrender Policy for Japan," in U.S. Department of State, *Occupation of Japan* (Washington: Government Printing Office, 1946), pp. 73–78, and *Political Reorientation*, II, 423–426. For the Australian attitude towards the establishment of Allied control organs see R. N. Rosecrance, *Australian Diplomacy and Japan, 1945–1951* (Melbourne: Melbourne University Press, 1962), pp. 10–56.

[6] Paul M. A. Linebarger, Chu Djang, and Ardath Burks, *Far Eastern Government and Politics: China and Japan,* 2nd ed. (Princeton: D. Van Nostrand, 1956), p. 453.

the Imperial Japanese Government (IJG) was intact and operating at the inception of the Occupation. Previous American plans for the establishment of military government in Japan (such as had been set up in Germany) were scrapped, and instead the Potsdam provisions were enforced by the Imperial Japanese Government under orders from SCAP. (The abbreviation SCAP was used to indicate either General MacArthur personally or his Headquarters generally.) SCAP written directives, known as SCAPIN's, were sent to the Central Liaison Office (CLO) of the IJG for implementation by the appropriate agency in the government. Often SCAP officials would suggest a program to Japanese officials, with the hint, stated or implied, that if the Japanese did not undertake the program on their own initiative a written SCAPIN would be forthcoming. Thus, it is frequently difficult to determine the precise extent of SCAP's role in specific postwar reforms. Following the termination of the Occupation on April 28, 1952, a spate of memoirs and exposés was published in Japan detailing the hitherto confidential relations between Japanese and American officialdom.

The Japanese government of the day would translate the SCAP order or suggestion into a bill which, after approval by SCAP, would be passed by the Diet, or the government might, when Diet approval would be too slow or uncertain, issue the SCAP-inspired measure in the form of an Imperial Ordinance (before May 3, 1947) or a Cabinet Order (after May 3, 1947). Some 520 such "Potsdam Ordinances" were issued by the government during the course of the Occupation. The conservative Governments of Shidehara and Yoshida were usually unenthusiastic about SCAP's reform policies and often sought to delay and water down their enforcement. After SCAP began to turn its back on reform in favor of political stability, economic recovery, and rearmament, the conservative second, third, fourth, and fifth Yoshida Cabinets proved quite cooperative. So-called military government teams attached to the U.S. Eighth Army in the prefectures were assigned the sole task of *reporting* to higher headquarters cases in which the SCAP policies were not being carried out. However, military government in the usual sense did not exist because of the SCAP procedure of working through the Imperial Japanese Government centered in Tokyo.

The United States could not indefinitely stave off British and Soviet demands for a greater voice in the Occupation. The December, 1945, meeting of Big Three Foreign Ministers in Moscow established a Far Eastern Commission (FEC) made up of eleven nations: Australia, Canada, China, France, India, the Netherlands, New Zealand, the Philippines, the Soviet Union, the United Kingdom, and the United States. Burma and Pakistan were added when they gained their independence. The Far Eastern Commission, meeting in Washington, would formulate Allied policy for the Occupation of Japan. It was intended that the Allied Council for Japan (ACJ), made up of China, the British Commonwealth, the United States, and the U.S.S.R., would advise SCAP and act as a watchdog for the Far Eastern Commission. Early in its existence, the American and Soviet representatives in the ACJ engaged in little else than propaganda and mutual vituperation, so that the Council had virtually no influence over the course of the Occupation.

The United States, like the United Kingdom, the U.S.S.R., and China, would enjoy the power to veto proposed decisions of the Far Eastern Commission. The United States also would have the power to issue interim directives to the Supreme Commander pending action by the Commission whenever urgent matters arose not already covered by the Commission's policies. However, "any directives dealing with fundamental changes in the Japanese constitutional structure or in the regime of control, or dealing with a change in the Japanese Government as a whole will be issued only following consultation and following the attainment of agreement in the Far Eastern Commission." Thus it would appear that constitutional reform in Japan could not be unilaterally carried out by American Occupation authorities. General MacArthur bitterly protested that he had not been consulted in setting up the Far Eastern Commission and the ACJ, which internationalized the Occupation.[7]

The "Japanese Bill of Rights"

The first great task of the Allied Occupation was to supervise the demobilization of over five million Japanese troops scattered throughout Manchuria, Korea, and Southeast Asia as well as Japan. The Emperor, on August 17, appointed his uncle, Prince Higashikuni, as Prime Minister so that the prestige of the imperial family would help to ensure an orderly surrender by the Army and Navy. On October 16, 1945, General MacArthur was able to announce that the Japanese Armed Forces throughout Japan had completed their demobilization and ceased to exist as such. These forces were "completely abolished."[8]

On October 4, MacArthur's Headquarters forwarded to the government a memorandum on "Removal of Restrictions on Political, Civil, and Religious Liberties (SCAPIN 93).[9] This directive, styled the "Japanese Bill of Rights" by SCAP officials, ordered the government to

[7] *Political Reorientation*, II, 744.
[8] *Ibid.*, II, 742.
[9] Text in *ibid.*, II, 463–465.

abrogate and suspend all laws and ordinances which maintained restrictions on freedom of thought, religion, assembly, and speech "including the unrestricted discussion of the Emperor, the Imperial Institution, and Imperial Japanese Government." All persons detained or imprisoned because of their thought, speech, religion, or political beliefs were to be released. All secret police organs and departments in the Home Ministry and the Police concerned with censorship and thought control were to be abolished. The Home Minister and the Chiefs of Metropolitan and Prefectural Police were to be dismissed.

The enforcement of the "Bill of Rights" seemed to be too difficult a task for the Higashikuni Cabinet, and it announced its resignation the following day.

On October 11, General MacArthur informed the new Prime Minister, Shidehara Kijūrō, "In the achievement of the Potsdam Declaration the traditional social order under which the Japanese people for centuries have been subjugated will be corrected." Specifically the reforms which MacArthur "expected" the government to institute were: (1) The emancipation of women by their enfranchisement, (2) the encouragement of the unionization of labor, (3) the opening of the schools to more liberal education, (4) the abolition of "systems which through secret inquisition and abuse have held the people in constant fear," and (5) the "democratization of economic institutions" by curbing monopoly and widening the distribution of income and ownership of the means of production and trade.[10] In close consultation with SCAP Headquarters, the Shidehara Government began drafting laws to enforce the sweeping social and political reforms demanded by Allied policy.

The ideological basis of ultranationalism and militarism had been the cult of the Throne, as elaborated by the state religion, Shinto. On December 15, 1945, SCAP Headquarters ordered that the state religion be disestablished.[11] SCAPIN 448 distinguished between State (or Shrine) Shinto, which was to be abolished altogether, and Sect Shinto, represented by thirteen officially recognized privately supported sects, which would be allowed to continue in existence. All financial support from public funds and all official affiliation with Shinto and Shinto shrines were to cease immediately. Private individuals would be permitted to contribute on a voluntary basis to the support of shrines hitherto maintained by the government. No Shinto doctrines could be taught in public-supported educational institutions. Shinto teachings would be deleted from public-school textbooks and teachers' manuals. "No official of the national, prefectural, or local govern-

[10] *Ibid.,* II, 741.
[11] SCAPIN 448, in *ibid.,* II, 467–469.

ment, acting in his public capacity" would be permitted to visit any shrine to report on his assumption of office or conditions of government or to participate as a representative of government in any Shinto ceremony or observance.

In addition to disestablishing the state religion, the SCAP directive also forbade the propagation by schools or any religious group of militaristic and ultranationalistic ideology. The forbidden ideology was defined as embracing teachings which advocate Japan's mission to rule over other nations by reason of the divine or special origin of the Emperor, the divine origin of the Japanese people, the divine origin of the Japanese islands, and any other doctrine which might delude the Japanese people into embarking on wars of aggression or which glorified the use of force as an instrument for the settlement of disputes with other peoples.

Two weeks after the Shinto directive, the Emperor, in his 1946 New Year's Message, stated that the ties between the Throne and the people had always stood on mutual trust and affection:

> They do not depend upon mere legends and myths. They are not predicated on the false conception that the Emperor is divine and that the Japanese people are superior to other races and fated to rule the world.[12]

The American-inspired Constitution of 1947 was intended to perpetuate the religious freedom introduced by SCAPIN 448. Article 20 of the new Constitution guaranteed freedom of religion to all and forbade the state from engaging in religious education or any other religious activity or giving privileges to any religious organization.

The Great Purge

The purpose of the purge was to remove and exclude from public office the leaders who had led Japan to ultranationalism and war and were therefore unfit to lead the nation in the paths of democracy and peace. On January 4, 1946, SCAP directed the Japanese government to plan for the removal and exclusion from office of persons who fell in the following categories: (A) those arrested as suspected war criminals, (B) commissioned officers in the Imperial Japanese Regular Army and Navy, commissioned and noncommissioned officers, enlisted men and civilians who had served in the Military or Naval Police or in secret intelligence, and high ranking civilians in the Ministry of War and Navy, (C) influential members of ultranationalistic, terroristic, or secret patriotic organizations, (D) persons influential in the activities of

[12] *Ibid.*, II, 470. See below, page 40, note 41.

the Imperial Rule Assistance Association and its related organizations, (E) officials of financial and development organizations involved in Japanese expansion, (F) governors of occupied territories, and (G) additional militarists and ultranationalists.[13]

The actual purge was administered by the Japanese government under the direction of SCAP. Holders and candidates for office of chokunin rank or higher were required to fill out comprehensive questionnaires in both English and Japanese (English version prevailing) concerning their past political activities and affiliations.[14] The purge ultimately involved the examination of literally millions of questionnaires and the purging of over 200,000 individuals. The enforcement of the purge was simplified by the fact that it was primarily an administrative rather than a judicial task. Individual motives and intentions were not delved into, so that while certain individuals may not have been in sympathy with the prevailing aims of the militaristic organization to which they had belonged, they were nonetheless automatically disqualified. Much of the confusion such as attended the administration of denazification in Germany was thus avoided.

SCAP's purge orders came in three waves. The first order (January, 1946) was concerned primarily with persons holding office in the central government, the second (January, 1947) was concerned with local and prefectural governments, information media, and business. The third important SCAP order came in the form of a letter from General MacArthur to Prime Minister Yoshida on June 6, 1950, in which he ordered the removal of the central committee of the Japan Communist Party from public office.[15] A short time later the purge of the editorial staff of the Communist newspaper *Akahata* was ordered. Of all the political leadership in Japan the Communists bore the least responsibility for Japan's aggressions, but they were resorting to violence to disrupt the Occupation.

Many prominent postwar politicians were disqualified from office at one time or another. Before becoming Prime Minister, Hatoyama, Ishibashi, and Kishi had been purged and depurged. Of the fifteen Cabinet Ministers who affixed their names to the Imperial Rescript promulgating the new Constitution, five were subsequently barred from office: Ōmura Seiichi, Uehara Etsujirō, Ishibashi Tanzan, Kanamori Tokujirō, and Zen Keinosuke.

The purge and depurge kept the political parties in constant turmoil, as the purge status of party leaders was a crucial factor in fac-

---

[13] SCAPIN 550, in *ibid.*, II, 482–488. *Ibid.*, 482–564, includes SCAPIN's and government ordinances from 1946 to 1948 relating to the purge.

[14] A copy of the questionnaire is given in *ibid.*, II, 486–488.

[15] Hans Baerwald, *The Purge of Japanese Leaders under the Occupation* (Berkeley and Los Angeles: University of California Press, 1959), p. 19.

tional politics. It was widely believed that the purge of some individuals, such as Hirano Rikizō, was politically motivated. The case of Hatoyama Ichirō was the most sensational. As president of the Liberal Party, which won a plurality of seats in the 1946 lower house election, Hatoyama was about to be recommended to the Emperor for the prime ministership by the outgoing premier. On the eve of Hatoyama's appointment, however, General MacArthur issued a formal directive (SCAPIN 919, May 3, 1946) banning Hatoyama from office because his past praise of Hitler's labor policies and Tanaka's foreign policy, among other things, meant that he fell under the vaguely worded Category G of the January 4 directive.[16]

Opinions vary as to the effect of the purge. It worked a hardship on many innocent individuals. It is said that "political bias had affected the work of the screening committees, slowing the progress of democracy and damaging the prestige of the Occupation."[17] As the Occupation policies became more conservative, a depurge was in full swing, and with the end of the Occupation, SCAP directives no longer applied. The application of the purge to Communists at a time when reactionaries were being depurged suggested that the policy had become a weapon of the Cold War. Nevertheless, the purge helped to clear the way for new leadership.[18]

The Tokyo War Crimes Trial

The Potsdam Declaration had provided that "stern justice shall be meted out to all war criminals," and the Allies agreed that the major Japanese war criminals would be tried by an international court. The International Military Tribunal for the Far East (IMTFE) was composed of eleven justices, one from each of the powers represented on the Far Eastern Commission. The principal charge against the twenty-eight "class A" war criminals was the commission of "crimes against the peace." The indictment included numerous violations of international law on the part of Japan for which the suspects were held responsible. As in the case of the Nuremberg trial, which received much more attention in Europe and America, there were controversial legal questions as to the responsibility of individuals for state acts.

The court met almost daily from May 3, 1946, to November 12, 1948. Matsuoka and Nagano died during the trial; Ōkawa was declared insane and not tried. All twenty-eight defendants save Ōkawa,

16 *Political Reorientation,* II, 494–495.
17 Harold S. Quigley and John E. Turner, *The New Japan: Government and Politics* (Minneapolis: University of Minnesota Press, 1956), p. 109.
18 Kazuo Kawai, *Japan's American Interlude* (Chicago: University of Chicago Press, 1960), p. 95.

an ultranationalist philosopher, had held high government and military offices. Among them were:

Prime Ministers: Hirota, Hiranuma, Tōjō, Koiso
Foreign Ministers: Hirota, Matsuoka, Tōgō, Shigemitsu
War Ministers: Minami, Araki, Itagaki, Hata, Tōjō
Navy Ministers: Nagano, Shimada
Finance Minister: Kaya
Education Ministers: Kido, Araki
Home Ministers: Hiranuma, Kido, Tōjō
Overseas Ministers: Koiso, Tōgō
Greater East Asia Ministers: Shigemitsu, Tōgō
Presidents, Planning Board: Hoshino, Suzuki
Ministers Without Portfolio: Hiranuma, Hoshino, Suzuki
Chiefs of Army General Staff: Tōjō, Umezu
Lord Keeper of the Privy Seal: Kido
President, Privy Council: Hiranuma
Ambassadors: Ōshima, Shiratori, Shigemitsu, Tōgō[19]

All were found guilty. Seven, including former Prime Ministers Hirota Kōki and Tōjō Hideki, were hanged, sixteen committed to prison for life, and two given shorter prison terms.[20] After his release from prison, Shigemitsu Mamoru became President of the Progressive Party (1952) and Foreign Minister in the three Hatoyama Cabinets.

There was much criticism that the Emperor was not indicted and tried. The reason usually given was that the Emperor was not constitutionally responsible in the Japanese system — he was simply a figurehead, and in spite of his personal views he had to do as his advisers told him. It was widely believed that the Americans spared the Emperor because his authority was necessary for administering the country and because his indictment might arouse popular opposition to the Occupation.

The Democratization of the Economy

In December, 1945, SCAP directed the government to initiate a land reform to end the many abuses of absentee landownership. Before the war, 46 per cent of the cultivated land was farmed by tenants.[21] Of the total number of farmers, 70 per cent were nonowners of part or all of the land that they tilled. Twenty-eight per cent of the

---

[19] Solis Horwitz, "The Tokyo Trial," *International Conciliation,* No. 465 (November, 1950), p. 497.
[20] Kawai, p. 22.
[21] SCAPIN 441, *Political Reorientation,* II, 575–576.

farmers owned no land at all.[22] Under the land reform program carried out under the supervision of MacArthur's staff, owners of land who were not themselves cultivating it were required to sell the land to the government in exchange for bonds. The government resold the land to tillers who paid for it in annual installments. The monetary inflation during the early Occupation meant that the purchasers bought their land very cheaply. Locally elected land commissions assisted in the administration of the program. By the end of 1950, only 10 per cent of the farm land was cultivated by tenants, while 90 per cent was cultivated by owners.[23] The land reform seems to have proved the most durable of the accomplishments of the Occupation.[24]

In order to end the control of the great monopolies over the Japanese economy, SCAP Headquarters ordered the dissolution of the Mitsui, Yasuda, Sumitomo, and Mitsubishi (Iwasaki) holding companies in the fall of 1945. A Holding Company Liquidation Commission was set up to take over the securities of the monopolies and resell them to the general public. Before the program had gotten well under way, however, American policy shifted from reform to recovery. Financial circles in the United States were highly critical of zaibatsu dissolution, and by 1949 it was feared that the economic disorganization which it would entail could sabotage the economic rehabilitation of Japan just when the Cold War was becoming more intense. The reform legislation was permitted to lapse, and before the Occupation was over the prewar forms of financial and corporate organization again predominated.[25]

The Allied policy of encouraging the unionization of labor had startling results. At the end of the war, unions were virtually nonexistent in Japan; in October, 1945, there were only six labor unions with a total of 3,866 members. Under SCAP stimulus, by October, 1946, 15,172 unions claimed a membership of 4,168,305.[26] The new unions rapidly fell under extreme leftist leadership and began to carry out political strikes. In order to check Communist labor leaders, General MacArthur at the eleventh hour issued an order calling off a general strike scheduled for February 1, 1947, which would have paralyzed the Japanese economy and possibly overthrown the Yoshida Government.

In the face of a new labor offensive in 1948, MacArthur's Head-

---

[22] *Agriculture in Japan* (Tokyo: Japan FAO Association, 1958), p. 53.
[23] *Ibid.,* p. 55.
[24] Hugh Borton, *Japan's Modern Century* (New York: Ronald, 1955), p. 417.
[25] Borton, p. 418.
[26] Oka Yoshitake, ed., *Gendai Nihon no Seiji Katei* [*The Course of Contemporary Japanese Politics*] (Tokyo: Iwanami Shoten, 1959), p. 10.

quarters directed the Ashida Cabinet to issue an ordinance denying the right of all government employees — national or local — to bargain collectively or to resort to strikes. The ordinance was later embodied in amendments to the National Public Service Law.[27] Since most of the railroads as well as communications systems were government owned, the number of workers denied the right to strike was substantial. The change of SCAP policy from strengthening unions to weakening them increased the militancy of the Communists and at the same time strengthened the hands of the more moderate labor leaders.

By 1949, it was evident that the Occupation had shifted its emphasis from democratic reform to defense against Communism.

First Efforts to Revise the Japanese Constitution

The Potsdam Declaration had called for the establishment of a "peacefully inclined and responsible government" in accordance with the "freely expressed will of the Japanese people." On October 4, 1945, General MacArthur strongly urged Prince Konoye Fumimaro, "Vice-Premier" of the Higashikuni Cabinet, to take the leadership in liberalizing the Japanese Constitution. Although Prince Konoye was not a member of the succeeding Shidehara Cabinet, on October 11 he obtained a commission from the Emperor to investigate "whether the Constitution needed revising and if so to what extent."[28]

Mr. George C. Atcheson, Jr., SCAP's Political Adviser, and three State Department people in Tokyo had a number of private conferences with Konoye and his advisers and indicated points in the Japanese Constitution which the Americans felt needed revision.[29] Although there was considerable agitation among the victorious Powers for the abolition of the Japanese monarchy, Mr. Atcheson did not demand the elimination of the Emperor system, but rather outlined democratic reforms which would make possible the retention of the throne.

During the period of the Atcheson-Konoye conversations, Mr. At-

[27] Evelyn S. Colbert, *The Left Wing in Japanese Politics* (New York: Institute of Pacific Relations, 1952), p. 272.

[28] Dr. Takagi Yasaka, a close associate of Konoye, gives a brief, authoritative account in English of Konoye's activities in connection with constitutional revision in *Toward International Understanding* (Tokyo: Kenkyūsha, 1945), pp. 114–123. See also Theodore McNelly, "Domestic and International Influences on Constitutional Revision in Japan, 1945–1946," (Columbia University doctoral dissertation, 1952, published on microfilm by University Microfilms, Ann Arbor, Michigan), Chapter II.

[29] Mr. Atcheson's advice to the Japanese is summarized in *Political Reorientation*, I, 91, and Takagi, p. 115n.

cheson, on October 17, received the following very important instructions from Secretary of State Byrnes:

There should be assurance that the Japanese Constitution is amended to provide for Government responsible to an electorate based upon wide representative suffrage. Provision should be made that executive branch of Government derive its authority from and be responsible to the electorate or to a full representative legislative body.

If Emperor institution is not retained constitutional safeguards against that institution will obviously not be required but provision should be made for (1) complete control by an elected congress of financial and budgetary matters, (2) guarantee of fundamental civil rights to all persons within Japanese jurisdiction, not repeat not to Japanese only, and (3) action by head of state only pursuant to authority expressly delegated to him.

If Emperor is retained following safeguards in addition to those enumerated above would be necessary: (1) a cabinet to advise and assist the Emperor should be chosen with advice and consent of and responsible to representative legislative body, (2) no repeat no vote [veto?] over legislative measures should be exercised by other bodies such as House of Peers or Privy Council, (3) Emperor should be required to initiate amendments to constitution recommended by cabinet and approved by legislative body, (4) legislative body should be permitted to meet at will, and (5) any ministers for armed forces which may be permitted in the future should be civilians and all special privileges of direct access to throne by military should be eliminated.[30]

The instructions left open the question of whether the Emperor was to be retained or not. The provision concerning "armed forces which may be permitted in the future" is notable because later General MacArthur was to insist that the Constitution renounce war and armed forces.

There was a widespread feeling among the Allies that Konoye, because of his alleged war guilt, should not direct constitutional revision in Japan. Furthermore, the office of the Lord Privy Seal, with which Konoye was connected, was not responsible to either the Diet or the Cabinet, so that there was no democratic basis for Konoye's efforts. It is said that the parleys of the American State Department people in Japan with Prince Konoye angered the Supreme Com-

[30] The State Department kindly permitted the present author to quote the three relevant paragraphs above, which make up part of the instructions of October 17. The instructions to Atcheson corresponded in spirit with the suggestions which he was giving the Konoye group, but there seem to have been variations in detail.

mander, and he directed them to cease communicating with Konoye. SCAP Headquarters on November 1 announced that MacArthur had not chosen Konoye to reform the Japanese Constitution.[31]

Prince Konoye and his advisers nevertheless continued their investigations and made reports to the Emperor late in November. Konoye advocated the alteration of the Constitution to strengthen the Diet but not to destroy the principle that sovereignty resided in the Emperor.[32] In December, SCAP Headquarters indicted Konoye as a war criminal, and he committed suicide just before being arrested by the Americans. Konoye's efforts to revise the Constitution, like his efforts to bring about a peace earlier in 1945, were primarily intended to preserve the Japanese throne.

In October, just as Konoye was beginning his investigations, General MacArthur directed the new Shidehara Cabinet to reform Japan's system of government. This would, he insisted, "unquestionably involve the liberalization of the Constitution."[33] However, Premier Shidehara publicly stated that it was unnecessary to alter the text of the Imperial Constitution in order to achieve democracy. He believed, as did many conservatives, that suitable legislation enacted by the Diet, such as laws expanding the franchise and the like, would be sufficient.[34] In response to MacArthur's prodding, Shidehara appointed a committee of scholars and bureaucrats headed by Minister of State Matsumoto Jōji to investigate "whether the Constitution needed to be revised and if so to what extent."[35] The Matsumoto group was very lukewarm toward any substantial changes in the Constitution, and

[31] *Political Reorientation* (I, 91n) states that, as a result of one interview with MacArthur and one interview with Atcheson, Konoye made the "unwarranted assumption that MacArthur had personally charged him with the work of revision of the Constitution, whereas in fact he was being spoken to not only in the most general terms, but merely as a responsible member of the Japanese Cabinet." However, nearly all of the Atcheson-Konoye conversations were held when Konoye was no longer a member of the Cabinet.

[32] The Konoye outline was published in the *Mainichi Shimbun* in late December, 1945, and is reproduced in Satō Isao, *Kempō Kaisei no Keika* [*The Progress of Constitutional Revision*] (Tokyo, 1947), pp. 275–277. English translation in McNelly, *op. cit.,* pp. 382–386. A more authentic Japanese version, together with the draft Constitution recommended to the Emperor by Dr. Sasaki, was published by the Commission on the Constitution in 1958.

[33] *Political Reorientation,* II, 741.

[34] *Yomiuri,* October 13, 1945, cited by Satō Isao, p. 31.

[35] An authoritative account in English of the work of the Matsumoto Committee is given by Satō Tatsuo, "The Origin and Development of the Draft Constitution of Japan," *Contemporary Japan,* vol. XXIV, Nos. 4–6, 7–9, 1956.

only toward the end of December did they actually decide to draft concrete proposals for revision.

The MacArthur Draft Constitution

On January 7, 1946, a few days after the decision of the Moscow Conference to establish the Far Eastern Commission, the State-War-Navy Coordinating Committee (SWNCC), composed of representatives of the Departments of State, War, and Navy in Washington, drew up a policy on "The Reform of the Japanese Governmental System." The purpose of the paper, usually designated SWNCC-228, was to "determine the constitutional reforms which the Occupation authorities should insist be carried out in Japan." On January 11 the paper was forwarded to MacArthur for his "information," but the phraseology made it clear that the United States government expected the Supreme Commander to carry out the policies contained in the paper.

The fourteen-page SWNCC document included the provisions of the State Department instructions to Atcheson of October 17 quoted above and a scholarly "Discussion" which analyzed the defects of the Imperial Constitution of 1889 and revealed the thinking behind the proposed revision. SWNCC-228 specified that "The Japanese should be encouraged to abolish the Emperor system or reform it along more democratic lines." However, "Only as a last resort shall the Supreme Commander order the Japanese Government to effect the above listed reforms, as the knowledge that they have been imposed by the Allies would materially reduce the possibility of their acceptance and support by the Japanese people for the future."

On January 30, the Far Eastern Advisory Commission (the predecessor of the Far Eastern Commission) visited MacArthur in Japan. The General indicated to the members that he was not then taking action on constitutional reform because the Moscow Agreement of December, which set up the FEC, had deprived him of authority in the matter. He said that he hoped the Constitution would be reformed in such a way that the Japanese would regard the resulting document as a Japanese product. A constitution imposed by bayonets, he said, could not outlast the Occupation.[36]

In January and February, 1946, the newly organized Liberal and Progressive Parties were advocating constitutional amendments to enhance the powers of the Diet without altering the principle that sovereignty resided in the Emperor. The Social Democrats advocated the principle that sovereignty resides in the state, while political au-

[36] Blakeslee, p. 44.

thority would be divided, the more important part being assigned to the Diet and a part being assigned to the Emperor.[37] The Communists demanded the trial of the Emperor as a war criminal and advocated the establishment of a Japanese People's Republic.

Cabinet Minister Matsumoto and his committee on constitutional reform began to work overtime, and on February 1 the *Mainichi Shimbun* published a version of the very conservative Matsumoto proposals.[38]

The Matsumoto group, unlike the Konoye group, had failed to get American advice before embarking on its investigation. General MacArthur found the Matsumoto proposals unacceptable because they were too reactionary. On February 3, he directed his Government Section to prepare immediately a constitution to serve as a "guide" for the Shidehara Cabinet as "the most effective method of instructing the Japanese government on the . . . principles he considered basic."[39]

The Supreme Commander directed that the "guide" provide that the Emperor be "at the head of the state" and that his powers be "exercised according to the will of the people." The draft was also to state that

> War as a sovereign right of the nation is abolished. Japan renounces it as an instrumentality for settling its disputes and even for preserving its own security. It relies upon the higher ideals which are now stirring the world for its defense and its protection.
>
> No Japanese Army, Navy, or Air Force will ever be authorized and no rights of belligerency will ever be conferred upon any Japanese force.[40]

Apparently the ban on war and arms had been originally suggested to MacArthur by Prime Minister Shidehara on January 24, 1946,[41] and was incorporated in the draft Constitution as a result of

[37] Japanese texts of Liberal, Progressive and Socialist party outlines are found in Satō Isao, pp. 274–297. English translations in McNelly, *op. cit.,* pp. 387–403.

[38] Japanese text in Satō Isao, pp. 281–288. English translation in *Political Reorientation,* II, 611–616.

[39] A rather frank account of the origins of the SCAP draft Constitution is contained in *Political Reorientation,* I, 101–112.

[40] The text of MacArthur's famous "Three Points" is given in *ibid.,* I, 102. The lawyers in Government Section did not include "even for preserving its own security" in their draft of February 13, 1946, nor did this phrase appear in subsequent versions.

[41] See Courtney Whitney, *MacArthur: His Rendezvous with History* (New York, 1956), pp. 257–258, and letter of General MacArthur to Dr. Takayanagi, Chairman of the Commission on the Constitution, December 10, 1958. Evidence exists to the effect that the no-war clause was suggested by

the General's enthusiastic advocacy. Such a provision had nowhere figured in the October 17 instructions to Atcheson, SWNCC-228, or the informal Matsumoto proposals. Indeed, all of these plans clearly contemplated the possible re-establishment of the armed forces. Although the documentary instructions from Washington to the Supreme Commander which have been cited leave open the question of fate of the Emperor, MacArthur could not remove the Emperor without the consent of the Joint Chiefs of Staff. Whether or not the final decision to retain the throne was made by General MacArthur, the preservation of the Emperor was his "fixed purpose."[42]

The Government Section worked in extreme secrecy between February 4 and 10 to produce its draft Constitution.[43] On February 13, 1946, General Courtney Whitney, Chief of Government Section, presented the draft Constitution to members of the Japanese Cabinet with the understanding that if they did not accept its essential principles, MacArthur would present it over their heads to the Japanese people. Whitney also said that if the Cabinet refused to adopt the principles of the MacArthur Constitution, the Americans could not guarantee "the person of the Emperor."[44]

Dr. Matsumoto felt strongly that General Whitney brought up the question of the "person of the Emperor" as a threat to indict the Emperor as a war criminal if the Japanese did not accept the American draft.[45] It seems certain, however, that Whitney intended no such

---

Shidehara as a means of preserving the Emperor system. (Commission on the Constitution, *Twenty-fourth General Meeting, January 21, 1959*.) It is said that Shidehara had drafted the Emperor's New Year's Rescript of January 1, 1946, primarily in order to make the Emperor more acceptable to Allied opinion. In that famous Rescript the Emperor renounced his divinity.

[42] Letter of General MacArthur to Dr. Takayanagi, of December 5, 1958. The "Basic Initial Post-Surrender Directive to the Supreme Commander for the Allied Powers for the Occupation and Control of Japan," of November 7, 1945, had stated, "You will not remove the Emperor or take any steps towards his removal without prior consultation with and advice issued to you through the Joint Chiefs of Staff." *Political Reorientation*, II, 429–439.

[43] The original mimeographed text of the Whitney draft Constitution, as presented to the Japanese Cabinet on February 13, 1946, was published in *Kokka Gakkai Zassi (The Journal of the Association of Political and Social Sciences)*, vol. LXVIII, No. 1 (September, 1945), p. 2, and in *Contemporary Japan*, vol. XXIV, Nos. 4–6 (1956), pp. 188–199.

[44] Satō Tatsuo, "Nihon Kempō Seiritsushi" ["History of the Formulation of the Japanese Constitution"], *Jurisuto*, No. 82. See also Satō Tatsuo, *Nipponkoku Kempō Tanjōki [Record of the Birth of the Japanese Constitution]* (Tokyo, 1957).

[45] Statement of the late Dr. Matsumoto to Liberal Party Constitution Investigation Committee, July 7, 1954. Other Japanese at the meeting did not

threat at all — he simply meant to advise the Japanese on what they would have to do to save the Emperor in the light of the objective situation. The trial of the Emperor as a war criminal and the abolition of the throne were widely advocated among the Allies. There was much criticism that the American Occupation of Japan was too soft toward the aggressors in World War II. Furthermore United States policy, expressed both in the October 17 instructions to Atcheson and in SWNCC-228, demanded that either (1) the throne be eliminated or (2) the prerogatives of the Emperor be greatly curtailed.

MacArthur had stoutly resisted Russian and Australian efforts to try the Emperor as a war criminal. He believed that if the Emperor were indicted, at least one million reinforcements would be needed in Japan, and military government would have to be set up throughout the whole country.[46] The Emperor had personally helped to bring about the Japanese surrender without the need for an Allied invasion of the Japanese homeland, and for the past five months the Emperor's government had been obediently enforcing American directives.

On February 21, MacArthur explained the situation in the FEC to Premier Shidehara. He reportedly complained that the FEC and its policies were making his position very difficult and he did not know how much longer he could remain at his post. He said that there was no essential difference between the Japanese and American draft constitutions. The purpose of the American draft, he asserted, was to preserve the Emperor. The Supreme Commander also emphasized the importance of constitutional disarmament in the light of international opinion.

The Cabinet was afraid that if it did not adopt the SCAP draft, the Far Eastern Commission might force it to adopt a republican constitution abolishing the throne.[47] Cabinet members also feared that if they did not accept the MacArthur draft, SCAP Headquarters would publish it and the newspapers would approve it. In this case, the Shidehara Cabinet might be forced to resign and a Cabinet which

---

interpret Whitney's statements in the same manner as Dr. Matsumoto. General Whitney does not refer to such a "threat" in his account of the famous February 13 meeting, although he mentioned "atomic sunshine." (Whitney, pp. 250 et seq.) General Whitney's letter to the Commission on the Constitution makes it clear that he had no intention of threatening to put the Emperor on trial. The Americans pursued humanitarian policies in Japan, he pointed out, rather than the harsh — even brutal — policies advocated by some Allied governments.

[46] Whitney, p. 284.

[47] Commission on the Constitution, *Fifth General Meeting, November 6, 1957*, p. 30.

supported the MacArthur Constitution would come into being. Politics in Japan would then veer sharply to the left.[48]

In response to much urging from both the Cabinet and the American side, Minister of State Matsumoto prepared an adaptation of the American draft and brought it to SCAP Headquarters on March 4. After Dr. Matsumoto's departure, Government Section officials suddenly insisted that final Japanese and English versions be prepared immediately for approval by higher authorities. There ensued, on March 4 and 5, a hectic 36-hour overnight session of Japanese and American officials to produce a text acceptable to the Americans. The final document conformed very closely to the original Government Section draft in both essentials and nonessentials. The most important of the concessions to Japanese views was that the Diet would consist of two chambers rather than of only one. The proposed Constitution would deprive the Emperor of all of his prerogatives and vest sovereignty in the people. It was replete with New Deal philosophy and was more radical than any of the proposals of the leading parties except the Communist. It reduced the Emperor's role to that of "the symbol of the State and of the unity of the people."

On the afternoon of March 5, Headquarters forwarded ten copies of the final English version to the Cabinet together with an inquiry as to whether or not the Cabinet would accept it before the day was over. If the Cabinet chose not to accept the draft, the American-proposed Constitution would be made public in the evening. It seemed to the Japanese officials that if the American side published the draft, the Japanese side could not very well avoid publishing it too. Late in the day Mr. Shidehara and his colleagues reached the decision that there was no alternative left but to adopt the draft Constitution as it then was.

In the evening, when the Prime Minister showed the proposed Constitution to the Emperor, his Majesty said he supposed that there was no other course, but hoped that it would be possible to preserve the court nobility and the imperial prerogative relative to the revision of the Imperial House Law. Nevertheless, Cabinet Ministers feared possible domestic and international repercussions if the draft were altered, and no action was taken on the Emperor's comments.

An hour or two later, Premier Shidehara told his Cabinet:

> We are making an extremely grave commitment in accepting such a Constitution as this. Perhaps this commitment will also bind our posterity. When this draft is made public, some will applaud and others will keep silence. The latter will undoubtedly be highly

[48] Commission of the Constitution, *Seventh General Meeting, December 4, 5, 1957*, p. 75.

indignant at bottom towards us. However, I believe that we are following the only possible course in view of the situation confronting us.[49]

Some ministers wiped tears from their eyes.

On March 6, 1946, the Cabinet published the American-inspired Constitution as its own proposal and made public an imperial rescript indicating the Emperor's approval of the democratic principles of the draft and implying that the Shidehara Government had drawn up the proposal on his orders. General MacArthur also published his "emphatic approval" of the document.

An "Induced Revolution"

The Far Eastern Commission was now faced with the *fait accompli* of a draft Constitution publicly approved by the Japanese Cabinet, the Emperor of Japan, and the Allied Supreme Commander. SCAP and Secretary of State James Byrnes maintained the thesis that the Japanese had originated the idea, that they had a perfect right to democratize their form of government, and that the Supreme Commander was only encouraging them in the laudable enterprise. Some members of the Far Eastern Commission were extremely indignant and felt strongly that MacArthur had exceeded his authority and infringed on the powers of the FEC in the matter of reforming the Japanese Constitution.[50] However, their position was weak because the American veto power in the Commission could prevent it from adopting policies opposed by the United States. Furthermore, the Commission was not empowered to deal with SCAP directly. It communicated its policies to the American State Department, which, through the Joint Chiefs of Staff, informed MacArthur. The Far Eastern Commission demanded that the Supreme Commander point out to the Japanese people that his approval of the draft Constitution did "not preclude favorable consideration of other proposals or drafts which may be submitted to the Diet for study and comparison."[51]

During the critical food shortage of May, 1946, a series of leftist-

[49] *Ibid.*, pp. 75 *et seq.*

[50] *Ibid.*, p. 405. The running controversy between MacArthur and the FEC over their respective powers concerning constitutional revision is detailed in Blakeslee, pp. 43–65.

[51] Text in *Political Orientation*, II, 658. In the same policy statement the FEC also expressed its desire that the Supreme Commander inform the Japanese government that the Commission would have to pass on the final draft of the Constitution to determine whether it was consistent with the Potsdam Declaration before it could be acted on by the Diet or become finally valid.

led mass demonstrations in Tokyo induced General MacArthur to issue a public "Warning Against Mob Disorder and Violence."[52] The Supreme Commander had been initially instructed by the United States government not to intervene in any efforts by the Japanese people to change their form of government by force, unless the security of Allied forces was endangered.[53] Nevertheless, he abhorred the thought of civil war in Japan,[54] and it was clear that any change in Japan's form of government would have to come about through nonviolent methods.

In July the Americans in the Far Eastern Commission were able to persuade the Commission to adopt the points contained in SWNCC-228 as FEC's "Basic Principles for a New Constitution."[55] The Communists were the only political party to oppose MacArthur's draft Constitution. They continued to advocate the trial of the Emperor as a war criminal, and the establishment of a Japanese People's Republic.[56] The Japanese Communists had an ally in the FEC: the Soviet representative, who also opposed the MacArthur Constitution.[57]

Conservatives in the Diet expressed fears that the draft Constitution would impair the traditional "national polity" (kokutai) by transferring sovereignty from the Emperor to the people.[58] It was also feared that the no-arms clause would endanger Japan's security. However, Diet members seemed to believe that the passage of the democratic Constitution was necessary to bring an early end to the Allied Occupation and approved the draft Constitution by nearly unanimous majorities.

The Australians and others in the Far Eastern Commission believed that the new Constitution was not an expression of the free will of the Japanese people.[59] In October, 1946, the Commission adopted a policy providing that both the Diet and the FEC "review the situation with respect to the Constitution" between May 3, 1948, and May 3, 1949, and that the Commission might require a referendum or other procedure to ascertain Japanese opinion on the Constitution.[60] But General MacArthur, always reluctant to recognize the prerogatives of the international body, did not inform the Japanese government of this

[52] Text in *Political Reorientation,* II, 750.

[53] "U.S. Initial Post-Surrender Policy for Japan," cited in note 5.

[54] Whitney, pp. 246–247.

[55] Text in *Political Reorientation,* II, 661.

[56] Text of Communist draft Constitution appears in Satō Isao, pp. 297–311.

[57] Blakeslee, p. 58.

[58] The Diet debate on the draft Constitution is described in Harold S. Quigley and John E. Turner, *The New Japan* (Minneapolis: University of Minnesota Press, 1956), pp. 127–163.

[59] Blakeslee, p. 58.

[60] *Political Reorientation,* II, 668.

policy until the Commission threatened to make the policy public.[61] The Diet did not formally review the Constitution during the specified period, nor was any plebiscite held. Japanese officials and the Supreme Commander felt that to review the Constitution under foreign pressure would undermine its prestige.

The struggle over the drafting and adoption of the Japanese Constitution may be regarded as a three-way affair. The conservative Japanese officials strove to preserve the imperial institution essentially unchanged. The Americans, both in Tokyo and in Washington, endeavored to preserve and reform the throne as a basis for stability and democracy. International communism, represented by the Japan Communist Party and the Soviet Union, sought to abolish the throne and establish a Japanese People's Republic.

SUGGESTED READINGS

Baerwald, Hans H. *The Purge of Japanese Leaders under the Occupation.* Berkeley and Los Angeles: University of California Press, 1959. Written by an American official directly connected with the purge.

Ball, W. Macmahon. *Japan: Enemy or Ally?* New York: The John Day Co., 1949. From a Commonwealth point of view.

Bisson, T. A. *Prospects for Democracy in Japan.* New York: The Macmillan Company, 1949.

Bisson, T. A. *Zaibatsu Dissolution in Japan.* Berkeley: University of California Press, 1954.

Blakeslee, George H. *A History of the Far Eastern Commission.* Washington: U.S. Department of State, Publication 5138, Far Eastern Series 60, 1953. On the formulation of Allied policy for the Occupation of Japan.

Borton, Hugh. *Japan's Modern Century.* New York: The Ronald Press Company, 1955. The author was closely associated with the formulation of American policy for the Occupation of Japan.

Brines, Russell. *MacArthur's Japan.* Philadelphia: J. B. Lippincott, 1948. Informed.

Dore, Ronald P. *Land Reform in Japan.* New York: Oxford University Press, 1959.

Fearey, Robert. *The Occupation of Japan: The Second Phase, 1948–1950.* New York: The Macmillan Company, 1950.

[61] FEC policy decision of December 6, 1946, in *ibid.*, p. 678. MacArthur's letter to Prime Minister Yoshida of January 3, 1947, in *ibid.*, p. 681.

Gayn, Mark. *Japan Diary*. New York: William Sloane Associates, 1948. Critical of SCAP's Occupation policies.

Hall, Robert King. *Education for a New Japan*. New Haven: Yale University Press, 1949. The author was an official in the Occupation.

Haring, Douglas G. *Japan's Prospect*. Cambridge: Harvard University Press, 1946. On the preparation for the Occupation.

Ito, Nobutaka. *New Japan: Six Years of Democratization*. Tokyo: The Peace Study Group, 1951.

Jones, F. C., Hugh Borton, and B. R. Pearn. *The Far East, 1942–1946*. London: Oxford University Press, 1955. Detailed.

Kawai, Kazuo. *Japan's American Interlude*. Chicago: University of Chicago Press, 1960. As an editor of the *Nippon Times* during the Occupation the author was exceedingly well informed on the effectuation of American policy.

Martin, Edwin M. *The Allied Occupation of Japan*. New York: American Institute of Pacific Relations, 1948. From an official point of view.

Montgomery, John D. *Forced to be Free*. Chicago: University of Chicago Press, 1957. Concerns the purges in Japan and Germany.

SCAP, Government Section. *The Political Reorientation of Japan*. Washington: Government Printing Office, (1949?), 2 vols. Authoritative. Contains a vast number of relevant documents.

Textor, Robert B. *Failure in Japan*. New York: John Day Co., 1951. Critical of American Occupation policies.

Whitney, Courtney. *MacArthur: His Rendezvous with History*. New York: Alfred A. Knopf, Inc., 1956. Contains information unavailable elsewhere; eloquently defends MacArthur's policies.

Wildes, Harry Emerson. *Typhoon in Tokyo: The Occupation and Its Aftermath*. New York: The Macmillan Company, 1954. Critical of MacArthur's policies. Contains many illuminating insights and suggestions.

❀ 3 ❀

The Throne and Popular Sovereignty

The Tennōsei

The Emperor in History

The usual title of the Japanese Emperor, Tennō (Heavenly Sovereign), was sometimes used by Chinese Emperors and is written with the same Chinese characters. In ancient times, it was common for the Chinese monarchs to claim divine ancestry, and it is not surprising that the Japanese ruler, of alleged similar lineage, should adopt a comparable title. Important princes who paid tribute to the Chinese Emperor were customarily entitled Wang (in Japanese, Ō). Thus the Korean king was a Wang. In 1897, when he wished to assert the independence of his kingdom against Chinese and Japanese claims of overlordship, he assumed the new title of Emperor, equal to that of the Chinese and Japanese monarchs, and set up a temple for his use in the worship of Heaven.

Whether during the ancient period, the feudal era, or the modern period of successively oligarchical, parliamentary, and military ascendancy, the Japanese Emperor has reigned but seldom ruled. Article I of the Meiji Constitution stated that Japan shall be "reigned over and governed by a line of Emperors," but in fact His Majesty had for centuries served as the titular chief executive rather than as the effective chief executive. Although reactionaries and Communists have asserted that the Emperor system (Tennōsei) is incompatible with democracy, the recent history of Japan seems to indicate that both oligarchy and democracy are possible with an Emperor at the head of the state. The Emperor, with extremely few exceptions, has not made any important political decisions in the past 750 years. He invariably

48

follows the advice of the effective government of the time, and that government must bear the brunt of responsibility for whatever decision has been made. The Emperor, therefore, has long been a constitutional monarch who can do no wrong.

The National Polity

According to the "orthodox" interpretation of the Meiji Constitution, such as that advanced by Hozumi Yatsuka and Uesugi Shinkichi, that part of the state system arising from location of sovereignty was the national polity (kokutai), and that part of the state system arising from the manner of the exercise of sovereignty was the form of government (seitai). The national polity was monarchical or republican depending upon whether sovereignty reposed in the monarch or the people. The form of government was constitutional or absolute depending upon whether there was separation of powers or concentration of powers. The essence of the state lay in the location of sovereignty. Although the manner of the exercise of sovereignty (the form of government) might be changed, the location of sovereignty (the national polity) might not be legally changed. So far as Japan was concerned, it might be legally permissible to alter the Cabinet or the Diet, which were matters related to the form of government, but it was absolutely not possible to alter the principle of imperial sovereignty, since that was a matter related to the national polity. The orthodox theory maintained that the principle that sovereignty rested with the Emperor was eternal and unchangeable, that is, "co-extensive with the Heavens and with the Earth."[1]

The Peace Preservation Law of 1925 forbade, among other things, advocating the alteration of the national polity. In interpreting this law, the Japanese Supreme Court (Taishin-in) defined kokutai as the principle that the Emperor, of a line unbroken for ages eternal, reigns and exercises sovereignty in Japan. Defined in this sense, kokutai was not a criterion for the analysis of state systems; rather it represented the peculiar characteristic of the Japanese Constitution, the idea that Japan, unique among the nations of the world, was blessed with a divine Throne and line of sovereigns which were unalterable.

In the mid-1930's, ultranationalists advocated a "Showa Restoration" which would remove the corrupt politicians from the government and restore direct rule by the Emperor. At the same time, militarists and reactionary politicians demanded a "clarification of the national polity." Professor Minobe Tatsukichi, of Tokyo Imperial University, who had long expounded the theory that the Emperor was an "organ

[1] Yamazaki Tanshō, *Tennōsei no Kenkyū* (Tokyo: Teikoku Chihō Gyōsei Gakkai, 1959), pp. 389–390.

of the state,"[2] was attacked as disloyal and forced to resign from the House of Peers. The narrow interpretation of kokutai, which held that the Emperor was sacred and ruled by mandate of his divine ancestors, became the official ideology of the state and was taught in the schools.[3] Democracy, socialism, and communism alike were held to be subversive of Japan's unique national polity. At the same time, the "Imperial Way" (Kōdō) and the theory of "Eight corners of the world under one roof," based on Shinto scriptures, were cited by statesmen to justify Japanese militarism and expansion. The Emperor system, thus exploited to justify totalitarianism and aggression, was understandably suspect in the minds of foreign observers as a rallying point of Japanese militarism.

Japan's Surrender and the Emperor System

The Potsdam Declaration

With the surrender of Germany in May, 1945, America turned her full attention to the defeat of Japan. It was hoped in Washington that the Japanese might be induced to surrender without the need for sending a huge Allied invasion force onto the mainlands of Japan to be met by fanatical defenders. A modification of the unconditional surrender formula was apparently in order. On May 8, President Truman issued a statement to the effect that if the Japanese submitted to the American demand for an unconditional surrender they would not be destroyed as a nation or condemned to prolonged suffering. This declaration did not include in it the promise, urged by Acting Secretary of State Joseph Grew, that unconditional surrender would not mean the elimination of the existing dynasty. The presidential statement was scornfully rejected by Japanese spokesmen, but Grew continued to advocate a declaration of our terms and a clarification of the American policy towards the Emperor in order to induce a Japanese surrender. Grew believed that Japanese alarm lest the revered imperial institution be destroyed would deter the Japanese from giving up the struggle and that unless this fear was quieted and they were able to save face they would fight to the bitter end. Furthermore, if after victory we should ban the imperial institution, the Japanese would try to restore it, and the effort would prevent resignation to defeat and reconciliation with the United States. In any case, Grew felt that a constitutional monarchy might be the most suitable form

[2] Minobe Tatsukichi, *Kempō Satsuyō,* 5th ed. (Tokyo: Yūhikaku, 1935), *passim.*

[3] An English translation of the basic textbook is Robert K. Hall, ed., *Kokutai no Hongi: Cardinal Principles of the National Entity of Japan,* trans. J. O. Gauntlett (Cambridge: Harvard University Press, 1949).

of government for Japan.[4] On May 28, following several great super-fortress raids on Tokyo, Grew submitted to the President a statement of our terms which he advocated be announced. This draft was to go through a number of versions before finally emerging as the Potsdam Proclamation.[5] The State, War, and Navy Secretaries all concurred in the need for issuing the kind of statement advocated by Grew, but for various reasons they decided to delay it until the summit conference of the Allied leaders in Potsdam, Germany.

There were some in the State Department who opposed the views of the Acting Secretary concerning the Japanese Emperor system. They held that the Emperor cult had enabled a coalition of aggressive military and civilian groups to control the Japanese people and to lead them to aggression and that to allow the system to survive would be to court danger for the future. Furthermore, they felt that it would be unjust and illogical to eliminate and punish other elements responsible for leading Japan into war and at the same time spare the Emperor.[6]

When the new Secretary of State, James Byrnes, left for Potsdam, early in July, he took with him a draft declaration which contained the following stipulations with regard to the future of the Japanese Emperor system:

> The occupying forces of the Allies shall be withdrawn from Japan as soon as these objectives [designated in other sections] have been accomplished and there has been established a peacefully inclined, responsible government of a character representative of the Japanese people. This may include a constitutional monarchy under the present dynasty if the peaceloving nations can be convinced of the genuine determination of such a government to follow policies of peace which will render impossible the future development of aggressive militarism in Japan.[7]

It was understood that the President would choose the time to issue the declaration after learning when the Russians were going to enter the war against Japan and the outcome of the first atom bomb test in New Mexico.

Before leaving Washington, Secretary Byrnes consulted former Secretary of State Cordell Hull about the advisability of issuing the pro-

[4] Herbert Feis, *Japan Subdued: The Atomic Bomb and the End of the War in the Pacific* (Princeton: Princeton University Press, 1961), p. 17.

[5] U.S. Department of State, *Foreign Relations of the United States, Diplomatic Papers: The Conference of Berlin (The Potsdam Conference)*, 2 vols. (Washington: Government Printing Office, 1960), I, 884–903.

[6] The views of Assistant Secretary of State Archibald MacLeish are set forth in *ibid.*, I, 895–897. Cf. also, Feis, p. 25.

[7] Feis, p. 26.

posed declaration. Hull pointed out that the paragraph which intimated that the Japanese would be allowed to preserve the Emperor and the monarchy would create serious differences if issued "now" and asked whether it would not be well to await the climax of allied bombing and Russian entry into the war.[8]

On July 18 at Potsdam, Admiral William D. Leahy sent Truman a memorandum indicating the view of the Joint Chiefs of Staff that from "a military point of view" the proposed proclamation was "generally satisfactory." However, the Joint Chiefs felt that the provision permitting Japan to retain "a constitutional monarchy under the present dynasty" should be clarified. The phrase might be misconstrued by extreme devotees of the Emperor as a commitment by the United Nations to depose or execute the present Emperor and install some other member of the Imperial Family. To the radical elements in Japan, the phrase might be interpreted as a commitment to continue the institution of the Emperor and Emperor worship. The Joint Chiefs therefore recommended that the passage in question be deleted and the following text substituted: "Subject to suitable guarantees against further acts of aggression, the Japanese people will be free to choose their own form of government."

Leahy's memorandum concluded, "From a strictly military point of view the Joint Chiefs of Staff consider it inadvisable to make any statement or take any action at the present time that would make it difficult or impossible to utilize the authority of the Emperor to direct a surrender of the Japanese forces in the outlying areas as well as in Japan proper."[9] When the Proclamation was finally issued at Potsdam on July 26, 1945, it made no clear commitment concerning the Emperor system. It stated: "The occupying forces of the Allies shall be withdrawn from Japan as soon as these [elsewhere stated] objectives have been accomplished and there has been established in accordance with the freely expressed will of the Japanese people a peacefully inclined and responsible government."

The Surrender

In the meantime, a peace movement in Japan had gained great impetus among the narrow circles of the Emperor's advisers in January and February, 1945, when the jūshin (former Prime Ministers) each singly had audiences with the Emperor, and many, but not all, urged an early termination of the war. The most interesting remarks were those of Prince Konoye, who emphasized the threat of Communism in a defeated Japan. "From the standpoint of maintaining

---

[8] U.S. Department of State, op. cit., II, 1267.
[9] Ibid., II, 1268–1269; Feis, p. 69.

Japan's imperial system, that which we have most to fear is not defeat itself but, rather, the threat inherent in the possibility that a Communist revolution may accompany defeat." He cited the subversive and aggressive activities of the Soviet Union in eastern Europe and the economic radicalism of much of the Japanese Army, many of whom, he said, thought that Communism was compatible with the Emperor system. He believed that Communists were at the bottom of the agitation to fight to the bitter end.[10] The Suzuki Government attempted without success to persuade the Soviet Union to receive a special mission headed by Prince Konoye in order to arrange Soviet mediation to end the Pacific War.

On July 28 Suzuki announced to the Japanese press that the Japanese Government had found nothing of important value in the Potsdam Declaration and that there was no other recourse but to ignore it entirely and resolutely fight for the successful conclusion of the war. This statement was interpreted by the Allies as an official rejection of the Potsdam "ultimatum." An atom bomb was dropped on Hiroshima on August 6 and on Nagasaki three days later. On August 8, the Soviet Government rejected a Japanese bid for Soviet mediation to end the war and declared war on Japan.

There was wide disagreement within the Suzuki Cabinet as to whether the Potsdam Proclamation should now be accepted, and if so with what reservations. Foreign Minister Tōgō Shigenori was a staunch advocate of peace, and urged that Japan accept the Proclamation "on the understanding that it did not include any demand for a change in the status of the Emperor under the national laws." At an Imperial Conference (Gozen Kaigi) of August 9, 1945, at which the Emperor was present, Baron Hiranuma Kiichirō, President of the Privy Council, said that Tōgō's phraseology did violence to the national polity by subordinating the Emperor to "national laws," and urged that the phrase be amended to "on the understanding that the Allied proclamation would not comprise any demand which would prejudice the prerogatives of His Majesty as a Sovereign Ruler."[11] War Minister Anami Korechika adamantly opposed surrender unless three additional conditions were added: that the Japanese forces be allowed to disarm and demobilize themselves, that there be no Allied occupation of Japan, and that all war criminals be prosecuted by the Japanese Government itself.

The Cabinet was hopelessly divided on the issue of peace. Under

[10] The Konoye "Memorial" is summarized in Robert J. C. Butow, *Japan's Decision to Surrender* (Stanford: Stanford University Press, 1954), pp. 47–50.

[11] Butow, p. 173.

normal circumstances a Cabinet so divided on a basic issue would resign, but a resignation of the Suzuki Government at so crucial a juncture in the international situation was unthinkable. Premier Suzuki,
who favored peace, had organized the Imperial Conference with the
deliberate intent of getting the Emperor to throw his weight on the
side of surrender. After a prolonged discussion, Suzuki bluntly asked
the Emperor, "Your Imperial Majesty's decision is requested as to
which proposal should be adopted . . . " The Emperor stated that end-
ing the war was the only way to restore world peace and to relieve the
nation from the terrible distress with which it was burdened.[12]

With the positive backing of the Emperor, it was possible for the
Suzuki Cabinet to make a decision for peace despite the opposition of
the Army. The Japanese government on August 10 issued a statement
to the United States indicating Japan's willingness to accept the Potsdam
terms "with the understanding that the said declaration does not comprise any demand which prejudices the prerogatives of His Majesty
as a Sovereign Ruler."

Admiral Leahy, the President's chief of staff, urged a prompt acceptance of the Japanese proposal, for he was convinced that it would
be necessary to use the Emperor in effecting the surrender.[13] Secretary
of War Stimson also urged a reply that would make clear that the
Japanese could retain the Emperor.[14] Secretary of State Byrnes,
however, was mindful of the policy of Roosevelt and Churchill that
the surrender should be unconditional, and conscious that it was need-
ful to consult the other Allies before modifying the Potsdam terms.[15]

The Byrnes reply to the Japanese offer to surrender included the
statements, "From the moment of surrender the authority of the Emperor and the Japanese Government to rule the state shall be subject
to the Supreme Commander of the Allied Powers who will take such
steps as he deems proper to effectuate the surrender terms. . . . The
ultimate form of government of Japan shall, in accordance with the
Potsdam declaration, be established by the freely expressed will of the
Japanese people." Thus the question of the Emperor system was left
in abeyance. The original Byrnes draft had included a provision that
the Emperor personally would be required to sign the surrender terms,
but this clause was dropped on the suggestion of the British.

The Japanese Cabinet was again badly split on the question of
whether to accede to Allied surrender terms. Foreign Minister Tōgō
favored acceptance, but Prime Minister Suzuki was inclined to reject
the Byrnes proposal since it did not explicitly accept the Japanese
condition concerning the Emperor. The Emperor favored immediate

[12] *Ibid.*, p. 176.   [13] *Ibid.*, p. 190.   [14] Feis, p. 120.
[15] *Ibid.*, pp. 122, 123.

peace and obtained the support of the imperial princes for this policy. At the Imperial Conference on August 14, the Emperor indicated that he agreed with the Foreign Minister that the Potsdam Declaration was not intended to subvert the national polity, and said, "unless the war be brought to an end at this moment, I fear that the national polity will be destroyed and the nation annihilated."[16]

All accounts agree that Emperor Hirohito's decision for peace was decisive in overcoming the opposition of the military to making peace. Never before in modern times had the Emperor taken a crucial part in the policy-making process. The Japanese made their definitive offer to surrender on August 14.

The Japanese Foreign Office believed that the national polity was not impaired by the surrender. The Emperor's surrender rescript of August 15, 1945, included the statement, "Having been able to safeguard and maintain the structure of the Imperial State [kokutai, the national polity], we are always with ye, our good and loyal subjects, relying upon your sincerity and integrity."

Following the surrender, there were persistent rumors that the Emperor would abdicate or that he would be tried as a war criminal. An abdication would have necessitated a regency, since Crown Prince Akihito was not yet of age. The Emperor first visited General MacArthur on September 27, 1945, and reportedly said, "I come to you, General MacArthur, to offer myself to the judgment of the Powers you represent as the one to bear sole responsibility for every political and military decision made and action taken by my people in the conduct of the war."[17] MacArthur was greatly impressed by this fine attitude on the part of His Majesty, but nevertheless did not order his indictment as a war criminal. To do so might provoke popular disturbances against the Occupation. Chief Prosecutor Joseph B. Keenan held that the Emperor was not considered guilty of participating in the "criminal conspiracy" for which the original panel of twenty-eight high-ranking Japanese went on trial. The head British prosecutor, Sir Arthur Comyns Carr, asked in his summation why the Emperor, who could stop the war in 1945, was unable to prevent it four years earlier. The Japanese answer was that he was permitted by tradition to vote for surrender because a deadlock had arisen in high circles; but opinion had been unanimous in favor of starting hostilities so he was "required" to remain silent.[18] Presumably, the American attitude towards Emperor Hirohito personally was influenced by the basic decision to use

[16] *Ibid.,* p. 130.

[17] Courtney Whitney, *MacArthur: His Rendezvous with History* (New York: Knopf, 1956), p. 286.

[18] Russell Brines, *MacArthur's Japan* (Philadelphia: Lippincott, 1948), p. 95.

the Throne as a basis of control and democratization. It would be undesirable to destroy the prestige of the Throne by submitting its occupant to severe indignities.

The New Constitution

As elsewhere noted, the position of the Emperor and the problem of the national polity were central issues in the enactment of the new Constitution as they had been during the surrender negotiations. It was widely held that the principle of popular sovereignty ran contrary to the national polity, which vested the power to rule ultimately in the Emperor, and that it was highly undesirable, if not illegal, to amend the Constitution to provide that sovereignty resides in the people rather than the Emperor. On the day the new Constitution came into effect, Shimizu Chō, constitutional advisor to the Emperor and Chairman of the Privy Council which approved the Constitution, drowned himself at Atami. His suicide note, among other things, said, "I have decided to die so that I from the spiritual world may help to protect our national polity and wish the safe-being of His Majesty."[19]

Popular Sovereignty in the New Constitution

From Divine Right to Popular Sovereignty

The fundamental difference between the old Constitution and the new is that the former was based upon the principle that the Emperor rules by divine right while the latter is based upon the principle of popular sovereignty.

In the Preamble to the Constitution of the Empire of Japan (1889) the Emperor Meiji declared, "The rights of sovereignty of the State, We have inherited from Our Ancestors, and We shall bequeath them to Our descendants."[20] Article I of the same Constitution provided that "The Empire of Japan shall be reigned over and governed by a line of Emperors unbroken for ages eternal," and Article IV stated, "The Emperor is the head of the Empire, combining in Himself the rights of sovereignty, and exercises them, according to the provisions of the present Constitution."

The new Constitution is a revolutionary document, for it signifies the transfer of sovereignty from the Emperor to the people. The Preamble of the Constitution of Japan (1947) states, "We, the Japanese people, . . . do proclaim that sovereign power resides with the

[19] Kanamori Tokujirō and Yamaura Kan-ichi, eds., *Nihon Seiji Hyakunen Shi* [*History of One Hundred Years of Japanese Politics*] (Tokyo: Jiji Shimpō Sha, 1953), p. 457.

[20] Text in Itō Hirobumi, *Commentaries on the Constitution of the Empire of Japan* (Tokyo: Insetsu Kyoku, 1889), pp. ix–xi.

people." Government is "a sacred trust of the people, the authority for which is derived from the people, the powers of which are exercised by the representatives of the people, and the benefits of which are enjoyed by the people. This is a universal principle of mankind upon which this Constitution is founded."

The Emperor no longer inherits authority from his divine ancestors, but, according to Article 1 of the new Constitution, derives his position "from the will of the people with whom resides sovereign power." There was no popular referendum in Japan concerning the retention of the monarchy such as was held in Italy in June, 1946. The will of the people to keep the Emperor was expressed by the enactment of the new Constitution by the people's representatives in the Diet. Presumably the Throne could be abolished in the future by simply amending the new Constitution.

Amendment Procedure

One of the most distinctive attributes of sovereignty is the constituent power, i.e., the authority to enact and amend the Constitution. The Emperor Meiji, on his own authority as occupant of a "Throne of a lineal succession unbroken for ages eternal," promulgated the 1889 Constitution as "a fundamental law of the State."[21] The Meiji Constitution was known as the *kintei kempō,* a "Constitution granted by the Emperor." Under Article LXXIII of that basic law, the Constitution was amended when a project to that effect was submitted to the Diet by Imperial Order and two-thirds of those present (two-thirds of the whole number of members had to be present) in each House passed the project. Only the Emperor possessed the power of initiating constitutional amendments. According to Prince Itō, "the right of making amendments to the Constitution must belong to the Emperor Himself, as he is the sole author of it."[22] Actually, until 1946, no serious effort was made to amend the Meiji Constitution, since it was almost universally regarded as perfect.

Under the new Constitution, the people, rather than the Emperor, exercise the constituent power. "We, the Japanese people, acting through our duly elected representatives in the National Diet, . . . do firmly establish this Constitution."[23] Amendments to the new Constitution are initiated by the Diet, through the concurring vote of two-thirds or more of all the members of each house, and then submitted to the voters for ratification, which requires the affirmative vote of a majority of the votes cast.[24]

The amendment process in Japan differs greatly from that in Great

[21] Constitution of the Empire of Japan, Preamble.
[22] Itō, p. 140.   [23] Constitution, Preamble.
[24] Constitution, Article 96.

Britain, which also has a parliamentary-cabinet system. In Britain, which is without a written constitution, there is no formal distinction between constitutional amendments and other laws. The Parliament, which is said to be sovereign, may amend the British constitution by following the usual procedure for enacting ordinary laws. In Japan, it is much more difficult for the Diet to change the Constitution. Two-thirds majorities are necessary in both houses, and the voters must also give their approval. Thus, even though majorities in both houses and a majority of the people want an amendment, it can be blocked by a minority of one-third in either house. In recent years, the Liberal-Democrats have devoted much attention to revising the Constitution, but they have been prevented from so doing by the Socialist minority in both houses. Because of the relative difficulty of the amendment process, it may be said that Japan's basic law is an example of a rigid constitution.

The constituent power passed from the Emperor to the people as a result of Japan's surrender to the Allies on September 2, 1945. Article 12 of the Potsdam Declaration, which the Japanese agreed to carry out, provided that the occupying forces of the Allies would be withdrawn when there had been established "in accordance with the freely expressed *will of the Japanese people* a peacefully inclined and responsible government [italics added]." Whether the Emperor had the legal right to alienate his constituent authority by means of an international agreement (i.e., the Instrument of Surrender) is a difficult question for experts in constitutional and international law. The procedure used to adopt the 1947 Constitution was to consider the new document as an amendment of the Meiji Constitution and enact it under the terms of Article LXXIII of the old basic law.

The "Symbol of the State"

The Functions of the Emperor

The Meiji Constitution had provided that "The Empire of Japan shall be reigned over and governed by a line of Emperors unbroken for ages eternal,"[25] that "The Emperor is sacred and inviolable,"[26] and that "The Emperor is the head of the Empire, combining in Himself the rights of sovereignty, and exercises them according to the provisions of the present Constitution."[27]

The new Constitution radically altered the theoretical status of the Emperor. "The Emperor shall be the symbol of the State and of the unity of the people, deriving his position from the will of the people

[25] Constitution of the Empire of Japan [1889], Article I.
[26] *Ibid.,* Article III.   [27] *Ibid.,* Article IV.

with whom resides sovereign power."[28] "The advice and approval of the Cabinet shall be required for all acts of the Emperor in matters of state, and the Cabinet shall be responsible therefor."[29] "The Emperor shall perform only such acts in matters of state as are provided for in this Constitution and he shall not have powers related to government. . . ."[30] Thus, the Emperor no longer rules by divine right but rather his reign is based upon the principle of popular sovereignty. He is now a constitutional monarch in theory as well as fact. It appears that the term "symbol of the State" may have been suggested by the British Statute of Westminster (1931) which provides that the British monarch is the symbol of the British Commonwealth.

Although the Emperor "does not have powers related to government," and therefore does not make political decisions, the Constitution requires him to perform specified formal duties, or "acts in matters of state" *with the advice and approval of the Cabinet.* Article 7 lists these functions:

[1] Promulgation of amendments of the constitution, laws, cabinet orders and treaties.

[2] Convocation of the Diet.

[3] Dissolution of the House of Representatives.

[4] Proclamation of general election of members of the Diet.

[5] Attestation of the appointment and dismissal of Ministers of State and other officials as provided for by law, and of full powers and credentials of Ambassadors and Ministers.

[6] Attestation of general and special amnesty, commutation of punishment, reprieve, and restoration of rights.

[7] Awarding of honors.

[8] Attestation of instruments of ratification and other diplomatic documents as provided by law.

[9] Receiving foreign ambassadors and ministers.

[10] Performance of ceremonial functions.

The Governance of the Imperial House

Under the terms of the Meiji Constitution, the Imperial House Law of 1889[31] which determined succession to the Throne, enjoyed higher

[28] The Constitution of Japan [1947], Article 1.   [29] *Ibid.,* Article 3.
[30] *Ibid.,* Article 4.
[31] Text in Supreme Commander for the Allied Powers, Government Section, *Political Reorientation of Japan: September 1945 to September 1948,* 2 vols. (Washington: Government Printing Office, n.d. [1949?]), II, 590–593. (These volumes will subsequently be referred to as *Political Reorientation.*) Also in Harold S. Quigley, *Japanese Government and Politics* (New York: Century, 1932), pp. 344–352; Itō Hirobumi, *Commentaries on the Constitution of the Empire of Japan* (Tokyo: Insetsu Kyoku, 1889), pp. 155–167.

status than ordinary statutes; it could not be repealed or altered in any way by the Imperial Diet. Only the Emperor, with the advice of the Imperial Family Council and the Privy Council, could amend this law. The Emperor did not depend upon parliamentary mandate for his position as did the Kings of England under the Act of Settlement (1701).

Under the new Constitution, however, the Imperial Throne is "succeeded to in accordance with the Imperial House Law *passed by the Diet* [italics added]."[32] The changed procedure for the enactment of the Imperial House Law exemplifies the shift from divine right to popular sovereignty. The Imperial Family has lost its autonomy. The new Imperial House Law[33] passed by parliament came into effect in 1947 simultaneously with the new Constitution.

The Imperial House Law, Kōshitsu Tempan, defines membership in the Imperial Family and Imperial House Council and provides for succession and the establishment of regencies. The Imperial Family was substantially reduced in size in 1947, when eleven princely families were relegated to the status of commoners. The Imperial Family consists of (1) the Empress, (2) the Grand Empress Dowager, (3) Shinnō, (4) the consorts of Shinnō, (5) Naishinnō, (6) Ō, (7) the consorts of Ō, and (8) Jo-ō. Shinnō (Imperial Princes) are legitimate sons and grandsons of an Emperor in the legitimate male line; Naishinnō (Imperial Princesses) are legitimate daughters and grand-daughters of an Emperor in the legitimate male line. Ō (Princes) are legitimate male descendants of an Emperor in the third and later generations in the legitimate male line; and Jo-ō (Princesses) are legitimate female descendants of an Emperor in the third and later generations in the legitimate male line. The Emperor and the members of the Imperial Family are not permitted to adopt children. The marriage of any male member of the Imperial Family must be passed by the Imperial House Council.

In ancient times the principles of succession were vague, save for the point that the claimant to the Throne must be a descendant of the Sun Goddess, and the death of an Emperor was as often as not the starting signal for a succession war. In the fourteenth century a dispute between the Southern and Northern Courts extended over several generations and threw the entire country into chaos. In the eighth century the reigning Empress Shōtoku became enamored of a Buddhist monk and was on the point of transferring her authority to him when an oracle asserted that the Throne could be occupied only by the descendants of Amaterasu. Since then only two women have ever

[32] The Constitution of Japan, Article 2.
[33] Text in *Political Reorientation*, II, 846–848.

been permitted to inherit the Throne. Under the Imperial House Laws of 1889 and 1947, there is no provision for female succession.

The Imperial House Law of 1947 provides that "the Imperial Throne shall be succeeded to by a male offspring in the male line belonging to the Imperial Lineage." The order of succession to the Imperial Throne within the Imperial Family is as follows: (1) the eldest son of the Emperor, (2) the eldest son of the Emperor's eldest son, (3) other descendants of the eldest son of the Emperor, (4) the second son of the Emperor and his descendants, (5) other descendants of the Emperor, (6) brothers of the Emperor and their descendants, (7) uncles of the Emperor and their descendants. If there is no member of the Imperial Family falling in any of the above categories, the Throne is passed to the member of the Imperial Family next nearest in lineage, precedence being given to the senior member of the senior line. The son of the Emperor who is the Imperial Heir is called Kōtaishi, and if there is no Kōtaishi, the grandson of the Emperor who is Imperial Heir is called Kōtaison. The Imperial Council may change the order of succession in case the Imperial Heir is affected with an incurable and serious disease or there is a serious hindrance. The Imperial Heir accedes immediately to the Throne upon the demise of the Emperor.

During the ascendancy of the Fujiwara, child Emperors occupied the Throne while their Fujiwara grandparents ruled as regents. Upon attaining majority, the Emperors almost immediately abdicated, so that regency was the rule rather than the exception during the Heian period. The mental incapacity of the late Emperor Taishō made necessary in 1921 a regency headed by Crown Prince Hirohito. The Imperial House Laws of 1889 and 1947 made no provision for abdication.

A Regency is established when the Emperor has not come of age (the Emperor comes of age at eighteen) or when the Emperor is affected with a serious disease or there is a serious hindrance to his performance of acts in matters of state. The Regency is established by decision of the Imperial House Council. Regents today must be members of the Imperial Family of age according to the following order: (1) Kōtaishi or Kōtaison (Imperial Heir), (2) Shinnō or Ō, the order of succession to the Throne applying, (3) the Empress, (4) the Grand Empress Dowager, and (6) a Naishinnō or Jo-ō.

The Imperial House Council is composed of ten members: two members of the Imperial Family, the Presidents and Vice-Presidents of the House of Representatives and of the House of Councillors, the Prime Minister, the head of the Imperial House Agency, the Chief Judge and one other judge of the Supreme Court. The Imperial Family members are chosen by election within the Imperial Family, and the judge other than Chief Judge by the judges of the Supreme

Court. Provision is made for reserve members. The Prime Minister presides over the meeting of the Imperial House Council.

The Imperial House Council of today is very different from the Imperial Family Council provided for in the old Imperial House Law. The former Imperial Family Council was composed of male members of age of the Imperial Family. It was presided over by the Emperor personally or a member of the Imperial Family delegated by him. The Lord Keeper of the Privy Seal, the President of the Privy Council, the Minister of the Imperial Household, the Minister of Justice, and the President of the Court of Cassation took part in the deliberations. Under the present system, the members of the Imperial Family are a tiny minority in the Imperial House Council, and may be outvoted by the representatives of the executive, legislative, and judicial branches of the government.

The Imperial House Council determines the exceptions from the usual order of succession to the Throne or Regency by two-thirds majority, and other questions by majority. The Council makes decisions respecting marriages of male members of the Imperial Family and the loss of membership in the Imperial Family.

The Office of the Lord Privy Seal was abolished in November, 1945, and the Imperial Household Ministry went out of existence when the new Constitution became effective. Neither the Lord Privy Seal nor the Imperial Household Minister was a member of the Cabinet, they were not responsible to the Diet, and they constituted very powerful, albeit thoroughly undemocratic, influences in the executive. Their functions have in large measure been taken over by the Imperial House Agency (Kunai-chō) which was established by the Imperial House Agency Law of April 18, 1947.[34]

The Imperial House Agency is under the jurisdiction of the Prime Minister. It has charge of state affairs relating to the Imperial House and the Emperor's acts in matters of state provided for by government ordinance. The Imperial House Agency also has custody of the Imperial Seal and the Seal of State. The personnel of the Agency include a Grand Steward, a Vice Grand Steward, a Private Secretary to the Grand Steward, a Grand Chamberlain, Chamberlains, a Master of Ceremonies, Secretaries of the Imperial House Agency, and technical officials.

The Finances of the Imperial House

Before the Pacific War, the Imperial House owned great tracts of land and large blocks of stock in leading financial and industrial institu-

[34] Text in *Political Reorientation*, II, 960.

tions. The Emperor was thus closely linked with the zaibatsu. In February, 1947, 3,330,000,000 yen of the total property of the Emperor, then amounting to 3,740,000,000 yen, was taken by the state as property tax.

Article 88 of the new Constitution provides that "All property of the Imperial Household shall belong to the State" and that "All expenses of the Imperial Household shall be appropriated by the Diet." Furthermore, no property can be given to or received by the Imperial House, nor can any gifts be made therefrom, without the authorization of the Diet.[35] Thus the Throne has lost the financial independence which it had enjoyed before the war, when it owned property and received a fixed income from the National Treasury which could not be reduced by the Diet.[36] The appropriation for the Imperial House is included in the budget and allocated according to the provisions of the Imperial House Economy Law,[37] other laws, and decisions of the Imperial House Economy Council and Imperial House Agency.

The Imperial House Economy Law provides that the budget appropriation for the Imperial House be divided into (1) the Inner Court Appropriation, (2) the Imperial Court Appropriation, and (3) the Imperial Family Appropriations. The Inner Court Appropriation applies to the daily expenditures of the Emperor, Empress, Grand Empress Dowager, Empress Dowager, Kōtaishi and his consort, Kōtaison and his consort, and other Imperial Family members belonging to the Inner Court. The Inner Court Appropriation is determined by law separately from other sums. It is the Privy Purse and is not administered by the Imperial House Agency. The Imperial House Economy Council may recommend a change in the Inner Court Appropriation to the Cabinet, which must report the recommendation to the Diet.

The Imperial Court Appropriation applies to all expenditures of the Court other than those of the Inner Court and is administered by the Imperial House Agency. The Imperial Family Appropriations are in the nature of annuities for members of the Imperial Family and payments to members of the Imperial Family who lose their status as members, made at the time that they leave the Imperial Family.

The Imperial House Economy Council is composed of eight members: the Presidents and Vice-Presidents of the two houses of the Diet, the Prime Minister, the Minister of Finance, the Head of the Imperial House Agency, and the Head of the Board of Audit.

[35] The Constitution of Japan, Article 8.
[36] The Constitution of the Empire of Japan, Article LXVI.
[37] Text in *Political Reorientation,* II, 849–850.

The Emperor Today and Tomorrow

The Imperial Family

The peerage created by Prince Itō in the 1880's is "not recognized" in the new Constitution, and there is no longer a House of Peers. The only official aristocracy remaining is the Imperial Family. The members of the former nobility have lost much of their influence and wealth. Few of their daughters could afford to play tennis, and the Crown Prince Akihito, who favors the sport, fell in love with and married the tennis-playing daughter of a businessman in the flour industry.

The first session of the Imperial House Council was held under the terms of the new Imperial House Law in October, 1947. The Council sanctioned the decision of fifty-one Princes and Princesses of eleven princely households to renounce their membership in the Imperial Family and become commoners. Today, the Imperial Family as formally defined is possibly the smallest it has been in history. It includes only the families of the Emperor and his three brothers, Princes Chichibu, Takamatsu, and Mikasa. The present Emperor (b. 1901) and Empress (b. 1903) have had two sons and five daughters, one of whom died in infancy and one of whom died in 1961. The remaining three daughters are no longer members of the Imperial Family since they are married to "commoners," although actually their husbands are members of high-ranking former nobility.

The present Emperor, Hirohito, is number 124 in a line of Emperors (and reigning Empresses), of whom the first sixteen are mythological. While Crown Prince, Hirohito made a trip to Europe visiting leading statesmen and royalty. He ascended the throne in 1926 after serving as Regent for five years on behalf of his demented father, Emperor Taishō. His hobby is marine biology, and newspaper photographs sometimes show him peering through a high-powered microscope. He has published several books on the marine life in Sagami Bay, and is credited with having discovered a number of new species.

During his lifetime the Emperor is referred to as Tennō Heika (His Majesty the Emperor), and after he dies he will be referred to as the Shōwa Emperor (Shōwa Tennō), since Shōwa (Enlightened Peace) is the name of his reign. In Japan, the name of the reign is used for designating years, so that 1963 in the Western system of reckoning is referred to as Shōwa 38.

Crown Prince Akihito, eldest son of the present monarch, was born in 1933. As a boy he attended the Peers School (Gakushūin) and was tutored during the Allied Occupation by Mrs. Elizabeth Vining, an American Quaker. In 1953 he represented the Emperor at the coronation of Queen Elizabeth II and toured Europe and America. He created a sensation in 1959 when he married a commoner in violation of all historical precedent. The "love match" symbolized the right of young people in postwar Japan to choose their own mates. The Crown Princess, *née* Shoda Michiko, is a young lady of unusual poise, charm, and intelligence who majored in English literature at the College of the Sacred Heart in Tokyo. In 1960, the couple was blessed with male progeny, Prince Hiro, so that the succession to the Throne seems well assured. In the same year, the Crown Prince and Princess visited the United States, Ethiopia, Iran, Nepal, and India.

The Future of the Emperor System

The decision of the American Occupation authorities to preserve but reform the monarchy in Japan represented a compromise among conservative, moderate, and radical views on the Throne which prevailed among the Allied Powers and the Japanese people. The new status of the Emperor shocked conservative legal theorists and pious Shintoists, but conservative peasants and villagers, baffled by academic debates about the national polity, were reassured to see that the Emperor, to all appearances, still held a prominent position in the state structure. Communists and some Socialists continue to regard the Throne with suspicion, but have on the whole discreetly refrained from making a frontal attack on the institution which would only result in increasing their unpopularity. The symbolic status of the Emperor is a *modus vivendi* which has thus far prevented the issue of the Throne from bedeviling the political life of the country — there is no Monarchist Party as in today's Italy and there is no Republican Party, albeit the Marxists are suspect. Substantive political issues have not been rendered insoluble nor has political stability been undermined by the injection of this constitutional issue.

Nevertheless, it must be said that the question of the national polity remains highly controversial, and the political leadership, both conservative and radical, is keenly conscious of the fundamental importance of the Throne in the ideological struggle. In Western countries, the Church has served as a basis for traditional morality and social harmony, but in Japan the moral influence exerted by Buddhism and Christianity is relatively weak. The familistic morality is based on Confucianism and ancestor worship. The Japanese state has traditionally been regarded as an enlarged family or clan, headed by the Emperor as its benevolent patriarch. Civil and military officials derived pride from exercising authority delegated to them by the Emperor. The obedience of the lower orders of the population to those higher in the hierarchy was regarded as obedience to the commands of the

Emperor. Reverence for the Emperor has been equated with patriotism and the moral obligations of the individual to his family and social superiors. To the Japanese conservative, the Throne represents the traditional Confucian morality and social stability; it appears as a mighty bulwark against the Marxist expropriation of private property, the subversion of the family, and juvenile delinquency.

The Throne, many conservatives feel, should be strengthened, and the condition of universal reverence for the monarchy which prevailed before Japan's defeat should be restored. They hold that the Emperor's position as a mere symbol of the state and of the unity of the people does violence to the historical tradition and the sentiment of the people. Some critics of the Constitution assert that the symbolic status, popular sovereignty, and denial of even nominal powers of government to the Emperor means that Japan is not a constitutional monarchy but a republic. In 1954, the conservative Liberal and Progressive Parties each organized committees for the study of constitutional revision. The main issue at that time was the disarmament clause, but both committees advocated the adoption of a completely new basic law which would restore the Emperor as constitutional head of the State.[38] Within two or three years after Japan regained her independence, Cabinet Ministers ceased participating in Constitution Day ceremonies. Premiers Hatoyama and Kishi were both strongly committed to constitutional reform. It is notable, however, that very few conservatives today advocate the outright denial of the principle of popular sovereignty. The Socialist Party has organized a People's League for the Protection of the Constitution, and thus far the parties of the left have managed to hold enough seats (slightly over one-third) in both houses of the Diet to veto any proposal to amend the Constitution.

On the grass roots level, a movement to restore Kigensetsu (National Foundation Day) has gained substantial momentum in Kyushu. Kigensetsu, February 11, is the traditional anniversary of the founding of the Japanese State by the first Emperor Jimmu Tennō in 660 B.C. Under the Occupation the old mythology had been culled from the textbooks, and is no longer being taught in the schools. Scientifically written history books have become best sellers. The younger brother of the Emperor, Prince Mikasa, who is Professor of History at Tokyo Women's College, is a strong advocate of the archeological study of Japan's origins and an outspoken opponent of the revival of Kigensetsu, which he holds to be based on erroneous conceptions of Japanese

[38] Miyazawa Toshiyoshi, *et al., Kempō Kaisei* [*The Amendment of the Constitution*] (Tokyo: Yūhikaku, 1956), pp. 160, 226.

history. He shares the fear of many Japanese that the old Shinto mythology may again be exploited by ultranationalists. He has recently edited a book on Japanese prehistory containing contributions by leading scholars.[39] Many conservative Japanese are shocked by the entrance of a member of the imperial family into the Kigensetsu controversy. The dispute concerning National Foundation Day exemplifies in Japan the struggle between scriptural authority and material evidence, between religion and science, between faith and reason, and between the political right and left.

The feeling has grown in some quarters that history should be taught in a way that would enhance patriotism and respect for Japan's historical institutions. It is ironic that the impetus for this tendency should come in part from the United States, which during the Occupation had done its best to emancipate Japan from nationalistic myths and militarism.[40]

While conservatives are trying to revive reverence for the Emperor and restore some of his constitutional prerogatives, journalists, academicians, and critics have been publishing articles in the popular press and learned journals which rationally analyze the imperial institution, often with an iconoclastic bias. Perhaps half of the material written on the Throne today would have been illegal under the stringent bans existing before World War II against criticizing the institution.

It seems possible that conservatives who today stir up the issue of the Emperor's constitutional prerogatives may in the long run be weakening their cause, because in the give-and-take of legal and political controversy over the Emperor's status, the mystery and awe upon which in the final analysis the Throne depends, is bound to be impaired. As James I of England pointed out in 1616, to dispute the mystery of the King's power "is to wade into the weaknesse of Princes, and to take away the mysticall reuerence, that belongs vnto them that sit in the Throne of God."[41]

In sensitive situations, the officials of the Imperial Household seem determined to maintain the political neutrality of the Emperor. As the Kishi government was making final preparations for President Eisenhower's visit to Japan, Imperial Household officials requested that the scheduled visit be called off, in the face of leftist threats to block the path of the automobile as it carried the Emperor and Presi-

[39] *Nihon no Akebono* [*The Dawn of Japan*] (Tokyo: Kobunsha, 1959).
[40] Shinobu Seisaburō, *Nihon Seiji Tokuhon* [*Reader on Japanese Politics*] (Tokyo: Tōyō Keizai Shinhōsha, 1960), p. 166.
[41] Speech in Star Chamber, quoted in Michael Curtis, ed., *The Great Political Theories from Plato and Aristotle to Locke and Montesquieu* (New York: The Hearst Corporation, 1961), p. 286.

dent from Haneda Airport to the Imperial Palace. In 1951, students at Kyoto University had stopped the limousine bearing the Emperor and demanded that rearmament be halted.

The existence of the Emperor, of course, has made it difficult for any other individual to capture completely the loyalty and adoration of the people as dictators have done elsewhere. At the same time, the Emperor has served as a check against Communism. He represents "the unity of the people" as opposed to class warfare. A principal reason for the unpopularity of Communism is the attacks which Communists have sometimes made on the Throne. If the Emperor succeeds in maintaining his political neutrality and if there is no revival of Shinto fanaticism, which would intensify leftist suspicions of the imperial system, it is probable that the Throne will continue to lend stability to the fledgling democracy in Japan.

Separation of Powers and Checks and Balances

From the time of Montesquieu, advocates of constitutional government have been prone to extol the principle of separation of powers as a barrier against tyranny. The Constitution of the United States, of course, provides a classic example of the application of this idea, and it is not surprising to find the principle embodied in the new Constitution of Japan. In its purest form, separation of powers implies that the executive, legislative, and judicial branches are all supreme and independent in their respective spheres. The new Japanese system of government, however, is primarily patterned after that of Britain, where there is *fusion* rather than separation of powers between the executive and legislative branches. In Japan today, as in Britain, the executive (Cabinet) is composed entirely or almost entirely of members of the legislature and is responsible to the lower house; the Cabinet is the executive committee of the parliament and is dependent upon the support of the parliament for its continued existence. There is thus no separation of powers in the sense that Americans use the term. On the other hand, the Japanese system bears a similarity to the American system in that the judicial branch may declare acts of the legislative and executive branches unconstitutional.

Under the Meiji Constitution there was, in theory, no real separation of powers because of the principle that "The Emperor is head of the Empire, combining in Himself the rights of sovereignty."[42] The transition from theoretical absolute monarchy to the parliamentary-cabinet system has not meant that fusion of powers has given way to thor-

[42] The Constitution of the Empire of Japan, Article IV.

ough-going separation of powers. Instead, fusion of powers has continued, but important changes in the distribution of power among the branches have occurred. The new Constitution proclaims that the Diet "shall be the highest organ of state power, and shall be the sole law-making organ of the State." Parliamentary supremacy ("parliamentary sovereignty") seems to prevail over the principle of separation of powers.

Some separation of powers exists, and there are important checks and balances in the new Japanese system. Dispersion of political authority has been made possible by depriving the Emperor of his unitary political authority. Figure 1, adapted from a Japanese high

Figure 1

**SEPARATION OF POWERS AND CHECKS AND BALANCES
IN THE JAPANESE CONSTITUTION**

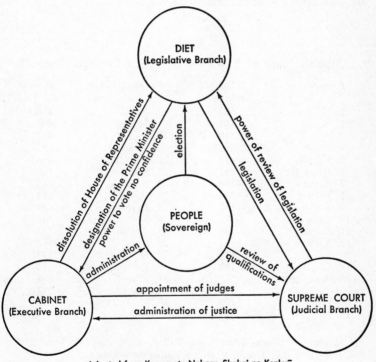

Adapted from Kawamata Noboru, Shakai no Kenkyū
[The Study of Society] (Tokyo: Obunsha, 1960), **P.70.**

school textbook, illustrates the system of separation of powers and checks and balances as it exists in Japan. Note how the Emperor, who has no "powers related to government," is conspicuously absent from the chart.

Although the new Constitution includes a chapter on local self-government, ever since the Meiji Restoration, local government has been relatively weak. In a federal system such as is found in the United States and Switzerland, constituent states exercise important constitutional powers which cannot be usurped by the central government. "States rights" provide protection for minority and sectional interests against the encroachments of the central authority. The Japanese system, on the other hand, is essentially unitary rather than federal. Prefectural governments do not have constitutions of their own, and they exercise authority largely subject to central direction. The lack of a federal system and the lack of separation of powers after the pattern of presidential democracy may open the possibility for centralization and executive domination.

Table 1

Japan's "Line of Emperors Unbroken for Ages Eternal"

Emperor	Year of Accession*	Emperor	Year of Accession
1. Jimmu	660 B.C.	17. Richū	400
2. Suizei	581	18. Hanzei	406
3. Annei	549	19. Ingyō	412
4. Itoku	510	20. Ankō	454
5. Kōshō	475	21. Yūryaku	456
6. Kōan	392	22. Seinei	480
7. Kōrei	290	23. Kenzō	485
8. Kōgen	214	24. Ninken	488
9. Kaika	157	25. Buretsu	498
10. Sujin	97	26. Keitai	507
11. Suinin	29	27. Ankan	531
12. Keikō	71 A.D.	28. Senka	535
13. Seimu	131	29. Kimmei	539
14. Chūai	192	30. Bidatsu	572
Empress Jingō		31. Yōmei	585
(Regent)	200	32. Sushun	587
15. Ōjin	270	33. Suiko (Empress)	592
16. Nintoku	313		

* Source: *The Orient Year Book, 1942* (Tokyo: The Asia Statistics Co., 1942), pp. 59–60. The first sixteen Emperors are legendary or semilegendary, and the dates traditionally given for their reigns are fanciful. The Yamato (Japanese) kingdom does not seem to have come into existence until about 0.

Emperor	Year of Accession	Emperor	Year of Accession
34. Jomei	629	80. Takakura	1168
35. Kōgyoku (Empress)	642	81. Antoku	1180
36. Kōtoku	645	82. Go-Toba	1185
37. Saimei (Empress)	655	83. Tsuchimikado	1198
38. Tenji	661	84. Juntoku	1210
39. Kōbun	671	85. Chūkyō	1221
40. Temmu	672	86. Go-Horikawa	1221
41. Jitō (Empress)	685	87. Shijō	1232
42. Mommu	697	88. Go-Saga	1242
43. Gemmei (Empress)	707	89. Go-Fukakusa	1246
44. Genshō (Empress)	715	90. Kameyama	1259
45. Shōmu	724	91. Go-Uda	1274
46. Kōken (Empress)	749	92. Fushimi	1287
47. Junnin	758	93. Go-Fushimi	1298
48. Shōtoku (Empress)	764	94. Go-Nijō	1301
49. Kōnin	770	95. Hanazono	1308
50. Kammu	781	96. Go-Daigo	1318
51. Heizei	806	97. Go-Murakami	1339
52. Saga	809	98. Chōkei	1368
53. Junna	823	99. Go-Kameyama	1383
54. Nimmyō	833	100. Go-Komatsu	1392
55. Montoku	850	101. Shōkō	1412
56. Seiwa	858	102. Go-Hanazono	1428
57. Yōzei	876	103. Go-Tsuchimikado	1464
58. Kōkō	884	104. Go-Kashiwabara	1500
59. Uda	887	105. Go-Nara	1526
60. Daigo	897	106. Ōgimachi	1557
61. Suzaku	930	107. Go-Yōzei	1586
62. Murakami	946	108. Go-Mizuno-o	1611
63. Reizei	967	109. Meishō (Empress)	1629
64. En-yū	969	110. Go-Kōmyō	1643
65. Kazan	984	111. Go-Sai	1654
66. Ichijō	986	112. Reigen	1663
67. Sanjō	1011	113. Higashiyama	1687
68. Go-Ichijō	1016	114. Nakamikado	1709
69. Go-Suzaku	1036	115. Sakuramachi	1735
70. Go-Reizei	1045	116. Momozono	1747
71. Go-Sanjō	1068	117. Go-Sakuramachi (Empress)	1762
72. Shirakawa	1072	118. Go-Momozono	1770
73. Horikawa	1086	119. Kōkaku	1779
74. Toba	1107	120. Ninkō	1816
75. Sutoku	1123	121. Kōmei	1847
76. Konoye	1141	122. Meiji	1862
77. Go-Shirakawa	1155	123. Taishō	1916
78. Nijō	1158	124. Present Emperor	1927[1]
79. Rokujō	1165		

[1]The present Emperor acceded to the throne on the death of Emperor Taishō on December 25, 1926, and was formally enthroned on November 10, 1928, following a period of mourning.

SUGGESTED READINGS

Brown, Delmer M. *Nationalism in Japan: An Introductory Analysis.* Berkeley and Los Angeles: University of California Press, 1955. The history of nationalism and the national polity.

Fujii, Shin'ichi. *Tennō Seiji* [in English, French, and German]. Tokyo: Yūhikaku, 1944. An analysis of the prewar constitutional position of the Emperor.

Hall, Robert K., ed. *Kokutai no Hongi: Cardinal Principles of the National Entity of Japan,* trans. J. O. Gauntlett. Cambridge: Harvard University Press, 1949. An official definition of the national polity.

Hozumi, Nobushige. *Ancestor-Worship and Japanese Law,* 2nd and rev. ed. Tokyo: Maruzen, 1912. Emphasizes the patriarchal basis of imperial authority.

Itō Hirobumi. *Commentaries on the Constitution of the Empire of Japan.* Tokyo: Insetsu Kyoku, 1889.

The Japan Advertiser. *Enthronement of the One Hundred Twenty-Fourth Emperor of Japan: Enthronement Edition of The Japan Advertiser.* Tokyo: The Japan Advertiser, 1928. A large collection of illustrated articles on the history and constitutional position of the Emperor.

Morris, Ivan. *Nationalism and the Right Wing in Japan: A Study of Post-War Trends.* London: Oxford University Press, 1960. Concerns efforts to revive prewar conceptions of the Emperor.

Ponsonby Fane, Richard. *The Imperial House of Japan.* Kyoto: Ponsonby Fane Memorial Society, 1959.

Stoetzel, Jean. *Without the Chrysanthemum and the Sword.* New York: Columbia University Press, 1955.

Ukai, Nobushige. "Constitutional Trends and Developments," *The Annals of the American Academy of Political and Social Science,* No. 308 (November, 1956), pp. 1–9.

Vining, Elizabeth Gray. *Windows for the Crown Prince.* Philadelphia: J. P. Lippincott Company, 1952.

4

The Cabinet

The Functions and Organization of the Cabinet

While the Emperor is the symbol of the *state* under the new Constitution, the Prime Minister is the head of the *government*. Since World War II the roles of the Prime Minister and Cabinet have grown vastly more important than they formerly were. The Meiji Constitution made only one or two references to Ministers of State (Daijin), and the words Cabinet (Naikaku) and Prime Minister (Sōri Daijin) did not appear once in the document. But the new Constitution devotes all of Chapter V to the organization and powers of the Cabinet. The Privy Council, the Elder Statesmen, the Imperial Household Ministry, the Lord Keeper of the Privy Seal, and the Imperial High Command no longer exist as rivals or superiors of the Cabinet within the executive branch.

Before the new Constitution went into effect, General MacArthur's staff regarded the Prime Minister as the effective chief executive and channeled their orders through him, thus enhancing his authority. When the Office of the Lord Keeper of the Privy Seal was abolished in November, 1945, the Prime Minister took custody of the Imperial Seal and control of official access to the Emperor. Under the new Constitution, the Emperor acts only on the advice of the Prime Minister and his Cabinet; the Prime Minister is the effective chief executive and is responsible only to the Diet and to his party.

The Cabinet as an institution was established in 1885, in anticipation of the enactment of the Imperial (Meiji) Constitution four years later. Under the Meiji Constitution the determination of the "organization of the different branches of the administration" was the prerogative of the Emperor, and in 1889 an Imperial Rescript described the organization and functions of the Cabinet.[1] The Emperor no longer exercises this

[1] Text in Supreme Commander for the Allied Powers, Government Section, *Political Reorientation of Japan: September 1945 to September 1948,*

73

power, and today the Diet, "the highest organ of state power," determines the main outline of Cabinet organization by law.[2]

Cabinet Functions

Under the old regime executive power belonged to the Emperor, and the Ministers of State simply advised the Emperor and exercised power delegated to them by His Majesty. But Article 65 of the 1947 Constitution provides that "Executive power shall be vested in the Cabinet," so that the Cabinet exercises executive authority in its own right. The Cabinet, in addition to other general administrative functions, is required by the basic law to (1) administer the law faithfully and conduct affairs of state, (2) manage foreign affairs, (3) conclude treaties with Diet approval, (4) administer the civil service according to standards established by law, (5) prepare the budget and present it to the Diet, (6) enact Cabinet orders (seirei) to execute the provisions of the Constitution and the law, and (7) decide on general amnesty, special amnesty, commutation of punishment, reprieve and restoration of rights.[3] All laws and Cabinet orders must be signed by the competent Minister of State and countersigned by the Prime Minister.[4]

In addition to the above powers, enumerated in Chapter V of the Constitution, the Cabinet exercises important functions connected with other organs of the government. It (1) advises the Emperor on "acts in matters of state,"[5] (2) designates the Chief Judge of the Supreme Court,[6] (3) appoints all judges of the Supreme Court (except the Chief Judge) and all judges of inferior courts,[7] (4) determines the convocation of extraordinary sessions of the Diet,[8] (5) convenes the House of Councillors in emergency session,[9] (6) expends monies from the reserve fund,[10] (7) submits final accounts of expenditures and revenues of the State,[11] (8) reports regularly to the Diet and the people on the state of national finances,[12] (9) proposes bills, budgets, and other measures to the Diet.[13]

---

2 vols. (Washington: Government Printing Office, n.d. [1949?]), II, 596 (these volumes will subsequently be cited as *Political Reorientation*), in W. W. McLaren, "Japanese Government Documents," *Transactions of the Asiatic Society of Japan*, Vol. XLII, Part 1, 1914, 232–233, and Harold S. Quigley, *Japanese Government and Politics: An Introductory Survey* (New York: Century, 1932), pp. 359–360.

2 *E.g.,* Cabinet Law, *Political Reorientation,* II, 851.
3 Constitution, Article 73.   4 Constitution, Article 74.
5 Constitution, Article 3.   6 Constitution, Article 6.
7 Constitution, Articles 79, 80.   8 Constitution, Article 53.
9 Constitution, Article 54.   10 Constitution, Article 87.
11 Constitution, Article 90.   12 Constitution, Article 91.
13 Constitution, Article 72; Cabinet Law, Article 5.

In practice a principal function of the Cabinet is *legislative,* since Cabinet Ministers initiate almost all of the bills which are enacted by the Diet.

The Cabinet performs its functions at Cabinet meetings presided over by the Prime Minister.[14] Since Meiji times, regular Cabinet meetings (teirei kakugi) are held every Tuesday and Friday morning. In addition, if necessary, special meetings (rinji kakugi) are frequently held. By long established custom, decisions are made by unanimous agreement, and the substance of Cabinet discussions are supposed to be kept secret.[15] It is customary for the Director of the Cabinet Secretariat and the Director and Deputy Directors of the Bureau of Legislation to attend Cabinet meetings, but they do not vote.[16]

Cabinet Organization

The Cabinet has grown in size and importance in the seventy-eight years of its existence. The first Cabinet of Prince Itō, in 1885, contained only ten men: the Prime Minister and the Ministers for Foreign Affairs, Home Affairs, Finance, Army, Navy, Justice, Education, Agriculture and Commerce, and Communications. Under the new Constitution, the number of Cabinet Ministers is determined by the Diet.

Today, under the Prime Minister, twelve Ministers head Ministries, and four Ministers, who are without portfolio, are known as State Ministers (Kokumu Daijin). The twelve Ministries are Justice, Foreign Affairs, Finance, Education, Welfare, Agriculture and Forestry, International Trade and Industry, Transportation, Postal Services, Labor, Construction, and Autonomy. In Ikeda's second Cabinet, as reconstructed in July, 1961, the Construction Minister served concurrently as Chairman of the Metropolitan Improvement Committee, and the Autonomy Minister served concurrently as Chairman of the National Public Safety Commission. The four State Ministers served as Directors of the Administrative Management Agency, the Hokkaido Development Agency, the Defense Agency, the Economic Planning Agency, and the Science and Technology Agency, and as Chairman of the Atomic Energy Commission.

The principal Cabinet committees are the Ministerial Council and the National Defense Council. The Ministerial Council (Kakuryō Shingikai) is made up of the Prime Minister, who is chairman, and the Foreign Minister, the Finance Minister, the Agriculture and For-

[14] Cabinet Law, Article 4.

[15] Naikaku Kambō [Cabinet Secretariat], ed., *Naikaku Seido Shichijū Nen Shi* [*History of Seventy Years of the Cabinet System*] (Tokyo: Okurashō Insatsukyoku, 1955), p. 177.

[16] Chitoshi Yanaga, *Japanese People and Politics* (New York: Wiley, 1956), p. 164.

estry Minister, the International Trade and Industry Minister, the Transportation Minister, and the State Minister who serves as Director of the Economic Planning Agency. The National Defense Council (Kokubō Kaigi) consists of the Prime Minister, who serves as chairman, the Foreign Minister, the Finance Minister, and the State Ministers serving as Director of the Defense Agency and Director of the Economic Planning Agency.

The auxiliary organs of the Cabinet are the Cabinet Secretariat and the Legislative Bureau. Their organization and that of the other necessary offices in the Cabinet are determined by law. The Cabinet Secretariat (Naikaku Kambō) is formally charged with "preparing the agenda of Cabinet meetings and other miscellaneous affairs of the Cabinet."[17] The Director of the Cabinet Secretariat, or Chief Cabinet Secretary, (Naikaku Kambō Chōkan) is responsible for the proper functioning of the Cabinet Secretariat. He is a principal political adviser to the Prime Minister especially during the formation of a government and he often makes announcements to the press on behalf of the Prime Minister and the Cabinet. He is at all times well informed on questions under discussion in the Cabinet, since the Secretariat prepares the Cabinet agenda.

The Legislative Bureau (Hōseikyoku) is "in charge of examining and drafting Cabinet bills and Cabinet orders, as well as examining drafts of treaties, and other legal matters."[18] All draft laws and Cabinet orders proposed by the Ministries must be submitted to the Legislative Bureau to be formally drafted. The substance of a bill is the responsibility of the Ministry, while its legal aspects are taken care of by the Bureau. The Director of the Legislative Bureau, like the Chief Cabinet Secretary, is authorized to attend Cabinet meetings but not to vote. The high legal competence of the Bureau ensures that Cabinet bills will command respect from a technical point of view and has contributed greatly to the strength of the executive branch in its dealings with the legislative.

The National Personnel Authority (Jinji-in), concerned with administering the civil service, and the Commission on the Constitution (Kempō Chōsakai), engaged in a long-term study of the Constitution, are extraministerial agencies created by acts of the Diet and administratively placed under the Cabinet. The Board of Audit (Kaikei Kensa-in) is independent of the Cabinet. In accordance with Article 90 of the Constitution, it audits the final accounts of the expenditures and revenues of the state.

17 Cabinet Law, Article 12.
18 Cabinet Law, Article 12.

Figure 2

THE ORGANIZATION OF THE EXECUTIVE BRANCH

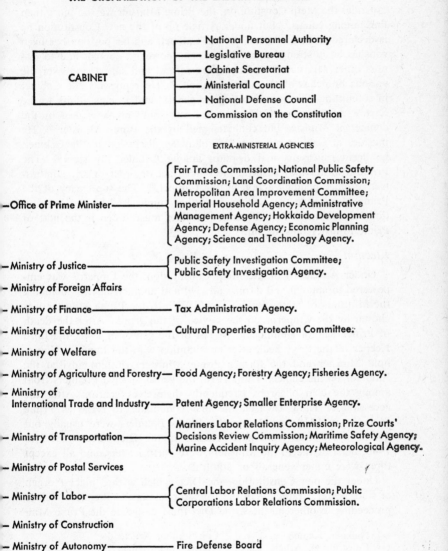

CABINET
— National Personnel Authority
— Legislative Bureau
— Cabinet Secretariat
— Ministerial Council
— National Defense Council
— Commission on the Constitution

EXTRA-MINISTERIAL AGENCIES

— Office of Prime Minister — Fair Trade Commission; National Public Safety Commission; Land Coordination Commission; Metropolitan Area Improvement Committee; Imperial Household Agency; Administrative Management Agency; Hokkaido Development Agency; Defense Agency; Economic Planning Agency; Science and Technology Agency.

— Ministry of Justice — Public Safety Investigation Committee; Public Safety Investigation Agency.

— Ministry of Foreign Affairs

— Ministry of Finance — Tax Administration Agency.

— Ministry of Education — Cultural Properties Protection Committee.

— Ministry of Welfare

— Ministry of Agriculture and Forestry — Food Agency; Forestry Agency; Fisheries Agency.

— Ministry of International Trade and Industry — Patent Agency; Smaller Enterprise Agency.

— Ministry of Transportation — Mariners Labor Relations Commission; Prize Courts' Decisions Review Commission; Maritime Safety Agency; Marine Accident Inquiry Agency; Meteorological Agency.

— Ministry of Postal Services

— Ministry of Labor — Central Labor Relations Commission; Public Corporations Labor Relations Commission.

— Ministry of Construction

— Ministry of Autonomy — Fire Defense Board

The Prime Minister

Powers

Under the Meiji Constitution, the Prime Minister was no more than first among equals,[19] but under Article 66 of the new Constitution he is declared to be the "head" of the Cabinet, and his position has been conspicuously strengthened. He has the power to appoint and to dismiss other Ministers[20] and exercises control and supervision over the various branches of the administration.[21] He represents the Cabinet in submitting bills and reporting on general and foreign affairs to the Diet.[22] All laws and Cabinet orders must not only be signed by the competent Minister but countersigned by the Prime Minister.[23] He presides at Cabinet meetings.[24] Following discussion in the Cabinet, he decides jurisdictional disputes among Cabinet Ministers.[25] The Prime Minister may suspend the official act or order of any administrative office pending action by the Cabinet.[26] The supremacy of the Prime Minister in the Cabinet is further emphasized by the constitutional requirement that the entire Cabinet must resign if the post of Prime Minister falls vacant.[27]

Election

Under Article 10 of the Meiji Constitution, the Emperor was empowered to appoint and dismiss all civil and military officers, including the Ministers of State. Before World War II, the Prime Minister was chosen by the Emperor on the advice of the genro. After the death of Prince Saionji Kimmochi, the last of the genro, in 1940, the Lord Keeper of the Privy Seal, after consultation with the Imperial Household Minister and the former Prime Ministers (jūshin) advised the Emperor on the choice. Until 1918, the genro selected Premiers from among the clan oligarchs (frequently themselves genro). After the accession of Hara Takashi, the first commoner to serve as Prime Minister, in 1918 and during the 1920's Premiers were usually but not always chosen from party leaders in the Diet. From 1932 to 1945, none of the Prime Ministers were party leaders, and all except three were either generals or admirals.

Under the new Constitution, the Diet, which is the "highest organ of state power," rather than the Emperor, elects the Premier. Before proceeding to other business, the Diet must designate the Prime Min-

[19] Naikaku Kambō, p. 174.
[20] Constitution, Article 68.
[21] Constitution, Article 72.
[22] Constitution, Article 72.
[23] Constitution, Article 74.
[24] Cabinet Law, Article 4.
[25] Cabinet Law, Article 7.
[26] Cabinet Law, Article 8.
[27] Constitution, Article 70.

ister from among its members by a resolution. If the House of Representatives and House of Councillors disagree and if no agreement can be reached in a joint committee of both houses, or if the House of Councillors fails to make designation within ten days after the House of Representatives has made designation, the decision of the House of Representatives is the decision of the Diet.[28] The Emperor "appoints" the Prime Minister as designated by the Diet.[29]

Although the constitutional procedure is quite clear, in practice the selection of a first Minister is sometimes an involved process. Before the election of the Prime Minister is held in the Diet, there is a great deal of maneuvering within and among the political parties. If no party has a majority in the House of Representatives, some kind of interparty agreement is necessary in order to choose a premier. For example, when the Socialist Party headed by Katayama Tetsu won a plurality in the 1947 election, all of the parties except the Communist agreed to form a four-party coalition headed by Katayama. As a result of this understanding, on May 23 Katayama was almost unanimously elected to the premiership. The Liberals then withdrew from the coalition agreement, and it took an entire week for Mr. Katayama to form a Government.

When the Katayama Cabinet resigned in 1948, the coalition parties planned to form a new Government under Ashida Hitoshi. The Liberals, under Yoshida Shigeru, urged that the principle of normal constitutional government required that when the Government resigns it should allow the opposition to form a Government rather than re-form the coalition. In this instance, the Liberals said, the Diet should designate Yoshida as Prime Minister.[30] On February 21, 1948, the House of Representatives elected Ashida and the House of Councillors elected Yoshida to the premiership. As provided by the Constitution, a joint committee of both houses met, but was unable to come to an agreement. The decision of the Representatives therefore became the decision of the Diet, and Ashida became Prime Minister of Japan.

For several years following the 1949 election, the Liberal Party held a comfortable majority in both houses and experienced no difficulty in electing and re-electing Mr. Yoshida as Prime Minister. In 1954 when the fifth Yoshida Cabinet resigned, no single party had a majority in the lower house, and it was again necessary to make some

[28] Constitution, Article 68.   [29] Constitution, Article 6.

[30] The Liberals were able to cite the "precedent" established in 1947, when, following the general election, the opposition Socialists became the plurality party. The Yoshida coalition Cabinet resigned in favor of a Socialist-led Cabinet even though the parties which had made up the Yoshida coalition still had a majority of seats. (Yoshida Shigeru, *The Yoshida Memoirs* [Boston: Houghton Mifflin, 1962], p. 83.)

interparty agreement on the premiership. Hatoyama Ichirō, president of the Democratic Party, promised the Left and Right Socialist members of the lower house that he would dissolve the Diet after becoming Prime Minister if they would vote for him. Hatoyama was then elected premier with the combined votes of his own party and the Socialists.

Since the advent of the two-party system in 1955, each party nominates its own leader for the Prime Ministership and then votes along party lines, so that the outcome of the election is a foregone conclusion. In 1956 when Hatoyama resigned, and in 1960 when Kishi resigned, much more attention was centered on the maneuvering among factions in the Liberal-Democratic Party to name a party president, who would certainly later be designated the premier, than on the formal election of the Prime Minister in the Diet. The term of office of the president of the Liberal-Democratic Party is two years, so that a premier could possibly lose his post because he fails to be re-elected party president. Thus, in 1959 and 1962, Liberal-Democratic Party presidential elections could conceivably have ousted Kishi or Ikeda, respectively, from the Prime Ministership.

SCAP and the Prime Minister

During the early part of the Occupation, General MacArthur's attitude towards Cabinet Ministers was usually crucial to their appointment and tenure in office. Thus, when the October 4, 1945, "Bill of Rights" directive called for drastic reforms and the resignation of the Home Minister, the Higashikuni Cabinet resigned *en bloc*. The appointment of Shidehara as Prime Minister was first cleared with General MacArthur, and the approval of SCAP Headquarters was obtained for the nomination of each Minister in Shidehara's Cabinet.[31] When Shidehara resigned following the 1946 election, it appeared that the president of the Liberal Party, which had a plurality in the lower house, would succeed him. However, at this crucial juncture, the Liberal Party leader, Hatoyama Ichirō, was suddenly and unexpectedly purged by direct order of General MacArthur, and the way was open for Foreign Minister Yoshida to become president of the Liberal Party and Prime Minister.

[31] Yoshida, p. 65. Courtney Whitney, in *MacArthur: His Rendezvous with History* (New York: Knopf, 1956, pp. 245–246) describes a conversation between General MacArthur and Foreign Minister Yoshida concerning a contemplated resignation of the Shidehara Cabinet and the reappointment of Shidehara. MacArthur is quoted as saying that after the contemplated resignation "Baron Shidehara may be acceptable to the Emperor for reappointment as Prime Minister, but he will not be acceptable to me." Yoshida, however, asserts that this account is in serious error. (Yoshida, pp. 67–68.)

In February, 1947, General MacArthur showed his lack of confidence in Prime Minister Yoshida by directing that a general election be held as soon as possible. As a result of the election, the Liberal Party of Mr. Yoshida lost its plurality in the lower house and Mr. Katayama succeeded to the premiership.

It is said that in 1948 after the fall of the Ashida Cabinet, SCAP Government Section (GS) opposed the accession of Yoshida, then president of the Democratic-Liberal Party, and favored the selection of Yamazaki Takeshi, secretary general of the same party, to head a coalition Government. Anti-Yoshida elements in the Democratic-Liberal Party and Democratic Party leaders tended to favor the election of Yamazaki, and a Democratic caucus voted to support him. About this time, SCAP's G-2 (Military Intelligence) Section, a rival of Government Section, vigorously protested against GS intervention in internal Japanese politics, and GS dropped the Yamazaki plan. Yoshida then persuaded Yamazaki to resign his seat in the Diet. When the vote was taken in the House of Representatives on October 14, 1948, Yoshida won the designation with 185 ballots in his favor as against 213 *blank* ballots.[32] Yoshida managed to retain the premiership until December, 1954. The friendly attitude of General MacArthur was one factor accounting for Yoshida's long tenure in office.

Before being elected Prime Minister, a man normally serves a stint as an ordinary Cabinet Minister or high party official. Some ministerial posts are more likely than others to lead to the premiership. The best stepping stones to the Prime Ministry have been the Ministries of Foreign Affairs and of Finance. Eight Prime Ministers had previously served as Foreign Ministers: Ōkuma, Saionji, Katō Takaaki, Shidehara, Hirota, Yoshida, Ashida, and Kishi. Six Premiers had formerly served as Ministers of Finance: Matsukata, Wakatsuki, Takahashi, Hamaguchi, Ishibashi, and Ikeda. Three had formerly served as Home Ministers: Yamagata, Hara, and Hamaguchi;, and three as Justice Ministers: Yamagata, Kiyoura, and Hiranuma. Saionji and Hatoyama had served as Education Ministers, Hara and Inukai as Communications Ministers, Kuroda as Agriculture and Commerce Minister, Takahashi as Commerce and Industry Minister, Ashida as Health and Welfare Minister, and Ikeda as International Trade and Industry Minister.[33]

Under the present Constitution, only civilians may serve in the Cabinet. Before 1946, sixteen Prime Ministers were career military men. From the Army came ten: Kuroda, Yamagata, Katsura, Terauchi, Tanaka, Hayashi, Abe, Tōjō, Koiso, and Higashikuni. The re-

---

[32] Soma Masao, *Sengo Seijishi* [*Postwar Political History*] (Tokyo: Sanichi Shobo, 1960), p. 171. Cf. also Yoshida, pp. 87–89.

[33] Watanabe Tsuneo, *Daijin* [*Minister*] (Tokyo: Kōbundō, 1959), p. 86.

maining six were from the Navy: Yamamoto, Katō Tomosaburō, Saitō, Okada, Yonai, and Suzuki.

Forming a Government

Following his election as Prime Minister, the new chief executive must appoint the members of his Cabinet, at least half of whom must be drawn from the Diet according to the new Constitution. Since Yoshida's time, nearly all the Ministers have been selected from the Diet. Because the Government must have the support of the Diet in order to have its proposals enacted into law, the political composition of the executive body is of primary importance.

Prewar Governments

Cabinets in prewar Japan were either (1) transcendental, (2) party, or (3) military-bureaucratic. Transcendental Cabinets (chōzen naikaku) were established by the genro aloof from political parties and did not contain party members. The first seven Cabinets (1885–1898) were all transcendental. Most of the Cabinets from 1898 to 1918 were headed by military or bureaucratic oligarchs, but included some party members.

Party Cabinets (seitō naikaku) were headed by party leaders, and the majority of the Ministers were party men. All of the Governments from 1918 to 1932 were party Cabinets except for the transcendental Cabinets of Katō Tomosaburō, Yamamoto, and Kiyoura. Military-bureaucratic Cabinets prevailed from 1932 to 1945. They were usually headed by generals or admirals, but occasionally by bureaucrats or aristocrats. Sometimes party men were included in these Cabinets. In the prewar Cabinets, the Ministers of Army and Navy were invariably generals and admirals respectively as required by an imperial ordinance of 1900, and the Ministers of Foreign Affairs were almost always career bureaucrats.

Postwar Governments

Governments in postwar Japan have been based on political parties, and are either coalition or one-party Cabinets. Coalition Cabinets (renritsu naikaku) are made up of members of two or more political parties which together have a majority in the lower house. When no single party has a majority, a Cabinet must depend on the support of more than one party for the passage of its bills, and a minority party may find it necessary to form a coalition rather than a single-party Cabinet. After World War II no single party was able to win a majority in the Diet until 1949, and coalition Governments were the rule. The first Yoshida Cabinet was a coalition of Liberals and Progressives headed by a Liberal. The succeeding Katayama Cabinet was a three-party coalition of Socialists, Democrats, and People's Cooperatives, headed by a Socialist. Its successor, the Ashida Government, was a coalition of the same three parties headed by a Democrat (Progressive). The third Yoshida Cabinet could have been a single-party government since Yoshida's Democratic-Liberals had a comfortable majority in the House of Representatives. Nevertheless, Democrats were brought into the Government in part, it is said, as the result of a suggestion by SCAP Headquarters, which wished to impose a check on the inflationary tendencies of the Democratic-Liberals.

There have been no coalition Cabinets since the third Yoshida Government largely because the two-party system inaugurated in 1955 has provided comfortable majorities in the Diet for Liberal-Democratic Governments. It is conceivable, but unlikely, that in a future election neither of the two great parties (Liberal-Democratic and Socialist) would win a majority. In such a contingency, the small Democratic-Socialist Party, the small Communist Party and a handful of independents would hold the balance of power in the House of Representatives. Either or both of the small parties might then make a bid for a place in a leftist or rightist coalition or extract other political concessions in exchange for their support.

One-party Cabinets (tandoku naikaku) have been formed when a political party wins majority or healthy plurality of the seats in the House of Representatives. The fourth and fifth Yoshida Cabinets were single-party regimes, as were all subsequent Cabinets. Under the two-party system all Governments have been one-party Cabinets made up of members of the Liberal-Democratic Party. As long as the Liberal-Democrats maintain their unity and preserve their majority in the lower house, they will doubtless continue to form one-party Cabinets.

If a single-party Cabinet does not control a majority in the Diet, its policies are apt to be defeated and it may be forced to resign. Occasionally a minority party has formed a Government following the resignation of a Cabinet and remained in power long enough to dissolve the Diet and supervise a general election. The second Yoshida Cabinet and first Hatoyama Cabinet are examples of such stop-gap Cabinets (chūkan naikaku).

In Japan, factions within parties are very powerful, and the competition for Cabinet posts is intense. As a consequence, a one-party Cabinet is in the nature of a coalition of factions of the ruling party. Each faction is made up of Diet members whose leader supports their nominations to candidacy, supplies them with funds, and sometimes finds Cabinet posts for them. The principal objectives of factions are the acquisition of money and political office, the supply of which is inadequate to satisfy everyone. It frequently takes several days for a premier to appoint a Cabinet, since it is necessary to avoid ruffling unduly the factions whose support will be needed by the Prime Minister in his relations with the Diet. The competition for the title of Daijin (Minister) and Seimu Jikan (Parliamentary Vice-Minister) is intense, for nearly every politician is more or less afflicted with daijinbyō (minister sickness). Nevertheless, sometimes faction leaders refuse to serve in a Cabinet, in order to signify their opposition to the Prime Minister. Often the rank of Parliamentary Vice-Minister is given a politician in order to give him prestige needed in a tight electoral race.

The only women ever appointed to the Cabinet were Mrs. Nakayama Masa, Welfare Minister in Ikeda's first Government and Miss Kondo Tsuruyo, State Minister and Director of Science and Technology Agency and Atomic Energy Commission in Ikeda's second Cabinet as reconstructed in July, 1962. Presumably women may serve in future Cabinets now that the precedent has been set, but traditional sentiment and factional politics will no doubt make female Ministers rare. The appointment of women to the Cabinet may serve to attract women voters to the government party.

The role of the throne in the formation of a Cabinet is, under the new Constitution, purely formal. The Emperor, as has been noted, appoints the Prime Minister designated by the Diet, and he attests the appointment of the other Cabinet Ministers, who are appointed by the Premier.

When newspapers list the members of a Cabinet they often include the Chief Cabinet Secretary, the Director of Administrative Affairs in the Office of the Prime Minister, and the Director of the Cabinet Bureau of Legislation. Actually the men holding these posts are not of ministerial rank and therefore do not fulfill a constitutional requirement for Cabinet membership, notwithstanding their important political and administrative functions.

Cabinet Changes

The turnover of ministerships in Japan is very high, because Cabinets have changed or been reformed since the war on the average of once a year. A single individual may become Prime Minister repeatedly, but every time he forms a new Government he is apt to find new men for most of the seats. Furthermore, during the lifetime of a single Cabinet, there are often substantial changes in personnel. The Prime Minister appoints and dismisses Cabinet members without the formal approval of the Diet. Premiers have made liberal use of their power to dismiss Ministers arbitrarily in order to strengthen their own political position and that of the Cabinet as a whole. Yoshida was famous, especially during his relatively long-lived third Government, for the "mass production" (masu puro) of Ministers. Twice Mr. Kishi and twice Mr. Ikeda made wholesale changes in the personnel of their Cabinets in such a way that the "reconstructed" Cabinets (kaizō naikaku) were virtually new ones. These reshuffles reflected changes in factional relations within the ruling Liberal-Democratic Party. The reconstruction of Kishi's second Cabinet in June, 1959, was a result of the House of Councillors election of that year. Technically, a reconstructed Cabinet cannot be considered a new Cabinet because the Prime Minister continues in office without undergoing the formalities of election by the Diet and appointment by the Emperor.

In July, 1961, following a conference in Washington with President Kennedy, Mr. Ikeda replaced ten of his sixteen ministers to ensure that every major faction within his party was represented. The reconstructed Cabinet was considered much stronger than it had previously been because a number of the faction leaders themselves accepted positions. The Ikeda faction received three posts, the Kishi, Satō and Kōno factions each got two, the Fujiyama, Miki, Ishii, and Ōno factions each received one. The remaining three ministerships were assigned to members of the upper house.

On July 17, 1962, following the 1962 House of Councillors election and Ikeda's re-election to the Liberal-Democratic Party presidency, the second Ikeda Cabinet was reconstructed a second time, as follows:

Prime Minister: Ikeda Hayato (Ikeda faction)
Justice Minister: Nakagaki Kunio (Ishii faction)
Foreign Minister: Ōhira Masayoshi (Ikeda faction)
Finance Minister: Tanaka Kakuei (Satō faction)
Education Minister: Araki Masuo (Ikeda faction, reappointed)
Welfare Minister: Nishimura Eiichi (Satō faction)
Agriculture-Forestry Minister: Shigemasa Seishi (Kōno faction)
International Trade and Industry Minister: Fukuda Hajime (Ōno faction)
Transportation Minister: Ayabe Kentarō (Fujiyama faction)
Postal Services Minister: Teshima Sakae (Fujiyama faction)
Labor Minister: Ōhashi Takeo (Ikeda faction)
Construction Minister: Kōno Ichirō (Kōno faction)
Autonomy Minister (concurrently Chairman, National Public Safety Commission): Shinoda Kosaku (Kishi faction)

State Minister (Director, Administrative Management Agency and Hokkaido Development Agency): Kawashima Shōjirō (Kishi faction, reappointed)

State Minister (Director, Defense Agency): Shiga Kenjirō (Miki faction)

State Minister (Director, Economic Planning Agency): Miyazawa Kiichi (Ikeda faction)

State Minister (Director, Science and Technology Agency and Chairman, Atomic Energy Commission): Kondo Tsuruyo (Miss) (Ōno faction)

The absence of all of the great faction leaders except Kōno from the reconstructed Cabinet suggested that the new Cabinet was lacking in stability and that another reshuffle of ministerial posts was not long distant. Newspapers speculated that the faction leaders were hoping to replace Ikeda after he had served his second two-year term as party president.

Responsible Government

The Cabinet is "collectively responsible to the Diet."[34] Article 69 of the Constitution provides that when the House of Representatives passes a resolution of no confidence in the Cabinet or rejects a confidence resolution, "the Cabinet shall resign en masse, unless the House of Representatives is dissolved within ten days."[35] According to Article 7, the Emperor, with the advice and approval of the Cabinet, dissolves the House of Representatives.[36] Thus when the lower house votes no confidence in the Government, the Government must either resign or advise a dissolution.

Dissolution of the House of Representatives

There has been much uncertainty concerning the scope of the Government's power of dissolution. Does the Prime Minister have to wait until the House of Representatives votes no confidence before asking the Emperor to dissolve the lower house?

In 1948, the question arose as to whether Mr. Yoshida could advise a dissolution without there first being a vote of no confidence. His party held that Article 7 provided sufficient authorization for dissolution independently of Article 69. If Article 7 could be so construed, it would mean that the Cabinet might dissolve the House of Representatives at any time politically advantageous to the Government party

[34] Article 66, Constitution of Japan.
[35] Article 69, Constitution of Japan.
[36] Article 7, Constitution of Japan. The Constitution makes no provision for the dissolution of the House of Councillors.

(or parties), even though a majority of the house might be opposed to dissolution. The manner in which prewar Governments had bullied the Diet by too frequent dissolution was fresh in the minds of many legislators. The opposition held that the lower house could be dissolved only if the house passed a resolution of no confidence. Occupation officials supported the view of the opposition, and mediated in the dispute. A compromise was worked out wherein the lower house voted no confidence in the Government and the Government then asked the Emperor for a dissolution.[37] Thus, in principle, the supremacy of the parliament provided for in the American-drafted Constitution was upheld. The victory of the Diet in this case was largely nominal: the Cabinet got the dissolution it wanted, and in the subsequent election the Government party (Democratic-Liberals) won an absolute majority.

Four years later, when the Allied forces had withdrawn, the Yoshida Government was able to have its way completely in the matter of dissolving the lower chamber, and effected a "surprise dissolution" (nukiuchi kaisan) without a prior vote of no confidence in Parliament.[38] The four-year terms of the Representatives were shortened by four months without their having any formal say in the matter.

In 1953, Premier Yoshida insulted the Diet by calling a member a stupid fool during the course of a debate, thus provoking a vote of no confidence. This was the second and last time that the House of Representatives passed a vote of no confidence in the Cabinet. The Government immediately obtained an imperial rescript dissolving the House of Representatives. In the subsequent election, Yoshida lost his absolute majority in the lower house, but managed to gain the distinction of being the only Prime Minister in Japanese history to be chosen to form a fifth Cabinet. The dissolutions of 1955, 1958, and 1960 were all effected without votes of no confidence.[39] The Cabinet now has the power to dissolve the lower house at will and since World War II has not once permitted the Representatives to serve out their full four-year terms.

In the 1960 crisis, the Socialists were in a minority and unable to vote no confidence in the Government. Nevertheless, they demanded both the resignation of the Cabinet and a dissolution of the House of Representatives. When the Kishi Government refused either to resign or dissolve the lower house, the Socialist members threatened themselves to resign from the Diet in order to deepen the crisis and thus

---

[37] Naikaku Kambō, pp. 188–189.
[38] Ibid., pp. 197–198.
[39] "Kaisan kara senkyo made: Kokkai kaisan ni futatsu baai," Asahi Janaru, Vol. 1, No. 43 (October 23, 1960), pp. 82–83.

force Kishi to do their will. They signed formal resignation papers for their party chairman, who would later submit them, if need be, to the Speaker of the house. The Government, of course, could call by-elections for seats which the Socialists might vacate, rather than dissolve parliament, and as things worked out, the Socialists did not make good their threat. After a number of general strikes and mass demonstrations, Kishi shortly announced his intent to resign, and the succeeding Ikeda Cabinet dissolved parliament without waiting for a vote of no confidence. The Cabinet may be under pressure to dissolve the lower chamber if the opposition organizes sufficiently large demonstrations and strikes. Of course, the opposition would presumably not wish too frequent dissolutions which would weaken their power in the Diet as was the case in former times. However, as shown in the 1960 affair, a demand of the opposition for a dissolution may be part of a larger movement of extraparliamentary forces to obstruct the will of the parliamentary majority. Socialists have frequently introduced non-confidence motions to harass the government. In discussing the responsibility of the Cabinet, account must be taken of the effectiveness of the extraparliamentary tactics of the Socialist opposition. It was political strikes and street demonstrations which forced Mr. Kishi's resignation and the establishment of a caretaker regime which would effect a dissolution.

The Resignation of the Cabinet

Under the new Constitution, the lower chamber has never been able to bring about the fall of a Cabinet with a resolution of no confidence, but the threat of one was sufficient in 1954. In December of that year, a nonconfidence resolution against Yoshida was introduced. It was evident that it would pass, and Yoshida, under the urging of his followers, resigned before the proposal was brought to a vote, rather than dissolve the lower chamber as had been his habit. Mr. Hatoyama, a leader of the opposition in the House of Representatives, succeeded to the premiership.

The principal cause of Cabinet resignations since 1947 has been the constitutional requirement (Article 70) that "the Cabinet shall resign en masse" upon the first convocation of the Diet after a general election of members of the lower house. Contrary to British custom, even though the government party wins the election, the Cabinet must resign. The victorious party, of course, may re-elect its leader as Premier. The following Cabinets resigned under Article 70: Yoshida's first, second, third, and fourth, Hatoyama's first and second, Kishi's first, and Ikeda's first (a total of eight).

The Constitution requires the Cabinet to resign when the post of

Prime Minister falls vacant. Hatoyama's third Cabinet and the Ishibashi Cabinet both resigned when the ill health of the premier made it unfeasible to remain in office. The coalition Governments of Katayama and Ashida fell because of dissension both within and among the parties making up the coalition.

Kishi's second Cabinet resigned when the strikes and demonstrations which were mounted against it became too overwhelming, and some of Kishi's rivals in his own party deserted him.

Extraparliamentary Factors

In Japan, two important extraparliamentary devices have been used to hasten the fall of Cabinets. These are popular demonstrations and terrorism. Street demonstrations against the Portsmouth Treaty in 1905 and the rice riots of 1918 precipitated the fall of the first Katsura Cabinet and the Terauchi Cabinet respectively. Since World War II, demonstrations and a threatened general strike directed against the first Yoshida Government apparently influenced MacArthur in calling for a general election, which resulted in a change of Cabinet. The resignation of the second Kishi Cabinet was clearly a consequence of strikes and demonstrations.

Assassination has been a commonly used political weapon from the beginning of Japanese history, when murder intrigues were not infrequent within the walls of the imperial court. Assassination became so conspicuous a political technique in Japan in the 1930's that one knowledgeable foreign observer wrote a description of the political system under the title, *Government by Assassination*.[40] Of Japan's thirty-eight different Prime Ministers, six lost their lives at the hands of terrorists during or after their terms of office. They were Itō (d. 1909), Hara (d. 1921), Hamaguchi (d. 1931), Inukai (d. 1932), Saitō (d. 1936), and Takahashi (d. 1936). Attempts were made on the lives of others, including Okada, Saionji, Suzuki, and Kishi. Governments which fell as the result of the assassination of the Prime Minister or members of his Cabinet were those of Hara, Hamaguchi, Inukai, and Okada. The motive and effect of assassinations in the 1930's were to discredit parliamentary government and party politics and strengthen the forces of military fascism.

The revival of rightist terrorism following World War II, especially the assassination on live television of Socialist Party Chairman Asanuma Inejirō in 1960, has aroused fears for the future of democracy and has been capitalized on by the Socialists to discredit conservative governments.

[40] Hugh Byas, *Government by Assassination* (New York: Knopf, 1942).

The Lifetime of Cabinets

Sixty different Cabinets have come into existence since the establishment of the system in 1885. Thus the average life of Japanese Cabinets is about fifteen months. Since May 3, 1947, when the new Constitution came into effect, there have been sixteen Cabinets, not counting the first Yoshida Government, which left office on May 22, 1947. The average tenure has been something less than a year. However, Yoshida headed five Cabinets, Hatoyama three, Kishi two, and Ikeda two, so that Prime Ministers frequently outlive their Cabinets.

Under the new Constitution, a general election for the lower house must be held at least once every four years, and the Cabinet must resign following a general election, so that it is impossible for a single Cabinet to remain in office longer than four years. Since 1885, the most durable Government was Katsura's third Cabinet, which lasted over four years and seven months. Itō's second Government holds second place, lasting over four years. Yoshida's third Government is third, with a tenure of three years and eight months. Itō served as Prime Minister longer than anyone else — a total of nine and a half years nonconsecutively.

The Civil Service

The Confucian tradition conferred high prestige upon the government official. The scholar-bureaucrats of imperial China were the political and social elite. Under the Meiji Constitution government officials were appointed and dismissed by the Emperor and acted in his name. Imperial ordinances rather than democratically enacted laws provided for the regulation of the imperial civil service. Premier Yamagata deliberately placed many high positions under the merit system in order to weaken political parties by depriving them of spoils. Top bureaucrats had higher court ranks than the members of the House of Representatives. Ambitious farm youths aspiring to worldly success sought entrance into the Law School of Tokyo Imperial University to qualify for government posts. The bureaucracy alone or in combination with the military tended to dominate the state. From 1890 to 1920, of 3,126 bills introduced into the Imperial Diet, 2,856 were Government bills and only 270 were initiated by the Diet itself.[41]

[41] Tsuji Kiyoaki, "The Cabinet, Administrative Organization, and the Bureaucracy," *The Annals of the American Academy of Political and Social Science,* Vol. 308 (November, 1956), 10–17.

Before World War II, the Japanese government service did not base its personnel administration on the relative evaluation and classification of the duties and responsibilities of positions, but conducted personnel assignments and transactions according to a rigid, complex system of assigning official rank to individual persons without particular reference to their posts of duty.[42]

The new Constitution provided that public officials were to be the "servants" — rather than the masters — of the people. The National Public Service Law[43] enacted in 1947 was intended to subordinate the bureaucracy to the elected representatives of the people and to ensure an efficient and democratic administration.

All national government personnel are divided into two groups: the regular government service, and the special government service. The regular government service includes all of the clerical and administrative employees of the national government except those classified as belonging to the special government service. The special government service embraces the members of the Cabinet, all positions appointment to which requires Diet approval, high officials in the Imperial Court, Judges, Ambassadors and Ministers, Diet employees, common laborers, and employees of Government Corporations (the Japan National Railways, the Japan Monopoly Corporation, and the Japan Telegraph and Telephone Public Corporation).

The National Public Service Law is concerned primarily with the regular government service. The National Personnel Authority (Jinji-in), which administers the National Public Service Law, was modeled after the Civil Service Commission of the United States and is largely independent of both the Diet and the Cabinet. The Authority is made up of three Commissioners, one of whom is the Chairman, appointed by the Cabinet with the approval of the Diet. The functions of the Authority are to supervise the preparation of civil service examinations, classify positions, promote employee training and welfare, deal with employee grievances, and recommend administrative and salary reforms to the Cabinet and Ministries. Government departments would like to regain the authority over personnel matters which they have lost to Personnel Authority, and the Government has tended to regard the Authority as a kind of internal opposition. At the same time, labor unions have frequently protested the salary recommendations advanced by the Personnel Authority. Thus, there has been incessant pressure

[42] *Political Reorientation,* I, 250.

[43] Text in *Political Reorientation,* II, 1022–1035. For an extensive discussion see Harold S. Quigley and John E. Turner, *The New Japan: Government and Politics* (Minneapolis: University of Minnesota Press, 1956), pp. 212–226.

from both right and left to abolish the institution which is sometimes referred to as a "love-child of the Occupation."[44]

Regular public servants have the right to organize and may authorize their union representatives to make requests to the National Personnel Authority concerning salaries and working conditions. However, as the result of amendments in the Public Service Law insisted on by General MacArthur in 1948, neither regular public servants nor the employees of Government Corporations have the rights to bargain collectively and to strike.

In 1959, there were a total of 1,657,581 national government employees, of whom 682,049 were in Government Corporations. They were divided among governmental agencies as follows:[45]

Diet	3,251
Courts of Justice	22,268
Board of Audit	1,178
Cabinet	878
Office of the Prime Minister	23,303
Ministry of Justice	44,650
Ministry of Foreign Affairs	2,004
Ministry of Finance	73,402
Ministry of Welfare	52,568
Ministry of Education	66,511
Ministry of Agriculture and Forestry	81,257
Ministry of International Trade and Industry	13,118
Ministry of Transportation	28,770
Ministry of Postal Services	267,457
Ministry of Labor	23,352
Ministry of Construction	16,725
Board of Defense	254,800
Government Corporations	682,049

In accordance with a local public service law passed by the Diet in 1950, the civil service of the prefectures and other local government units is locally administered along the same general lines as the national civil service. Prefectural and other local personnel commissions correspond in organization and function to the National Personnel Authority. National law denies the rights of collective bargaining and striking to local government as well as to national government employees. The number of local government employees totals 1,391,000.[46]

[44] *Asahi Nenkan, 1962,* p. 287.

[45] Japanese Government, Ministry of Foreign Affairs, *Statistical Handbook of Japan* (Tokyo, 1961), p. 104.

[46] Japanese Government, Ministry of Foreign Affairs, *The Japan of Today* (Tokyo, 1961), p. 15.

The Bureaucratic Spirit

The provisions of the new Constitution assure that the executive branch is responsible to the Diet, which represents the people, rather than to the Emperor. The Cabinet is thus a democratic rather than an oligarchic institution. Furthermore, Article 15 of the Constitution provides that "all public officials are servants of the whole community and not of any group thereof." Cabinet ministers and other officials are no longer officers of the Emperor using the authority delegated by the Throne to rule the people; they are public servants. The old attitude summed up in the motto, "Respect for officials and scorn for the people" (*kanson minpi*) has presumably been replaced by the egalitarian idea.

However, many historical, social, and political factors militate against democratic attitudes and behavior. Confucianism has normally exalted the role of the bureaucrat. The most promising sons of rural landlords have traditionally aspired to high position in government and the prestige that it brings to himself, his family, and his community. The brightest students in the great Imperial (now National) Universities major in law and public administration in order to pass the examinations for public office.

During the Meiji period the government bureaucracy, rather than private initiative, introduced Western technology and business methods. After government enterprises were put on a paying basis they were sold to private companies. Business still depends greatly on the bureaucracy for advice and favors of all sorts. The economy as well as the politics of the country have long been under bureaucratic direction. Ordinary politicians do not enjoy the measure of respect that high government officials command. The bureaucrat is respected because of his education, technical knowledge and skill, his reputation for impartiality, and his power.

Under the new Constitution, it is necessary to be a member of the Diet in order to become Prime Minister, and half of the remaining Ministers must be Diet members. Today the bureaucrat who aspires to Cabinet position must enter politics. Furthermore, when an official finds that further promotion is unlikely or that he must retire on an inadequate pension, he is apt seriously to consider a political career. He has already proved his administrative competence, and he enjoys a measure of prestige in his home community where people regard him as a home-town boy who made good, and they take a personal interest in his political career. During the long regime of Yoshida, bureaucrats streamed into the Liberal Party. Thus Japanese politics differs drastically from politics in America, for in Japan one of the best ways to begin a political career is to enter the civil service. Most of the post-war Prime Ministers in Japan have had long careers in the civil service, but never in the history of the United States has the career bureaucracy produced a President. Shidehara, Yoshida, Ashida, Kishi, and Ikeda were career civil servants before becoming premier.

A Case of Tender Feeling

Finance Minister Ikeda told a news conference that if five or ten small businessmen go bankrupt and commit suicide it just can't be helped. Here Ikeda concentrates on his abacus, while small business protests. Japanese newspapers, like newspapers elsewhere, carry political cartoons. (Source: Nasu Ryosuke, *Yoshida kara Kishi e* [*From Yoshida to Kishi*] [Tokyo: Mainichi Shimbunsha, 1959], p. 3.)

Bureaucrats naturally regard their own opinion as more informed than that of the layman, and Cabinet Ministers with bureaucratic origins often take a scornful attitude towards legislators, the press, and the general public. Ikeda Hayato was notorious for his lack of tact before he became Prime Minister. While Finance Minister he said in a plenary session of the Diet that "It can't be helped if five or ten small businessmen involved in blackmarketing commit suicide because of bankruptcy." This cold-hearted attitude provoked a vote of no confidence in Ikeda, forcing him to resign from the Cabinet.

Table 2

Japanese Cabinets

Clan and party affiliations of Prime Ministers are indicated in parentheses.

1.	December 22, 1885	Itō Hirobumi (Chōshū), *First*
2.	April 30, 1888	General Kuroda Kiyotaka (Satsuma)
3.	December 24, 1889	General Yamagata Aritomo (Chōshū), *First*
4.	May 6, 1891	Matsukata Masayoshi (Satsuma), *First*
5.	August 8, 1892	Itō Hirobumi (Chōshū), *Second*
6.	September 18, 1896	Matsukata Masayoshi (Satsuma), *Second*
7.	January 12, 1898	Itō Hirobumi (Chōshū), *Third*
8.	June 30, 1898	Ōkuma Shigenobu (Hizen, Kenseitō), *First*
9.	November 8, 1898	General Yamagata Aritomo (Chōshū), *Second*
10.	October 19, 1900	Itō Hirobumi (Chōshū, Seiyūkai), *Fourth*
11.	June 2, 1901	General Katsura Tarō (Chōshū), *First*
12.	January 7, 1906	Prince Saionji Kimmochi (kuge [court noble], Seiyūkai), *First*
13.	July 14, 1908	General Katsura Tarō (Chōshū), *Second*
14.	August 30, 1911	Prince Saionji Kimmochi (kuge, Seiyūkai), *Second*
15.	December 21, 1912	General Katsura Tarō (Chōshū), *Third*
16.	February 20, 1913	Admiral Yamamoto Gombei (Satsuma), *First*
17.	April 16, 1914	Ōkuma Shigenobu (Hizen), *Second*
18.	October 9, 1916	General Terauchi Masatake (Chōshū)
19.	September 29, 1918	Hara Takashi (Seiyūkai)
20.	November 13, 1921	Takahashi Korekiyo (Seiyūkai)
21.	June 12, 1922	Admiral Katō Tomosaburō
22.	September 2, 1923	Admiral Yamamoto Gombei (Satsuma), *Second*
23.	January 7, 1924	Kiyoura Keigo
24.	June 11, 1924	Katō Takaaki (Kenseikai), *First*
25.	August 2, 1925	Katō Takaaki (Kenseikai), *Second*
26.	January 30, 1926	Wakatsuki Reijiro (Kenseikai), *First*
27.	April 20, 1927	General Tanaka Giichi (Seiyūkai)
28.	July 2, 1929	Hamaguchi Osachi (Minseitō)
29.	April 14, 1931	Wakatsuki Reijiro (Minseitō), *Second*
30.	December 13, 1931	Inukai Tsuyoshi (Seiyūkai)
31.	May 26, 1932	Admiral Saitō Makato
32.	July 8, 1934	Admiral Okada Keisuke
33.	March 9, 1936	Hirota Kōki
34.	February 2, 1937	General Hayashi Senjūrō
35.	June 4, 1937	Prince Konoye Fumimaro (kuge), *First*
36.	January 5, 1939	Hiranuma Kiichirō
37.	August 30, 1939	General Abe Nobuyuki
38.	January 16, 1940	Admiral Yonai Mitsumasa

39.	July 22, 1940	Prince Konoye Fumimaro (kuge), *Second*
40.	July 18, 1941	Prince Konoye Fumimaro (kuge), *Third*
41.	October 18, 1941	General Tōjō Hideki
42.	July 22, 1944	General Koiso Kuniaki
43.	April 7, 1945	Admiral Suzuki Kantarō
44.	August 17, 1945	Prince Higashikuni Naruhiko
45.	October 9, 1945	Shidehara Kijūrō (Shimpotō)
46.	May 22, 1946	Yoshida Shigeru (Jiyūtō), *First*
47.	May 24, 1947	Katayama Tetsu (Shakaitō)
48.	March 10, 1948	Ashida Hitoshi (Minshutō)
49.	October 15, 1948	Yoshida Shigeru (Minshu-Jiyūtō), *Second*
50.	February 16, 1949	Yoshida Shigeru (Minshu-Jiyūtō), *Third*
51.	October 30, 1952	Yoshida Shigeru (Jiyūtō), *Fourth*
52.	May 21, 1953	Yoshida Shigeru (Jiyūtō), *Fifth*
53.	December 10, 1954	Hatoyama Ichirō (Minshutō), *First*
54.	March 19, 1955	Hatoyama Ichirō (Minshutō), *Second*
55.	November 22, 1955	Hatoyama Ichirō (Jiyū-Minshutō), *Third*
56.	December 23, 1956	Ishibashi Tanzan (Jiyū-Minshutō)
57.	February 25, 1957	Kishi Nobusuke (Jiyū-Minshutō), *First*
	(July 10, 1957	Reconstructed)
58.	June 13, 1958	Kishi Nobusuke (Jiyū-Minshutō), *Second*
	(June 18, 1959	Reconstructed)
59.	July 19, 1960	Ikeda Hayato (Jiyū-Minshutō), *First*
60.	December 10, 1960	Ikeda Hayato (Jiyū-Minshutō), *Second*
	(July 18, 1961	Reconstructed)
	(July 17, 1962	Reconstructed)

SUGGESTED READINGS

See Suggested Readings listed at end of Chapter 6.

❋ 5 ❋

The Diet

The House of Representatives Electoral System

Since Japan is a unitary state, the qualifications for voting and the electoral system are determined by the national government rather than, as in the United States, by state governments. The principal electoral laws for the House of Representatives have been those of 1889,[1] 1900, 1919, 1925, 1945, and 1947.[2] In 1950, a Public Offices Election Law, subsequently amended at intervals, laid down provisions for elections of members of both houses of the Diet and of prefectural and municipal officials.

There are no primary elections or nominating conventions in Japan. A person becomes a candidate for either house of the National Diet simply by notifying the chairman of the local election board and filing a deposit of 100,000 yen ($277.00). The money is not returned unless the candidate polls one-fifth of the valid votes cast divided by the number of seats to be filled from the district. Independent candidates as a rule have little chance to be elected, so that it is normally necessary to be officially sponsored by a political party and to run as a party candidate. Party nominations are made by an election committee in the central headquarters of the party.

In 1890 in the first election for the newly established House of Representatives, only 1.10 per cent (450,852) of the total population of Japan (39,902,000) were allowed to vote. A voter had to be a male at least 25 years of age, who paid more than 15 yen direct

[1] "Law of the Election of the Members of the House of Representatives," in Itō Hirobumi, *Commentaries on the Constitution of the Empire of Japan* (Tokyo: Insetsu Kyoku, 1889), pp. 195–246.

[2] "The Law for the Election of Members of the House of Representatives," in Government Section, Supreme Commander for the Allied Powers, *Political Reorientation of Japan: September 1945 to September 1949,* 2 vols. (Washington: Government Printing Office, n.d. [1949]), II, 822–845. (These volumes will subsequently be referred to as *Political Reorientation.*)

national tax for more than one year, or paid an income tax for more than three years. It was also necessary to have official as well as actual residence within a prefecture for more than one year.

In 1902 the tax qualification was lightened, with the result that the electorate was doubled in number. The tax requirement was reduced to 3 yen direct national tax and the residence period was reduced to six months in 1919, so that in the following year there were slightly over 3,000,000 qualified voters in a total population of about 56,000,-000. The early twenties witnessed a hard-fought struggle for "universal suffrage" (i.e., suffrage for adult *males*), and in 1925, the Diet passed a Universal Suffrage Act, which conferred the right to vote on all males over 25 years of age. Nearly 10,000,000 of the 12,500,000 qualified voters cast their vote in the 1928 election, the first in which universal manhood suffrage applied.

Although women still did not have the right to vote, it appeared that it would not be long before this right was granted. Unfortunately, the Peace Preservation Law and the weak position of the Diet with respect to the military oligarchy which ruled Japan in the 1930's more than counterbalanced the democratic features of the electoral system.

In October, 1945, General MacArthur directed the Japanese government to provide for female suffrage in the forthcoming general election. The Diet revised the electoral law to give the vote to women and reduce the voting age from 25 to 20. In April, 1946, women voted for the first time in Japanese history. Article 44 of the 1947 Constitution provides that "The qualifications of . . . electors shall be fixed by law. However, there shall be no discrimination because of race, creed, sex, social status, family origin, education, property or income." This article applies to both houses of the Japanese Diet, so that the democratic basis of the upper house as well as the lower house is apparently assured.

In the 1890 election, the country was divided into small districts, each sending one, or in some cases two, members to the House of Representatives. The system has been changed from time to time, but that in use since 1925, excluding the 1946 election, has been the "medium-district system" (chū senkyoku sei). The country is divided into 117 election districts, each sending from three to five members to the House of Representatives. In addition, since 1955, the district of Amami Ōshima elects one Representative. Each voter casts his ballot for *only one* candidate. The candidates receiving the highest numbers of votes win. Thus, for example, in the Shizuoka Prefecture third district, which is entitled to four seats in the House of Representatives, the four candidates receiving the highest number of votes win the four seats. In this system, a party which commands only a minority of the votes in the district may win one or two seats. The Japanese system is a form of "limited voting," i.e., the individual elector is permitted to vote for fewer candidates than the total number of seats to be filled for his electoral district.

The Japanese medium-district system makes possible a very rudimentary form of proportional representation (PR). Ideally, of course, proportional representation allots the seats of a district to parties in proportion to the votes that they receive. In the Japanese system, however, candidates of the same party find themselves competing against one another for votes. Thus in 1953 Kishi Nobusuke and his brother Satō Eisaku both competed for Liberal votes in the same district in Yamaguchi. Notwithstanding this disadvantage, both were elected.[3] A member of the Socialist Party might receive many more votes than he needs to win and deprive a fellow Socialist of necessary votes. However, if the Socialist voters divide their votes among too many Socialist candidates, the Socialists might win very few or no seats. It is therefore necessary for the political parties to see to it that they put up the optimum number of candidates in each district. Party leaders try not to put up too many candidates, which would scatter the vote excessively, or too few candidates, which would result in wasting votes. Generally, Socialists do better in four- or five-man districts than in three-man districts.

In the 1960 election, there were 940 candidates for the 467 seats, or slightly more than two candidates for each seat. The Liberal-Democrats nominated 399 candidates, the Socialists 186, the Democratic-Socialists 105, the Communists 118 (one in each district), minor parties 34, and independent candidates came to 98.[4] From these figures it is evident that it would be impossible for any one party to win all of the 467 seats, since none put up that many candidates. Furthermore, the only party which could hope to win a majority (234 seats) in the new Diet was the Liberal-Democratic. The voters had, in effect, a choice between either a Liberal-Democratic Cabinet or some kind of coalition Cabinet.

In 1960 it was assumed that interest in the election would be unusually high because of the turmoil of the preceding summer concerning the "forcible passage" of the Security Pact, the cancellation of the Eisenhower visit, and the assassination by a rightist of the Socialist secretary general Asanuma. Among the issues were foreign policy and the preservation of parliamentary government. However, the turn-out of voters was 73.5 per cent, a decline from the 76.9 per

[3] Dan Kurzman, *Kishi and Japan: The Search for the Sun* (New York: Ivan Obolensky, 1960), pp. 276–277.

[4] *Japan Times*, November 20, 1960.

cent of the preceding 1958 election. Voter participation in Japan, nevertheless, compares favorably with that in the United States, where 64.3 per cent of the adults over 21 voted in the presidential election in 1960.[5]

In 1960 the Liberal-Democrats with 57.6 per cent of the votes won 63 per cent of the seats. The Socialists, with 27.5 per cent of the votes, won 31 per cent of the seats. In terms of the votes that they had received, the two large parties got more seats than they deserved. On the other hand, the election was disastrous for the Democratic-Socialist Party. With 8.8 per cent of the votes it won only 3.6 per cent of the seats. Under strictly proportional representation it would have won 41 seats. Instead, it won only 17, and there was a question as to whether with so few members it could qualify as a bargaining group in the Diet. The Socialists were the best election strategists, because it took them only 75,000 votes to win each seat, while it took the Liberal-Democrats about 76,800 votes for each of its seats. The Democratic-Socialists did the worst, since it took an average of 204,000 popular votes to win each of their seats.[6]

In Japan as elsewhere, politicians like to tinker with the electoral system to make it work most advantageously for them. Just before or just after an election, the majority party or majority coalition wants to change the rules of the game in its favor, and the opposition strongly objects. In 1956 Liberal-Democratic Prime Minister Hatoyama submitted a bill to the Diet providing for the small-district system. He alleged that the medium-district system prevented the proper development of the two-party system since there was the possibility that a third or fourth party might be formed, making necessary coalition Cabinets. Furthermore, he held that elections under the present system cost too much money.

The opposition charged that the Prime Minister's real motive in advocating small districts was to decrease Socialist strength, which had to gather its votes from relatively large districts. The small-district system would have an additional advantage for the Liberal-Democrats because it would reduce factional struggles within the party for nomination and for election. It was also widely understood that a change in the electoral system might work sufficiently to the advantage of the Liberal-Democrats so that they would win the two-thirds majority in the lower house necessary to amend the Constitution. The Hatoyama electoral bill ("Hatomander"), however, was rejected be-

[5] Philip E. Converse, Angus Campbell, Warren E. Miller, Donald E. Stokes, "Stability and Change in 1960: A Reinstating Election," *The American Political Science Review,* Vol. LV, No. 2 (June, 1961), p. 269.

[6] *Japan Times,* November 24, 1960.

cause of opposition not only from the Socialists but also from the anti-mainstream faction in the Liberal-Democratic Party which feared that the electoral reform would strengthen the mainstream faction of the party. While the Liberal-Democrats tend to advocate the small-district system, the Socialists have advocated large districts with proportional representation.[7] However, following the 1960 election, in which the Socialists won more seats per vote than the other parties, the Socialists became less dogmatic in their advocacy of proportional representation. In the light of the record, it may be assumed that considerations of political expediency rather than abstract theory will continue to determine the nature of the electoral system.

The House of Councillors Electoral System

The House of Peers, as noted in Chapter 1, had been created by Prince Itō to win the support of the aristocracy to the centralized monarchy and to check democratic excesses in the lower house. This aristocratic body, as constituted under the Imperial Ordinance of the House of Peers of 1889,[8] several times revised, contained in 1941 the following categories of members: (1) 16 Princes of the Blood, (2) 18 Princes, (3) 37 Marquises, (4) 18 Counts, (5) 66 Viscounts, (6) 64 Barons, (7) 125 imperial nominees, (8) 4 Imperial Academy members, (9) 64 high taxpayers, a total of 412 members.[9] Just before the House of Peers was brought to an end by the new Constitution, its membership had fallen to 373.[10] The Counts, Viscounts, and Barons were representatives elected by the members of their respective orders. The highest taxpaying members were elected from and by the 100 or 200 persons in each prefecture, depending upon its size, who paid the highest direct national taxes on land or on industrial or commercial property. The term of office was for seven years except for the members of the Imperial Family, Princes, Marquises, and imperial nominees, all of whom served for life.

At the time of the drafting of the new Constitution in SCAP Government Section, it was made known that General MacArthur favored a unicameral legislature. There was a strong feeling in the Section that the House of Peers should be done away with and nothing resembling it should be put in its place. Furthermore, there was strong objection to any form of functional or corporate upper house (i.e., an upper

[7] Shinobu Seisaburō, *Nihon Seiji Tokuhon* (Tokyo: Tōyō Keizai Shimpōsha, 1960), pp. 163–166.

[8] English text in Itō, pp. 168–171, and *Political Reorientation*, II, 596–597.

[9] *The Orient Year Book: 1942* (Tokyo: The Asia Statistics Co., 1942), p. 372.

[10] *Political Reorientation*, I, 181.

house representing vocational or economic groups).[11] The Americans held that no upper house corresponding to the United States Senate was necessary in Japan, because Japan was not a federation of states each of which required representation in the national legislature.[12] Japanese officials proposed that a House of Councillors be established to "consist of members elected for the various districts or professions and members appointed by the Cabinet upon resolution of a committee consisting of members of both Houses."[13] An upper house, the Japanese felt, was necessary as a check against hasty, ill-considered measures supported by a majority party in the lower house.[14]

A compromise between the Japanese and American points of view emerged with the establishment of a House of Councillors, the members of which would, according to the Constitution, be elected for six years, election for half of the members taking place every three years. The precise composition of the House of Councillors was left vague by the Constitution. However, like the lower house, it would consist of "elected members, representative of all of the people," and there could be "no discrimination because of . . . social status, family origin, education, property or income." Although the electoral system would be determined by ordinary law, it would seem difficult, in the light of the Constitution, to make the House of Councillors a vocational, corporate, or aristocratic chamber.

The House of Councillors consists of a total of 250 members, of whom 150 represent prefectural constituencies, and 100 represent the national constituency, i.e., are elected by the nation at large. Since the terms are staggered, every three years 75 members are elected in the prefectural constituencies, and 50 members elected in the national constituency. Each of the 46 prefectures is entitled to from two to eight seats in the House of Councillors, the more populous prefectures having more seats than the less populous. In House of Councillors elections, each voter votes for one candidate in the prefectural constituency and for one candidate in the national constituency. As in the case of the lower house elections, the candidates receiving the most votes win.[15] The purpose of the large electoral districts was to ensure that the political composition of the House of Councillors would be dissimilar from that of the House of Representatives. It was hoped that

[11] *Ibid.*, I, 103.

[12] Matsumoto Jōji, "Nihonkoku Kempō no Sōan ni tsuite" [Concerning the Drafts of the Constitution of Japan], Kempō Chōsakai, *Kenshi Sōdai Nijūhachi Go* [*Materials on the Constitution,* General No. 28], (October, 1958), pp. 11–12.

[13] *Ibid.*, II, 626–627.

[14] Matsumoto Jōji, p. 12.

[15] *Political Reorientation,* I, 183.

the large prefectural and national constituencies would provide an opportunity for persons of wide reputation to win political office without having to become involved in the rough-and-tumble of partisan politics and that Councillors, who are required to be at least 30 years of age, as contrasted with the Representatives who need be only 25, would be superior in dignity, experience, and impartiality to the Representatives. After fifteen years of operation, however, the House of Councillors is not greatly different from the House of Representatives either in terms of age or politics. The strength of the two main parties is about identical in each house.

There is as much possibility to gerrymander with the House of Councillors districts as with the lower house districts. Conservatives sometimes allege that the national constituency should be abolished since most of the candidates in the national constituency are completely unknown to the voters and there is lack of interest in the election. On the other hand, the Socialists have advocated that all of the seats of the House of Councillors be based on the national constituency, each party receiving a number of seats proportional to its votes. In the national constituency arrangement, candidates who enjoy the support of national organizations have a great advantage over those who do not. Socialist candidates are often supported by nation-wide labor unions, whereas conservative candidates usually cannot get support from more than four or five prefectures at most. When people vote according to personalities of the candidates they are apt to vote conservative; when they vote according to party platform, the Socialist party stands more chance than it would otherwise.[16] Given the present balance of political forces both within and without the Diet, it seems rather unlikely that either the Liberal-Democrats or the Socialists will be able to change the electoral systems for the two houses of the Diet.

The Organization of the Houses

The terms of the members of the lower house are fixed by the Constitution at four years, subject to being shortened as the result of a dissolution. Since World War II the members of the House of Representatives have never served out full four-year terms. The term of office of Councillors is six years, with the terms of half of the members expiring every three years. The House of Councillors is not subject to dissolution.

Each house elects a Speaker and a Vice-Speaker. Ideally the Speaker should be politically neutral. However, in 1946, Speaker

[16] Shinobu, pp. 164–165.

Higai Senzo attempted to prevent a committee from reporting on a bill in the lower house. The Socialists moved a vote of no confidence in the Speaker, but the motion was defeated. When the Socialists threatened to boycott further deliberations until the Speaker resigned, Higai quit, and a new Speaker was elected.[17] Neutrality is virtually impossible of achievement since the Speaker is bound to make himself *persona non grata* to one party or another when he makes decisions respecting partisan quarrels over procedure.

The first main business of each house after an election is to choose its Speaker and Vice-Speaker. In June, 1958, when it appeared that the majority Liberal-Democratic Party would elect both of its candidates to these positions, the objections of the Socialists resulted in delaying the election of the Speaker until the second day of the session, but the Liberal-Democratic candidates won both posts. In December, 1960, the Socialists and Democratic-Socialists strenuously objected to the re-election as Speaker of Kiyose Ichirō, who was supported by the Liberal-Democrats. Faced with a possible Socialist boycott of the Diet, Ikeda Hayato, president of the Liberal-Democratic Party, consented to negotiations between party leaders to work out an understanding. A compromise between the majority party and the other parties provided for the election of the conservative candidate, Kiyose, for Speaker, and a Socialist, Kubota Tsurumatsu, for Vice-Speaker. When the house convened, the Liberal-Democrats (a majority) voted for Kiyose, and the Socialists cast blank ballots so that Kiyose was elected. The Liberal-Democrats and Socialists both voted for Kubota for Vice-Speaker. This squabble over the speakership had its basis in the factionalism of the Liberal-Democratic Party and the political crisis of the preceding session of the Diet. Miffed because his faction would not be represented in the forthcoming Ikeda Cabinet, Ishii Mitsujirō had refused Ikeda's request that he run for Speaker. Kiyose was left as the only other Liberal-Democratic possibility; however, Kiyose, as Speaker, had called police into the Diet in the preceding May, and thus antagonized the Socialists. The willingness of the two parties to compromise on the speakerships was their contribution to the "normalization of the Diet," a cause to which both parties had proclaimed emphatic devotion in the November campaign.

As in the United States, each house is organized into committees to consider proposed legislation. The first houses under the new Constitution each had 21 standing committees (jōnin iinkai). The number was subsequently reduced to 16. There are in each house standing committees on (1) Cabinet, (2) local administration, (3) judicial af-

---

[17] Supreme Commander for the Allied Powers, *Monthly Summation of Non-Military Activities in Japan,* August, 1946, p. 27.

fairs, (4) foreign affairs, (5) finance, (6) education, (7) welfare and labor, (8) agriculture, forestry and fisheries, (9) commerce and industry, (10) transport, (11) communications, (12) construction, (13) budget, (14) accounts, (15) steering, and (16) discipline. Most of these committees correspond to ministries in the executive branch.

There are also special committees for the study of particular problems or proposals. For example, in the House of Representatives of the thirty-fourth Diet there were (1) the Special Committee for the Study of the Revision of the Public Offices Election Law, (2) the Special Committee on Policy for the Promotion of Science and Technology, (3) the Special Committee on Coordinated Land Development, and (4) the Special Committee on the Japan-United States Security Treaty.

Committee chairmen are chosen on the basis of partisan political considerations. The seniority system, which prevails in the United States Congress, is not followed. Since 1958, chairmanships have been monopolized by the government party. Memberships in each committee are allocated to parties on the basis of party strength in the house.

The Diet committees hold public hearings, make investigating trips, including travel abroad, have the power of subpoena, and may use the services of the National Diet Library. Several investigating committees have become quite famous, especially the Committee on Illegal Disposal of Government Property, organized in 1947, and the Special Committee on Administrative Supervision.

There has been criticism that the standing committees are too much inclined to support the legislative proposals of the Government. However, it is difficult to see how the committee members could act in a completely independent fashion without breaking party discipline and possibly forcing the resignation of the Cabinet. The coalition Cabinet of the Socialist Prime Minister Katayama Tetsu was forced to resign in 1948 partly because of the defeat which it suffered in the budget committee led by the committee chairman, a Socialist, who disagreed with the Government's fiscal policies. The government party members of a committee, out of loyalty to their party, are more or less duty bound to see to it that their party platform is legislated into reality, and the Government party is not embarrassed. The opposition members of a committee often resort to filibusters, boycotts, and occasionally to riots in order to prevent committee approval of a Government bill. It is notable that in Great Britain, where the parliamentary-cabinet system operates most smoothly and efficiently, standing committees are tame institutions and on the whole support the Government. The principal functions of the committee system in Japan are (1) to educate the public, since committee meetings are usually open and well publicized by the press, and (2) to provide an arena for criticism and obstruction by the opposition.

The Legislative Process

The Diet, according to the Constitution, is "the sole lawmaking organ of the State."[18] Its function thus resembles that of the Congress of the United States, in which are vested all legislative powers granted by the United States Constitution. However, the legislative power of a parliament in a parliamentary system such as the Japanese is very different from that in a presidential system such as the American. In the parliamentary system, if the legislature rejects a measure deemed vital by the executive, a political crisis arises which may result in either the resignation of the cabinet or the dissolution of the parliament with new elections, or both. Thus, in the parliamentary form of democracy, the legislative process is fraught with vastly greater political significance than in a presidential democracy, and bills are not considered on their merit alone but in terms of the politically crucial relation between the legislature and the executive. In the parliamentary system, a principal function of the legislature is to supervise the executive.

If the parliament frequently disregards the wish of the cabinet concerning important measures, and if the cabinet cannot dissolve the parliament, ministerial instability such as characterized the French Third and Fourth Republics will result. On the other hand, if the cabinet normally enjoys the support of a comfortable majority, i.e., if the cabinet and the majority in the parliament are of the same political party or harmonious coalition of parties, there is apt to be no serious difference of views on legislation, and the parliament tends to be a "rubber stamp" for bills presented by the cabinet. The result is a so-called "cabinet dictatorship," such as is sometimes said to exist in Great Britain. When this situation arises in Japan it is apt to be labeled by the opposition as the "tyranny of the majority."

In Japan, "voting in the House of Representatives runs strictly along party lines."[19] The Government party (or parties) normally vote for government bills, the opposition party (or parties) vote normally against them. Bills introduced by individual Diet members often require budgetary outlays not provided for in the budget, thus endangering the government's fiscal policy. It has been found necessary to develop some procedure whereby the Government party and

[18] Constitution, Article 41.

[19] Nobutaka Ike, *Japanese Politics: An Introductory Survey* (New York: Knopf, 1957), p. 184.

Cabinet may curb the introduction of pork-barrel legislation catering to special interest groups and particular localities. Consequently, under the third Hatoyama Cabinet, the political affairs research committee of the Liberal-Democratic Party and the Cabinet undertook to clear individual members' bills.[20] The policy organs of the ruling Liberal-Democratic Party have therefore become an important factor in the legislative process.

How are laws made? Bills (hōan or hōritsu-an) may be introduced by the Prime Minister, representing the Cabinet, or, infrequently, by a member of either house. The Speaker of the house to which the bill is introduced as a rule refers the bill to the appropriate standing committee or a special committee of the house. When a bill is considered urgent, committee examination may be omitted by decision of the steering committee. After study and approval by a committee, the bill is submitted to a plenary session of the house for deliberation and a vote. In the event of a tie, the Speaker casts the deciding vote. After approval by one house, the bill is sent to the Speaker of the other house where it must again be submitted to deliberation in committee and plenary sessions. When passed by both houses the bill becomes law.

If the House of Councillors rejects a measure passed by the Representatives or fails to take action on the measure within sixty days (time in recess excepted), the House of Representatives may override the veto of the House of Councillors by a two-thirds majority. In the event of a difference of view between the House of Representatives and the House of Councillors, the former may call for a meeting of a joint committee of both houses to deliberate on the measure.[21]

The procedure for the enactment of the budget and for the approval of treaties is different from that for other legislation. The budget or treaty must first be submitted to and approved by the House of Representatives. The Representatives' decision is that of the Diet (1) when the House of Councillors makes a decision different from that of the Representatives and when no agreement can be reached even through a joint committee of two houses, or (2) when the House of Councillors fails to take action within thirty days (period of recess excluded) after the receipt of the budget or treaty passed by the

[20] Hattie Kawahara Colton, "The National Diet After Independence," *The Annals of the American Academy of Political and Social Science,* Vol. 308 (November, 1956), pp. 25–26. See also Dr. Colton's article, "The Working of the Japanese Diet," *Pacific Affairs,* XXVIII (December, 1955), pp. 363–372, reprinted in Lyman Jay Gould and E. William Steele, eds., *People, Power and Politics: An Introductory Reader* (New York: Random House, 1961), pp. 374–384.

[21] Constitution, Article 59.

Representatives.[22] A dramatic application of this provision occurred in 1960, when the Japan-America Security Pact, after approval by the House of Representatives, was not deliberated upon in the House of Councillors because of the decision of the latter not to deliberate without the Socialists, who were boycotting the house. Tens of thousands of demonstrators surrounded the Diet building awaiting the "automatic approval" (shizen shōnin) of the treaty, which would occur at midnight, June 18, thirty days after the Liberal-Democrats in the House of Representatives had approved the treaty in the absence of the Socialist members. The parades, the speeches, the shouts and the placards of the multitude were of no avail against the inexorable ticking of the clock.

Bills which apply to only a single local entity must be approved by a majority vote of the people of the entity before becoming law.[23]

The Diet may initiate amendments to the Constitution when two-thirds of all of the members of each house vote in favor of the proposed amendment. The proposal must then be ratified by a majority vote of the people in order to become part of the Constitution.[24] Thus far, the 1947 Constitution has not been amended because none of the much publicized proposals for constitutional change has been supported by a sufficient majority in either house.

When the House of Representatives is dissolved, the House of Councillors is closed at the same time. In case of a national emergency, the Cabinet may convoke the House of Councillors in emergency session to take provisional measures which become null and void unless agreed to by the House of Representatives within ten days after the next session of the Diet opens.[25] This provision of the Constitution was invoked in 1952 and again in 1953.[26]

Under the old Constitution, the sanction of the Emperor was necessary before a bill could become law.[27] Under the present Constitution, the assent of the Emperor is unnecessary, and the Emperor has no power to veto the bill. Instead, the Constitution simply states that the Emperor promulgates laws.[28]

Obstructionism

With the polarization of Japanese politics into two ideological camps, the one conservative, the other radical, parliamentary process in Japan has deteriorated to the point that it sometimes appears

[22] Constitution, Articles 60, 61.
[23] Constitution, Article 95.
[24] Constitution, Article 96.
[25] Constitution, Article 54.   [26] *Asahi Nenkan, 1960,* p. 233.
[27] Constitution of 1889, Article VI.   [28] Constitution, Article 7.

that democratic government itself is in danger. Certain measures proposed by the conservative majority have been so unacceptable to the Socialist minority that they feel that extralegal methods may justifiably be used to obstruct the objectionable bills, many of which would reverse the democratic reforms of the Occupation. The conservative-sponsored electoral bills (1947, 1956), the Subversive Activities Prevention Bill (1952), the Police Bill (1954), the Police Duties Revision Bill (1958), the United States-Japan Security Pact (1960), and the Anti-Violence Bill (1961) were held by the Socialist opposition to be in clear violation of the spirit and letter of the democratic Constitution. The passage of these measures by the Government using its majority in the Diet, would, it was held, endanger the existence of democracy itself.

Since the coming into being of the two-party system in 1955, there has been a gross imbalance of political forces in the Diet, the Liberal-Democrats holding nearly two-thirds of the seats, the Socialists and their allies holding slightly over one-third in each house. There is little prospect that a general election in the near future would result in a change in this balance of forces. The Liberal-Democrats dominate the executive, legislative, and judicial branches of the government. In order to prevent the "tyranny of the majority," the minority believes that it must use obstructionist tactics.

In the United States Senate, a minority may obstruct the will of the majority by using a filibuster which prevents a vote from being taken on the measure which the minority opposes. Other devices for the protection of minorities are the presidential veto, judicial review of legislation, and states' rights, all of which place limits on the power of the majority in the national legislature.

In Japan, there is no executive veto, practically speaking, since most of the bills laid before the Diet have been either sponsored or approved by the Cabinet. The Supreme Court is distrusted as partisan. There are no states' rights, since the political system is unitary rather than federal. The Socialists make frequent use of the filibuster both in committees and in plenary session to prevent votes from being taken before the expiration of parliamentary sessions and to defeat motions to extend the session. Another device is the suwarikomi, or "sit-down" (literally, sit and fill up). On a number of occasions, Socialist members of the lower house, sometimes aided by their secretaries, have blocked the corridors of the Diet to prevent the Speaker of the House of Representatives from calling the meeting to order. In 1954, 1960, and 1961 the Speaker called in police physically to remove the Socialists who were preventing him from convening the house. The suwarikomi is also used by demonstrators around the Diet building and in labor and other disputes. The advantage for the sit-downers is that they may obstruct the orderly process of law without incurring the onus of committing violence. It is the police who are blamed for starting trouble when they try to remove sit-downers.

The parliamentary opposition may resort to a riot within the august chambers of the Diet to prevent a vote from being taken. In 1961, when the speaker called for a vote on the Anti-Violence Bill, the tumult was so great that neither he nor the members voting could be heard. He nevertheless announced on the microphone that the bill was passed and sent it to the House of Councillors. There the Liberal-Democrats were reluctant to provoke Socialist violence, and the Socialists were willing to compromise. It was agreed to suspend discussion of the controversial measure until the next session of the Diet. The prospects of passing the bill now seem dim, as the Government considers other legislation more urgent and does not want to invite trouble by resuming deliberation on such a controversial measure.

A bicameral system provides more scope for obstruction than a single-chamber system. If the opposition cannot defeat a measure in one house, it can try again in the other.

Another obstructive device is the boycott. An opposition boycott cannot of itself prevent the formation of a quorum, which is one-third of the membership in each house. However, by nonattendance, the Socialists can make the majority party appear to be behaving "undemocratically" if the latter votes on a measure in the absence of the opposition. The Socialists have on frequent occasions boycotted both committee meetings and plenary sessions of both houses. An extreme form of the boycott was suggested by the threat of the Socialists members to resign their seats in parliament if the government refused to do the bidding of the Socialists. This occurred in 1960, when the Socialists demanded that the Cabinet resign and dissolve the Diet.

The mobilization of great mass demonstrations around the Diet protesting against a government bill creates the impression that the "people" are against the proposal, especially if the newspapers support the demonstrators, which is sometimes the case. Political strikes, usually led by the Sōhyō labor federation, are also an important political weapon of the Socialists. In some instances, the strikes or demonstrations are illegal or are violent, but usually they are not. Sometimes extremists, either Communists or rightists, attempt to make political capital by instigating or provoking violence; public opinion, however, tends to react negatively against excessive violence. When bloodshed does occasionally occur, the left accuses rightists of provocation (often a true charge) or the police of "brutality." The government blames the violence on Communist agitators and declares its determination not to give in to mob rule. Both sides in the political crisis are usually bitter and self-righteous. The struggle is basically ideological and frequently the immediate issues are lost sight of by the participants, all of whom are zealous to "protect democracy" and "parliamentary government" as they interpret the terms. The conservatives are normally unable to organize mass demonstrations. Instead, they are embarrassed by the notorious activities of small rightist terrorist organizations, which promote assassination and start fights with peaceful leftist demonstrators. Attempts by the government to limit demonstrations are of course labeled by the opposition as attacks on basic democratic freedoms and are met with more demonstrations. However, in order to mount demonstrations and strikes sufficient to bring about the defeat of a given bill, the issue must be one that gets the support of the press and seizes the imagination of the populace. Such issues are fairly few in number but arise about once every other year.

The obstructive and extraparliamentary tactics of the left against the parliamentary majority have been notably successful in several instances. Premier Hatoyama's electoral reform bill of 1956 was defeated. In 1958, Prime Minister Kishi withdrew the Police Duties Revision Bill but did not resign as was demanded. In 1960 Kishi promised to resign and later did, but managed to obtain approval of a controverted treaty in spite of mass demonstrations and repeated political strikes. In 1961, the controversial Anti-Violence Bill was shelved by the Ikeda Government. In the light of the effectiveness of their extralegal obstructive technics, it seems unlikely that the Socialist Party and Sōhyō labor federation will willingly give them up, notwithstanding the pious injunctions of government officials and well-meaning foreign observers.

The Powers of the National Diet

The Japanese Diet is the oldest parliament in Asia, having been in continuous existence since 1890. But as indicated in Chapter 1, the role of the Diet in policy-making before the end of World War II was much restricted. The executive branch represented the bureaucratic and military oligarchy and normally was not responsible to the parliament. About the most that the Diet could do was to defeat Government bills. The Diet did not have the power to convene on its own initiative, to disapprove of treaties, to declare war, or to initiate constitutional amendments. The Diet could pass, reduce, or reject the Government-prepared budget, but could not increase it. If the parliament rejected the budget, the budget of the previous year could be put into effect by the Government. The members of the lower house had lower court rank than many government officials, and their pay was about half that of Vice-Ministers. The Speaker of the House of Representatives was not elected by the Representatives, but rather was chosen by the Emperor from three members nominated by the house. The Government, if it wished, could prorogue the Diet, i.e., suspend a session for up to fifteen days. Between 1930 and 1935, the House of Representatives sought desperately to amend the Law of the Houses of 1889[29] to enhance the independence, power, and prestige of the Diet. Three times the lower house passed a reform bill, and three times the measure was rejected by the House of Peers, which made common cause with the oligarchic executive to prevent democratization.[30]

In the postwar Constitution the Diet was not only designated the "sole lawmaking organ of the State" but was declared to be "the highest organ of state power." The Japanese parliament would be "sovereign" like its British counterpart. It was given the powers normally possessed by legislatures in Anglo-Saxon democracies, and was organized along the lines of the Congress of the United States. The British type of parliamentary-cabinet system occupied an important place in the thinking of the Japanese and American reformers of the political system. There are, however, a number of important differences between the Japanese system and the British system. In Japan the upper chamber of the legislature is not virtually powerless like the House of Lords. In Japan there is an elaborate system of powerful committees unlike those in Britain. In Japan, from 1945 to 1955 there was a multi-party system rather than a two-party system, and it was frequently necessary to form coalition cabinets.

The American reformers seem to have thought of the Japanese Diet as a truly legislative chamber like the Congress of the United States, and at the same time thought of the parliament as having complete power over the executive. It was natural, in view of the past experience in Japan with executive dictatorship, to look to the legislature as the principal instrument of democratic government. However, the Americans apparently assumed the existence of a system of local autonomy and of a self-regulating free enterprise economy which would prevent excessive centralization of power in the national capital. They seem not to have foreseen the rise of ideological struggle in Japan, which would make it very difficult for the Diet to resolve class conflict, and the tendency towards a two-party system which would make it less likely for the parliament to check the executive. Nor did they clearly anticipate the possibility that the majority in the democratically elected Diet might enact reactionary legislation which would compromise democratic freedoms.

[29] English text in Itō, 172–194, and *Political Reorientation*, II, 597–602.
[30] *Political Reorientation*, I, 153–156.

It is also possible that the Americans had an only partial under-standing of cabinet government as it has actually operated in Great Britain in the twentieth century. "The omnipotence of the House of Commons, the absolute responsibility of the ministers to parliament — these ideas are so mystical that they can be explained only in terms of nostalgia for the nineteenth century."[31]

In 1955 when the two-party system replaced the multi-party system in Japan, the subordinance of the Cabinet to the Diet began to dis-appear. A vote of no confidence in the Cabinet became unlikely because party loyalty inhibited the majority from voting its own government out of office. In Japan, therefore, the legislature does not govern, nor does the Cabinet. The Liberal-Democratic Party governs. Liberal-Democrats in the Cabinet propose legislation, and Liberal-Democrats in the Diet pass it. The checks are the anti-mainstream faction within the Liberal-Democratic Party, the Socialist Party, the press, public opinion, or-ganized labor, and the student movement. This is not to say that the system is a one-party totalitarian dictatorship. The electorate may choose to vote the Liberal-Democrats out of office and vote the So-cialists in. For the time being, in light of the social influence and economic power of the conservatives, such an eventuality seems im-probable unless the Socialist Party tempers its program sufficiently to attract a majority of the voters.

The turmoil of Japanese parliamentary life is in part the result of conflicting conceptions of the proper roles of the Cabinet and the Diet in the political process and of the relation of majority rule to minority rights. Clear precedents and rules have not been established so that excessive time and energy are spent on procedural disputes, which are sometimes solved only by brawling or introducing the police or abdicating to street demonstrators. However, even if the rules were clear, the legitimacy of "bourgeois" parliamentary democracy is not universally accepted, so that extraparliamentary tactics are frequently resorted to, especially by left-wing Socialists, in order to "protect democracy" or to achieve ideological ends.

SUGGESTED READINGS

See Suggested Readings listed at end of Chapter 6.

[31] Don K. Price and Harold J. Laski, "A Debate on the Parliamentary and Presidential Systems," Roy C. Macridis and Bernard E. Brown, eds., *Comparative Politics: Notes and Readings* (Homewood, Illinois: Dorsey Press, 1961), p. 374.

6

Political Parties and Pressure Groups

The Liberal Party (1945–1955)

The conservative political parties which came forth in 1945 were essentially resuscitations of the prewar political parties which had been dissolved in 1940 at the time of the formation of the Imperial Rule Assistance Association by Prince Konoye. Members of the prewar Seiyūkai formed the Jiyūtō (Liberal Party), while the prewar Minseitō members joined the Shimpōtō (Progressive Party). The leadership of both of these parties was drastically affected by the purges of 1946 and 1947 and by the depurge which began in 1949. They were forever rent with factionalism and continual secessions of groups under disgruntled leaders. During the Occupation, when government policies were determined by SCAP, party labels and platforms meant little compared with factional and personal allegiances. In 1955, when the Socialist Party reunified, the two conservative parties stepped up their own efforts to unite, and in November, 1955, joined to form the Liberal-Democratic Party (Jiyū-Minshutō), which has since been the ruling party in Japan.

The founder of the Liberal Party, Hatoyama Ichirō, originally hoped to bring into a single conservative party all antimilitary, constitutionally liberal elements in the Diet, especially those who were fellow members of the Dōkō Kai, an anti-Tōjō group in the Diet between November, 1941, and May, 1942. The Dōkō Kai had been made up of Seiyūkai, Minseitō, and Shakai Taishūtō (Social Mass Party) people. Only former Seiyūkai members, however, joined Hatoyama's postwar Liberal Party; the rest chose to form parties of their own. When the second postwar Diet opened on November 26, 1945,

114

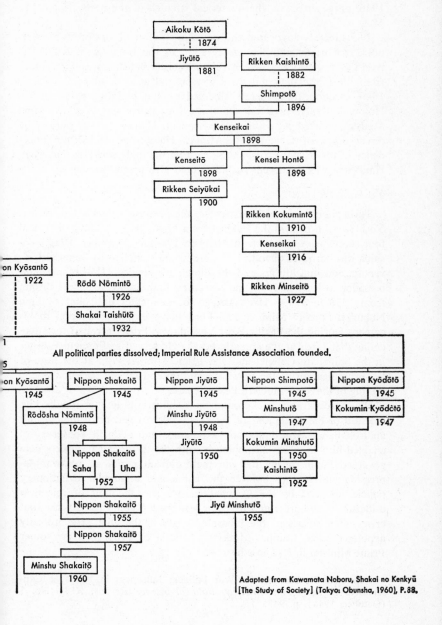

Figure 3

THE EVOLUTION OF POLITICAL PARTIES

Adapted from Kawamata Noboru, Shakai no Kenkyū
[The Study of Society] (Tokyo: Obunsha, 1960), P. 88.

the Liberal Party included 46 members in the House of Representatives and held second place among political parties. Following the January, 1946, purge directive, the numerical strength of the party dropped to 18.[1]

The Liberals advocated the popular election of prefectural governors, free trade, and the preservation of the Emperor system. The rival Progressive Party, led by Prime Minister Shidehara, suffered more from the purge than did the Liberals, and as a result of the April, 1946, election the Liberals emerged as the plurality party in the House of Representatives. On the eve of being appointed as Prime Minister to head a coalition Government, Hatoyama was purged by direct order of General MacArthur. Hatoyama yielded the presidency of the party to Yoshida Shigeru on the understanding that when Hatoyama was depurged Yoshida would give up the presidency.

Yoshida Shigeru

Throughout most of its existence, the party was dominated by Mr. Yoshida, who headed the Cabinet from May, 1946, to May, 1947, and four successive Cabinets from October, 1948, to December, 1954. Yoshida was born in Tokyo in 1878, graduated from Tokyo Imperial University, and in 1906 entered the diplomatic service. He became Ambassador to Italy in 1930 and served as Ambassador to Great Britain from 1936 to 1939. His marriage to a daughter of Count Makino Nobuaki, Foreign Minister and Lord Privy Seal, was a boon to his career. During the Pacific War, Yoshida was briefly arrested for advocating that Japan make an early peace. He served as Foreign Minister in the Shidehara Cabinet and was Prime Minister both at the time of the promulgation of the new Constitution and on the occasion of the signing of the San Francisco Peace Treaty.

His bureaucratic background and autocratic temper made him scornful of the politicians in the Diet, and he ruled his Cabinets with an iron hand. His diplomatic experience and staunch conservatism enabled him to work harmoniously with the American occupiers. He governed Japan during the extremely difficult period of postwar depression and had to enforce the harsh and unpopular deflationary policies dictated by the Occupation. He was the butt of relentless criticism by the press and by labor leaders, but could usually ride out crises on the basis of the Liberal strength in the Diet. He probably appointed more Cabinet Ministers (a total of 118) than any other Prime Minister in Japanese history.

[1] Kenneth E. Colton, "Pre-War Political Influences in Post-War Conservative Parties," *The American Political Science Review*, XLII, No. 5 (October, 1948), p. 945.

In the general elections of January, 1949, the Liberal Party (then known as the Democratic-Liberal Party) became the first party after World War II to win an absolute majority of the seats in the House of Representatives. It won a majority again in the 1952 election. Following his depurge in 1951, Hatoyama insisted that Yoshida step down from the party presidency. When Yoshida stubbornly clung to his position in spite of his promise to Hatoyama, the latter formed an opposition faction within the party. At the time of the 1953 election he organized his "Hatoyama Liberal Party" and won 35 seats at the expense of the Liberals, who lost their absolute majority. As a result of corruption involving his immediate associates, the Hatoyama issue, and the rising nationalist feeling, the "pro-American" Yoshida began to lose the support of substantial sections of his party. His fifth Cabinet resigned on December 7, 1954, and the leadership of the Liberals passed to the party's former vice-president, Ogata Taketora. Ogata died shortly, but Yoshida is today influential in the councils of the Liberal-Democratic Party and remains a force to be reckoned with in Japanese politics.

The Democratic (Progressive) Party (1945–1955)

When it was first organized on November 16, 1945, the Progressive Party claimed to include about 288 Diet members. The vast majority of these, however, had been connected with the quasi-totalitarian Great Japan Political Society (Dai Nippon Seiji Kai), the 1945 successor to the Imperial Rule Assistance Political Society. As a consequence, the 1946 purge deprived the party of all but 32 of its Diet members. Most of the members of parliament who remained after the purge had belonged to the prewar Minseitō.[2]

Shidehara Kijūrō

Shidehara Kijūrō had been Foreign Minister in the Kenseikai and Minseitō Cabinets of Katō, Hamaguchi, and Wakatsuki in the 1920's and early 1930's and had distinguished himself for his "conciliatory" policy towards China. He was therefore presumed to be acceptable to the victorious Allies and was appointed Prime Minister in October, 1945. He was the leader of the Progressive Party at the time of the election of 1946. The Progressives were junior partners in the first Yoshida Cabinet. In 1947, Ashida Hitoshi left the Liberals to join the Progressives in forming an ostensibly new party, the Democratic Party (Minshutō). The Democrats advocated "reformed capitalism" and ideologically stood somewhere between the Liberals and Social-

[2] *Ibid.*, pp. 943–945.

ists. The Democrats participated in the coalition Cabinet of the Socialist Prime Minister Katayama in 1947, and in the following year, Ashida headed a Cabinet which included Socialists as well as Democrats. In the meantime, during the controversy over coal nationalization in 1947, Shidehara and some friends left the Democratic Party to form the conservative Dōshi Club. In 1948, the Dōshi Club coalesced with Yoshida's Liberals to form the Democratic-Liberal Party.

Ashida Hitoshi

Ashida Hitoshi was a graduate of Tokyo Imperial University who entered the foreign service in 1912. He was counsellor in the Turkish and Belgian Embassies in 1929 and 1930 and retired from the diplomatic service in 1932. In the same year he was elected to the House of Representatives, where he served until his death in 1959. He was president and editor of the *Japan Times*, an English-language daily published in Tokyo before the war, and his well-known liberal views qualified him to serve as Welfare Minister in the Shidehara Cabinet and Foreign Minister in the Katayama Government. He became president of the Democratic Party in 1947 and was Prime Minister in 1948. A series of scandals rocked the Ashida Government, and it resigned in October, 1948, after a troubled existence of only seven months.

Inukai Ken succeeded Ashida to the presidency of the party. Following the Democratic-Liberal Party landslide in 1949, the Democrats split over the question of whether to participate in the third Yoshida Cabinet or to go into the Opposition. The coalitionist faction joined Yoshida's Democratic-Liberals. In 1950, the remaining Democrats coalesced with the People's Cooperative Party to form the National Democratic Party (Kokumin Minshutō), under the presidency of Tomabeji Gizō.

In 1952, the party took the name Reform Party (Kaishintō), and Shigemitsu Mamoru, who had recently been released from Sugamo Prison, where he had served a sentence as a war criminal, became the president of the party. He had been Foreign Minister in the wartime Cabinets of Tōjō and Koiso and had signed the 1945 Instrument of Surrender. The party was again internally divided on the question of cooperation with the Yoshida Cabinet.

Hatoyama Ichirō

In November, 1954, the Reform Party was reorganized to include the Liberal Hatoyama Ichirō and his faction and numerous depurgees. Hatoyama was elected president and Shigemitsu vice-president. The reorganized party took the name of Japan Democratic Party (Nippon Minshutō). The Japan Democrats were now even more conservative than the Liberals and wished to demonstrate their independence of America. They declared that their purposes were to "clean up the nation's political life; to achieve complete independence and correct the various reforms inaugurated under the Occupation; to carry out an autonomous people's diplomacy to reduce international tension and to help rehabilitate Asia; to stabilize the people's livelihood through over-all planning and to strengthen racial unity and enhance morality."[3]

The resignation of Yoshida's fifth Cabinet in December, 1954, made necessary the designation by the Diet of a new Prime Minister. Since no party had a majority, an interparty understanding would be needed to elect a premier. The left-wing and right-wing Socialists gave their votes to Hatoyama on the understanding that he would dissolve the Diet and call for new elections after taking office. The first Hatoyama Cabinet, therefore, was a caretaker Cabinet, lasting only three months. The Democrats won a plurality in the February, 1955, elections.

The Liberal-Democratic Party

Conservative Union

The reunification of the Socialist Party in October, 1955, was a great stimulus to the union of the Liberal and Democratic Parties, whose leaders had begun working towards this goal during the last year or so of the Yoshida regime. The Liberal-Democratic Party (Jiyū-Minshutō, frequently abbreviated to Jimintō) came into existence on November 15, 1955.[4] It was understood that the former Democrat, Hatoyama, would remain Prime Minister and that Ogata Taketora, of the old Liberal Party, would later become president of the new party. Kishi Nobusuke, a principal organizer of the new party, became secretary-general.[5] For the first time since the war, the two-party system prevailed in Japan. The new Liberal-Democratic Party had a comfortable majority in the Diet and was evidently in a position to enact its legislative proposals. Since its formation, it has been the Government party.

The Liberal-Democratic Party has been quite as ridden with factionalism as were the two parties from which it was formed. It has,

[3] Hugh Borton, *et al., Japan Between East and West* (New York: Harper, 1957), p. 17.

[4] English-language newspapers in Japan very often use the term "Tories" to designate the Liberal-Democrats. Of course, the Japanese conservative party has a very different history from the Conservative Party of Great Britain.

[5] Dan Kurzman, *Kishi and Japan: The Search for the Sun* (New York: Ivan Obolensky, Inc., 1960), pp. 289–291.

therefore, not always been able to show a united front against the opposition. In December, 1956, Hatoyama resigned as Prime Minister and president of the Liberal-Democratic Party because of ill health. Ogata, who had originally been expected to succeed Hatoyama, had died in January, 1956. As a compromise between the supporters of Kishi and Kōno Ichirō, Ishibashi Tanzan, a former purgee who had been Finance Minister in the first Yoshida Government, was elected party president and designated Prime Minister. After only two months as premier, he also retired because of ill health. Kishi, who had been serving as "Acting Premier" and Foreign Minister, was designated Prime Minister in February, 1957, and chosen party president the following month.

Kishi Nobusuke

Satō Nobusuke was born in Yamaguchi Prefecture in southwestern Japan in 1896. One of a family of ten children, he was adopted by an uncle who could support his education, and his name was changed to that of his uncle, Kishi. After a brilliant record at Tokyo Imperial University, Kishi Nobusuke became a leading bureaucrat in the Ministry of Agriculture and Commerce. As an advocate of greater controls over the economy, he was a leader of the "new bureaucrat" faction. In 1932, he was appointed Vice-Minister of Industry in the Manchoukuo Government, where he fostered cooperation between the Japanese military and the Japanese zaibatsu. In 1941, he became Minister of Commerce and Industry in the Cabinet of Tōjō Hideki and was a signer of the declaration of war against the United States. At the end of the war he was arrested as a war crimes suspect by the Allied authorities, but the Tokyo war crimes trial ended before Kishi was brought before the court. In 1952, he was depurged.

Kishi's brother, Satō Eisaku, was a leader in Yoshida's Liberal Party when the former was released from prison and helped Nobusuke to enter the party in 1953. Kishi was expelled from the Liberal Party because of his anti-Yoshida intrigues. He helped to organize first the Japan Democratic Party and then the Liberal-Democratic Party. Owing largely to the fortuitous illnesses of Hatoyama and Ishibashi and the sudden death of Ogata, Kishi became Prime Minister in 1957. Shortly after the Girard incident, in which an American G.I. killed a Japanese woman, he visited President Eisenhower and addressed a joint session of Congress. Although he was not able to obtain the return of the Ryukyu and Bonin Islands to Japan, he persuaded the Americans to withdraw their ground forces from Japan.

Kishi's capacity for fund raising and backstage maneuver account for much of his success in politics. To the political left and to much of the center he has become a symbol of all that is worst in Japanese political life: a "war criminal" and a self-seeking politician more solicitous of the well-being of the capitalists who finance him than of the common people. He was one of the most widely disliked Prime Ministers in Japanese history and a scapegoat for popular frustrations. Americans, of course, were prone to regard him as a repentant convert to democracy and dependable advocate of the anti-Communist alliance.[6] During his administration, notwithstanding the existence of gross economic inequalities, Japan became more prosperous and attained a higher average standard of living than ever before in her history. Kishi was forced to resign as a result of Socialist opposition and mass demonstrations on the one hand and the ambitions of rival faction leaders in his own party on the other.

Ikeda Hayato

A principal rival of Kishi, Ikeda Hayato, was born in 1899 in Hiroshima Prefecture, the youngest son of a sake-brewer. He graduated from Kyoto Imperial University and distinguished himself as a tax expert in the Finance Ministry. He first won a seat in the Diet in 1949 and became Finance Minister in the third Yoshida Cabinet. There he enforced the stringently deflationary Dodge Plan and a policy of close economic cooperation with the United States. He was one of the six Japanese who signed the Japanese Peace Treaty in San Francisco in 1951. In addition he served as Minister of International Trade and Industry in the fourth Yoshida Cabinet, Minister of Finance in the Ishibashi Cabinet and first Kishi Cabinet, Minister without portfolio in the second Kishi Cabinet, and Minister of International Trade and Industry in the second Kishi Cabinet (reconstructed). He was notorious for his bureaucratic cold-heartedness and lack of tact and, in 1952, was forced to resign his ministerial post as a result of a vote of no confidence provoked by an undiplomatic remark.

Ikeda has close ties with financial circles. At "the most corrupt convention in the . . . short history"[7] of the Liberal-Democratic Party, on July 14, 1960, he was elected to succeed Kishi as party president with the support of Yoshida Shigeru and Satō Eisaku over the strong opposition of the vice-president, Ōno Bamboku, and the executive board chairman, Ishii Mitsujirō. Five days later, the Diet designated him as Prime Minister. His first and second Cabinets, with a few notable exceptions, were made up of rather obscure Liberal-Democrats,

[6] "Like his country, he has experienced a conversion from totalitarianism to democracy almost as incredible as the conversion of St. Paul." (*Ibid.*, p. 7.)

[7] *Time Magazine,* July 25, 1960, p. 26.

while powerful faction leaders did not personally participate. Following his visit to Washington in the summer of 1961, Ikeda reconstructed his Cabinet to include nearly all of the great faction leaders: Kōno Ichirō, Satō Eisaku, Fujiyama Aiichirō, and Miki Takeo, although Kishi Nobusuke and Ishii Mitsujirō were missing. With the support of most of the great politicians of the Liberal-Democratic Party, it appeared that Ikeda was at the height of his power. Ikeda was re-elected party president following the House of Councillors election in July, 1962. The Ikeda Cabinet, as reconstructed in that month, did not include any of the great faction leaders except Kōno, and there was speculation that Ikeda's days as Prime Minister were numbered.

Ikeda advocates the welfare state and a strong economy based on private enterprise, which is necessary to finance the welfare state. His policy is to double the national income within ten years, and if the rapid rate of economic expansion maintained during his first two years in the premiership is kept up, this goal may be attained.

Factions

The internal struggles of the conservative party are of particular significance, since that party and its predecessors have supplied the Government with Prime Ministers consistently since 1948 and presumably will continue to do so for some years to come. The leader of the conservative party, then, is Prime Minister of Japan, and whoever aspires to the premiership must first work for hegemony within the party. Newspapers and magazines frequently carry detailed, but not always edifying, articles on factional struggles. A Diet handbook published in 1961 lists the strength of the factions of the Liberal-Democratic Party in the House of Representatives as follows:

Ikeda Hayato faction: 55
Satō Eisaku faction: 43
Kishi Nobusuke faction: 42
Kaya Kōsen group: 5
Ichimada Hisato group: 5
Fujiyama Aiichirō faction: 40
Kōno Ichirō faction: 34
Ōno Bamboku faction: 32
Miki Takeo-Matsumura Kenzō faction: 33
Ishii Mitsujirō faction: 23
Ishibashi Tanzan faction: 4
Ishida Hirohide faction: 6
unaffiliated: 2[8]

[8] *Kokkai Benran* (Tokyo: Nihon Seikei Shimbunsha, 1961), pp. 310–313.

The factions supporting the party president are known as "mainstream" (shuryūha), and the opposition factions are known as "anti-mainstream" (han-shuryūha). There is apt to be a showdown, when, every two years (sometimes sooner), the national party convention must elect a president.

The Liberal-Democratic Party factions are based principally upon personal loyalties and enmities, often antedating the Pacific War, rather than on differences concerning policy. Various factors serve to define groups in the conservative camp. Those with bureaucratic backgrounds tend to side against those without such experience. Former purgees have been arrayed against those who had not been purged. Former Liberals may oppose former Democrats. Old school ties and blood relationships may be a factor. However, no hard-and-fast rules can be laid down, and politicians sometimes desert one faction in favor of another or organize their own factions. The politician relies on his faction leader to provide campaign funds and to obtain the party nomination for a Diet seat or Cabinet post. The relation between a faction leader and his followers resembles the relation of oyabun and kobun (boss and henchman), frequently depicted in popular samurai movies, where the feudal loyalties one owes to one's overlord are exalted.

Politicians depend more upon their personal supporters and factional leaders than upon the party for funds and help in electioneering. As a result, the party organization is neglected, and the party lacks grass roots. Factional rivalries are especially keen during general elections, where there is much competition within the party for nominations and funds, and when, because of the electoral system, men in the same party often run against each other.

The Socialist Party

The Socialist Party (Shakaitō) was organized in November, 1945, from remnants of the prewar Laborers and Farmers Party (Rōnōtō), the Farmers Party (Nōmintō), and the Socialist Mass Party (Shakai Taishūtō). None of these parties had ever enjoyed substantial electoral success before the war, partly because of government suppression of their activities, especially after the passage of the 1925 Peace Preservation Law. Prominent organizers of the postwar Socialist Party were Kagawa Toyohiko, the Christian socialist leader, Abe Isoo, the founder of the Japan Socialist Party in 1901, and Takano Iwasaburō of the former Socialist Mass Party. Almost every shade of utopian, Fabian, and Marxian socialism was represented in the membership. At the time of its formation, the Socialist Party claimed 17 members in the Diet, but most of them were purged in 1946. In the election for the lower house held in the same year, the Socialists won nearly 18 per cent of the votes and 92 seats. The Socialists welcomed the liberal SCAP-draft Constitution and voted for it in the Diet in 1946.

From the beginning, the postwar Socialists have rejected Communist efforts to form a united front, but in late 1946 and early 1947, they joined in mass rallies calling for the resignation of the Yoshida Cabinet, which was becoming increasingly unpopular as the result of its failure to solve the economic crisis. In the 1947 electoral campaign, the Socialists advocated the state control of coal, iron, steel, and fertilizer industries, preparatory to state ownership. Although the Yoshida administration succeeded in passing an electoral law unfavorable to the parties of the left, the Socialists managed to win a plurality of 143 seats in the House of Representatives. Over a month was required to form a Cabinet, originally intended to be a four-party coalition (Socialists, Liberals, Democrats, and People's Cooperatives), but at the last minute the Liberals backed out.

Katayama Tetsu

Katayama Tetsu, chairman of the Socialist Party, headed the coalition Cabinet. Katayama was a Christian labor lawyer, college lecturer, and author of books on law, and had been elected several times to the Diet in the 1930's. He was not an aggressive and dynamic leader, but his broad tolerance and unquestioned honesty were necessary to hold widely divergent factions in the party together. As a concession to other parties in the coalition, left-wing Socialists were excluded from the Cabinet. The Prime Minister had a difficult, and as it ultimately proved, impossible job to keep left-wing Socialists and the Democrats both happy at the same time. The Socialists proposed the nationalization of the coal industry, but had to modify their stand because of the reluctance of the other parties of the coalition. After much wrangling in the Diet and within the coalition parties, a mild Temporary Coal-Mining Bill was passed.

A great controversy broke out over the dismissal of the Socialist Minister of Agriculture and Forestry, Hirano Rikizō, whose subsequent purge was widely believed to be politically motivated. The Cabinet appeared unable to meet the economic problems which it faced, and when the left-wing Socialists opposed the financial policies of the Katayama administration, the only Socialist-led Government in Japan's history came to an end. Left-wing as well as right-wing Socialists participated in the short-lived Ashida Government, but the Socialist Party was compromised by the implication of some of its leaders in the financial scandals which came to light at that time.

The 1949 election was disastrous for the Socialists, whose strength in the House of Representatives dropped from 143 to 48. The issue of the peace settlement split the party into a right wing, under the leadership of Asanuma Inejirō and a left wing led by Suzuki Mosaburō. The right-wing Socialists supported the San Francisco Peace Treaty but opposed the Security Treaty with the United States, while the left wing, which advocated a peace with the Soviet Union and Communist China as well as with the non-Communist nations, opposed both pacts. In October, 1955, the Socialists reunited into a single party with Suzuki as chairman of the central executive committee and Asanuma as secretary-general. The party won 166 seats in the 1958 election and, following a rightist secession, won 145 seats in 1960.

Personal and ideological factions have been a constant threat to the unity of the party. Ideologically, the Socialists include dyed-in-the-wool orthodox Marxists who advocate the revolutionary overthrow of capitalism as well as revisionists, radical and moderate labor leaders, humanitarians, neutralists, and assorted do-gooders. The question of relations with the Communist Party is often troublesome, the left-wing Socialists being more prone to united front activities than the right. Being too heavily dependent on the radical Sōhyō labor confederation for support, the Socialists often pursue policies which alienate other elements of the population. In 1959, a right-wing faction led by Nishio Suehiro seceded and formed the Democratic-Socialist Party.

In 1961 and 1962 there was much internal debate concerning "structural reform," advocated by the personable Eda Saburō with the support of the younger elements in the party. Structural reform was never very clearly defined, but seemed to imply that it was not necessary to await a take-over of the government by the Socialists in order to ameliorate the lot of the people; rather, the Socialists would seek to force concessions favorable to the people from the conservative government. Sasaki Kōzō attacked structural reform as "revisionism" and a betrayal of sound Marxist principles. Eda, who is a popular television personality, has recently served as secretary-general of the party.

Factionalism prevents the party from presenting a clear, constructive program to the voter. The Socialist Party is the second strongest party in what is essentially a two-party system. However, under the present electoral scheme, the Socialists do not have enough confidence to nominate candidates for even half of the seats in the lower house. Thus it has not been mathematically possible for the Socialists to win a majority in the House of Representatives.

The main support for the Socialists comes from organized labor (Sōhyō), white-collar employees, intellectuals, and lower civil servants. The Socialists have very little appeal to farmers, who fear that the radical ideology might result in the collectivization of agriculture.

Wedded Bliss

In October, 1955, the right- and left-wing Socialists reunited to form a single party. Suzuki Mosaburō was elected chairman and Asanuma Inejirō secretary-general. Here the two leaders are depicted as an old-fashioned married couple, the wife (Asanuma) walking behind the husband (Suzuki) and carrying a paper umbrella, labeled "Socialist Party." (Source: Nasu Ryosuke, *Yoshida kara Kishi e* [*From Yoshida to Kishi*] [Tokyo: Mainichi Shimbunsha, 1959], p. 64.)

Much of the party's support is in the nature of protest against the economic hardships which many people in Japan suffer notwithstanding the postwar recovery. Also, many moderates vote Socialist to register their opposition to the "reactionary" proposals of the conservatives, such as rearmament, centralization of control over the police and education, and constitutional revision. So long as the conservatives are prevented from winning a two-thirds majority in either house of the Diet, the amendment of the Constitution can be prevented. Although there seems little likelihood in the foreseeable future that the Socialists will be able to win a parliamentary majority, it is significant that in the 1960 election the parties of the left (Socialist, Democratic-Socialist, and Communist) won over 39 per cent of the total of the votes cast. Thus, although the parliamentary strength of the Socialist Party has remained fairly constant over the past ten years, there has been a slow and steady increase in the total number of "progressive" voters.

The 1960 party platform provided that the task of the party at the present stage of the development of Japanese capitalism is to bring into being a socialist society by democratically and peacefully reforming the capitalist society to accomplish the peaceful revolution. The peaceful revolution would be carried out by obtaining an absolute majority in the Diet in accordance with democratic forms and without the use of violence or armed force. A socialist administration would first be established and stabilized and the capitalist society would be converted into a socialist society. The party also assumed the task of restoring and defending the independence of Japan. It would bring about the complete independence and territorial sovereignty of Japan, abrogate the United States-Japan Security Treaty and Administrative Agreement, revise unequal treaties, and resume autonomy in diplomacy. The party claimed to be a class-mass party, with its nucleus the working class, and to be a union of toiling classes made up of farmers, fishermen, small and medium commercial and industrial enterprisers, intellectuals and others constituting the great majority of the people. Both during and after the realization of socialism, the freedoms of speech, assembly, association, and faith would be promoted thoroughly. The party would welcome free criticism by the people, and the existence and criticism of opposition parties. The return and rotation of authority would be determined by the free will of the people.[9]

The Japanese Socialist Party is much more radical than socialist parties in European countries. Whereas the Socialist International is committed to opposition to Communist expansion and the support of NATO, the Japanese Socialists advocate a policy of neutrality and have declared their friendship with the Chinese Communists and opposition to "American imperialism." The Japanese Socialists are committed to "peaceful revolution" to overthrow capitalism and establish socialism, but have not unequivocally renounced the use of extraparliamentary methods to achieve their goals.

Kawakami Jōtarō

Kawakami Jōtarō was born in Tokyo in 1889 and after graduating from Tokyo Imperial University taught at Rikkyo, Meiji, and Kansai Universities. He was active in the proletarian political parties before

[9] *Asahi Nenkan, 1961*, pp. 219–220.

World War II. During the war he was a director of the Imperial Rule Assistance Association and became an active organizer of the Imperial Rule Assistance Political Society. He helped to organize the postwar Socialist Party, but was purged in January, 1946. Following his depurge he became chairman of the central executive committee of the right-wing Socialist Party. During the anti-Security Pact struggle, in June, 1960, as he was collecting signatures for a petition near the Diet building, he was stabbed by a right-wing fanatic. Following the assassination of Asanuma Inejirō, Kawakami was elected chairman of the central executive committee.

Socialist Party Organization

The political parties of the left are similarly organized on the top level. Each has a national convention (taikai), made up of delegates of local party units and of affiliated organizations. The convention elects a central executive committee, a chairman of the central executive committee and a secretary-general. The convention normally adopts a party platform. The central executive committee handles the affairs of the party between conventions and supervises the secretariat. The secretariat is assisted by a number of committees and bureaus, each of which is normally headed by a member of the central executive committee. The national party headquarters is in Tokyo. Here the party officials, and its bureaucrats, and journalists — the parties sponsor newspapers and magazines — carry on their activities in close proximity to the Diet.

The political leadership in all of the Japanese parties is, on the whole, old and experienced, and personal and group rivalries within the parties may sometimes be traced back to the period before World War II. The competition for top party posts is intense, and may, in extreme cases, result in the secession of a dissident faction. Sometimes, in order to avoid internecine warfare, it is necessary to leave certain top party posts vacant or to set up some kind of regency for an extended period.

The Socialist Party has been defective in local organization. In large measure organized labor makes up for this deficiency. In the 1958 election, 73 per cent of the Socialist candidates sponsored by Sōhyō were elected, 68 per cent of the Socialist candidates sponsored by Zenrō, the other leading labor federation, were elected, and 84 per cent of the Socialists jointly sponsored were elected. At the same time, Socialist candidates not sponsored by organized labor did very badly.[10] The Japanese Socialist Party today has come to be widely re-

[10] Robert A. Scalapino and Junnosuke Masumi, *Parties and Politics in Contemporary Japan* (Berkeley and Los Angeles: University of California Press, 1962), p. 98.

garded as a mere appendage of the labor movement. Nevertheless, there are recent indications that the Socialist Party has been increasingly successful in recruiting members and getting votes from farmers and small businessmen. The prefectural organizations seem to be relatively indifferent to the doctrinal disputes which seem very important on the national level.[11]

The party had 50,150 members in 1960. In the lower house election of that year its candidates drew 10,901,280, or 27.55 per cent, of the votes cast.

The Democratic-Socialist Party

The reunification of the Socialist Party in 1955 by no means eliminated the ideological and personal feuds that had constantly plagued the Socialist movement even in the prewar era. In the 1959 House of Councillors election, the Socialists received a million votes less than they had won in the 1956 election. There ensued much unhappiness among many party members with the principles and policies sponsored by the leadership. The Socialist International, which included most of the Socialist parties of the world, had been discarding the Marxian doctrine of basing the Socialist Party on a single class and had assumed an increasingly strong anti-Communist attitude. The Japan Socialist Party, on the other hand, was quite out of step with the trends of the world Socialist movement. It advocated a policy of neutrality and appeared to support anti-Americanism and pro-Communism. Furthermore, it seemed too willing to resort to unparliamentary tactics. The failure of the Socialist Party to win popular support outside of organized labor was apparently making it impossible to win majorities in the two houses of the Diet.

In October, 1959, a group within the Japan Socialist Party led by Nishio Suehiro, who had been Vice-Premier in the Ashida Government, issued a statement that "there is an urgent desire in Japan for a democratic socialist party which, while abiding by parliamentarism, will fight both extreme leftists and rightists and promote the general welfare of all sections of the working people, without special favor or partiality to labor unions." The members of the "Socialist Reconstruction League" led by Nishio formally seceded from the Socialist Party to organize a "genuine" Socialist Party.

The Democratic-Socialist Party (Minshu Shakaitō) was formally founded at a meeting in Tokyo on January 24, 1960. The nucleus of the party was made up of about fifty erstwhile Socialist members of the

[11] LeRoy B. Weed, "Organization of the Shakaito: A Study, Especially at the Prefectural Level, of the Membership, Components and Leadership of the Social Democratic Party of Japan" (Master's thesis, Wayne State University, 1962).

Diet. The moderate *Zenrō* labor confederation threw its support to the new party. Nishio Suehiro was elected chairman of the executive committee, Sone Eki, secretary-general, and Mizutani Chōsaburō, chairman of the parliamentary group. Former Prime Minister Katayama became supreme adviser, and Suzuki Yoshio became chairman of the control committee. The party leaders proclaimed their opposition to capitalism and totalitarianism of both left and right and their determination to emancipate all members of society from oppression and exploitation and to establish a society which would guarantee respect for the individual and the free development of the human character. The new party would be a people's party rather than a class party as advocated by the left wing of the Socialist Party and the Sōhyō leaders.

The Democratic-Socialists opposed the new Japan-United States Security Treaty on the ground that it would strengthen the military alliance between the two countries. However, during the course of the anti-treaty struggle, the Democratic-Socialists, consistent with their policy of defending parliamentary government, refused to resort to boycott and violence to oppose the treaty as did the Socialists. The Democratic-Socialists were therefore widely accused of being half-hearted and insincere in their opposition to the Security Pact and of playing into the hands of the conservatives.

Nishio Suehiro

Nishio Suehiro was born in Shikoku in 1891. After leaving primary school, he worked in the Osaka Arms Factory. In 1915, he joined the Yūaikai (Friendly Society), the first trade unionists' organization in Japan, and soon became an official in that organization. He was arrested several times for his labor activities and became secretary-general of the Japanese Federation of Labor (Sōdōmei) and a member of the central executive committee of the Social Democratic Party. In 1928 he was elected to the House of Representatives in the first general election under universal suffrage. He was again elected to the lower house in 1937 representing the Socialist Mass Party (Shakai Taishutō). In 1940, he attempted to form a National Workers Party (Kinrō Kokumintō), which was immediately banned by the Government. Like some other socialist leaders, he joined the Imperial Rule Assistance Association and later the Imperial Rule Assistance Political Society, which supported Premier Tōjō.

After the war he helped to organize the Socialist Party and served as Minister of State and Chief Cabinet Secretary in the Katayama Cabinet and Minister of State and Vice-Premier in the Ashida Government. In 1948, he was arrested in connection with the financial scandal, which precipitated Ashida's resignation, but was exonerated ten years later. In October, 1959, when the Socialist Party Convention was considering a proposal to expel Nishio for his criticism of its extreme leftist tendencies, he walked out of the meeting with his followers and declared his intention to found a new party.

At the first meeting of the party in January, 1960, Nishio told his supporters:

> The Socialist Party suffers from the illusion that a Marxist revolution is possible in Japan. The conservative Liberal-Democratic Party degenerates into political agents of big business.
>
> The goal of our party is to give political expressions to the aspirations of a vast segment of the nation including impoverished farmers, fishermen, and small businessmen whose voices have not been heeded by either the Liberal-Democrats or the Socialists.
>
> We recognize that the society in which we live today is a capitalistic one. We do not propose to overthrow it overnight but will try to change it gradually by piling up patiently one small reform upon another, one improvement upon another.
>
> I propose that we practice political tolerance. Totalitarianism, either left or right, stifles opposition.
>
> Our party intends to achieve socialism through democratic methods, and the essence of democracy is the belief in the value of dissension and of efforts of persuasion.[12]

In the campaign for the November, 1960, election, the Democratic-Socialists stressed their devotion to orderly parliamentary government as contrasted with the unparliamentary tactics of the Liberal-Democrats and the Socialists.[13] They advocated an economic program that would make all Japanese into members of the middle class. However, as previously noted, the 1960 election for House Representatives was a disaster for the Democratic-Socialists. Although they won 8.8 per cent of the votes, they won only 3.6 per cent of the seats. The party representation in the lower house dropped from 40 members to a mere 17, and even former Premier Katayama went down in defeat. In 1961, the Democratic-Socialists cooperated with the Liberal-Democrats in the formulation of the Anti-Violence Bill, thus alienating themselves from much of the left. Nevertheless, when the bill was brought up in the House of Councillors, certain leading Liberal-Democrats allowed it to be blocked by the Socialists, much to the chagrin of the Democratic-Socialists, whose political future was closely tied to the measure.

[12] As summarized by the *Japan Times,* January 25, 1960.
[13] The author is deeply indebted to Mr. Nishio for the privilege of discussing with him on August 3, 1960, the program of the Democratic-Socialist Party.

In Japan's bipolarized politics, the Democratic-Socialists seem to have fallen between two poles. They have managed to exert a slight mediatory influence between the Liberal-Democratic and Socialist Parties, but on the whole their hard lot stands as a warning to those who would blithely form splinter parties. The Japanese seem fairly committed to the two-party system. The Democratic-Socialists lost 5 of their 16 seats in the 1962 House of Councillors election, and their future seems very dim.

The Japan Communist Party

"Peaceful Revolution"

In October 4, 1945, MacArthur ordered the Japanese government to release the Japanese who had been imprisoned for political offenses, and among those freed were the veteran Communist leaders Tokuda Kyūichi and Shiga Yoshio. The Communists reorganized the party and immediately made themselves widely unpopular by demanding the trial of the Emperor as a war criminal and the abolition of the Emperor system. In January, 1946, Nosaka Sanzō (Okano Susumu) returned from Yenan, the Chinese Communist capital, where he had been engaged in the Communist indoctrination of Japanese prisoners of war. Nosaka urged that the Party make itself "lovable" and tone down the anti-Emperor agitation. Communists rapidly infiltrated the nascent labor unions. They emphasized peaceful rather than violent revolution, and in the April, 1946, election won five seats in the House of Representatives.

The Communists had hailed the Allied Occupation troops as liberators, and it appeared to many Japanese that General MacArthur, in giving the Communists freedom to speak, organize mass demonstrations, and publish their newspapers, favored the communization of Japan. But following the "Food May Day" demonstration of May 19, 1946, MacArthur and the Emperor both issued warnings against violent demonstrations. The Communists drew up a constitution for the establishment of a Japanese People's Republic and were the only group in the Diet to vote against the draft Constitution supported by General MacArthur. Communists in the labor movement led in organizing a general strike to be carried out on February 1, 1947. The Communists were apparently aiming at the overthrow of the Yoshida Cabinet and the formation of a people's front government in which they would participate. At the eleventh hour, the Supreme Commander for the Allied Powers issued an order to the labor leaders to call off the strike, and when they reluctantly did so, the Communist leadership lost much prestige.

In 1947 and 1948, the failure of the Socialists in the Katayama Cabinet to socialize the economy and solve urgent economic problems and the scandals which besmirched the Ashida coalition discredited the Socialist and Democratic Parties. As the voters turned away from the moderate left and center, a polarization of Japanese politics occurred. In the 1949 election, the Liberals under Yoshida won an absolute majority, and the Communists won 10 per cent of the votes and 35 seats, to become the fourth largest party in the House of Representatives. No doubt an important factor was that the Communist Party appeared to many voters as the only real opposition party, since the Liberals, Democrats, and Socialists had all been carrying out the policies of the Supreme Commander. A vote for the Communists was a protest vote not only against the bourgeois parties and half-hearted Socialists, it was also a vote against the policies of the Occupation. Occasionally, labor disputes, in which Communist agitation figured prominently, resulted in violence. For example, during the railroad strike in 1949, Shimoyama Sadanori, president of the Japanese National Railways, was found lying across the tracks in Tokyo, murdered and with one arm and both legs cut off. There were two instances of derailments in which people were killed. General MacArthur began to urge Yoshida to outlaw the Communist Party. The Prime Minister, notwithstanding his strong anti-Communist attitude, took the view that to outlaw the party on the authority of SCAP would not provide a permanent solution and that proposed legislation banning the party would meet serious obstacles. Yoshida preferred to rely on the voters to repudiate the Communist Party, whose activities made it increasingly unpopular.[14]

Cominform Criticism and Violent Revolution

The legal labor union and parliamentary activity of the Communists seemed to be paying off. Nosaka and other Communist leaders had repeatedly emphasized their faith in the possibility of a "peaceful revolution" to achieve socialism. But in January, 1950, the Japan Communist Party was suddenly shaken by an article in the organ of the Cominform, *For a Lasting Peace: For a People's Democracy,* which attacked Nosaka Sanzō as a servant of American imperialism with a bourgeois attitude.[15] The Cominform accused Nosaka of spreading the false notion that peaceful transition to socialism was possible in Japan during the Occupation.

[14] Yoshida Shigeru, *The Yoshida Memoirs: The Story of Japan in Crisis* (Boston: Houghton Mifflin, 1962), pp. 234–236.

[15] Murakami Kanji, *Nihon Kyōsantō* [*Japan Communist Party*] (Tokyo: Hobunsha, 1956), pp. 69–79.

Nosaka's "theory" has nothing whatever in common with Marxism-Leninism. Actually . . . [it] is an undemocratic, antisocialist theory . . . [which] serves only the imperialist occupiers in Japan and the enemies of independence. . . . Consequently . . . [it] is simultaneously an anti-patriotic, anti-Japanese "theory."[16]

The Cominform criticism seemed to confirm the views of leftist elements in the Japanese Communist Party, such as Shiga Yoshio, who had for some time been warning against "right-wing opportunism." The success of Communist armed revolution in China and Southeast Asia raised serious doubts in the minds of many Japanese Communists as to the efficacy of their soft line. Sharp factional disputes arose within the party, especially between the "internationalists" and the "mainstream faction," but following a purge of dissident elements, the party rallied around its triumvirate — Tokuda, Nosaka, and Shiga, in that order. The Communists embarked on a campaign against "American imperialism," which, they said, was converting Japan into a military base, restoring fascism and the police state in Japan, and subjugating the Japanese economy to the dictates of Wall Street monopoly capitalism. On May 30, 1950, Communist-inspired demonstrators stoned and mauled American military personnel in Tokyo, and when the Japanese arrested were tried by Allied authorities, the Communist daily *Red Flag* referred to the culprits as "patriots."

On June 6, 1950, the Supreme Commander forwarded a letter to Premier Yoshida directing him to purge from political life the twenty-four members of the central committee of the Japan Communist Party.[17] Seventeen editors of the *Red Flag* were also disqualified. Instead of reporting regularly to local authorities as they were required to do under the purge order, some of the central committee members went "underground," i.e., into hiding, and some escaped to the Asiatic continent. MacArthur's action was only one phase of the great "Red Purge." The Japanese government, information media, and industry took informal steps to remove Communists and fellow travelers from their jobs. In 1949, 10,793 were removed from government posts. By October, 1950, 690 persons in broadcasting, news agencies, and news-

[16] Rodger Swearingen and Paul Langer, *Red Flag in Japan: International Communism in Action 1919–1951* (Cambridge: Harvard University Press, 1952), p. 199.

[17] Portions of the letter are cited in Hans H. Baerwald, *The Purge of Japanese Leaders under the Occupation* (Berkeley and Los Angeles: University of California Press, 1959), p. 19, and in Courtney Whitney, *MacArthur: His Rendezvous with History* (New York: Knopf, 1956), pp. 309–310.

papers had been dismissed, and 9,514 workers in private industry had lost their jobs, making a total of 20,997 dismissals.[18]

When war broke out in Korea on June 25, 1950, and the *Red Flag* and other Japanese Communist publications turned out propaganda favoring the cause of the North Korean Communists, the Japanese Communist papers were banned. There is ample evidence that the Communists were planning an armed uprising against the "American imperialists" in Japan so that American troops could not be spared to fight in Korea.

The Communists made political capital of the unpopular repressive measures of the Yoshida regime, and took a conspicuous part in the demonstrations against the Subversive Activities Prevention Bill. On May 1, 1952, they instigated a riot on the Palace Grounds against the measure, and in the course of the disturbance blood flowed and American automobiles were set afire.

In the October, 1952, election, the Communists, whose violent tactics had alienated the people and whose leaders had been banned from public life, lost all of the seats that they had held in the House of Representatives. The Communist Party was never outlawed in Japan during the postwar period. Probably one reason for this fact is that since 1949 the party has not had enough success at the polls to necessitate such a measure. The very leftist Socialist Party steals the thunder of the Communists without the onus of appearing to be subject to foreign direction.

Peaceful Coexistence

In 1955, after the Korean War and the Occupation had ended, the Japanese Communist leaders came out of hiding. The Soviet Union began peace talks with Japan and Nosaka resumed the "peaceful revolution" line. Tokuda Kyūichi had died in Peking in 1953, and Nosaka was the undisputed leader of the party. One Communist was elected to the House of Representatives in the 1953 election, two in 1955, one in 1958, and three in 1960. There has always been at least one Communist in the House of Councillors and following the 1962 election there were four.

The platform adopted at the 1961 party congress holds that Japan is at present ruled by United States imperialism and its obedient ally, Japanese monopoly capitalism. Although Japan is a highly developed capitalist country, it is in fact a dependency under partial occupation by American imperialism. Japan is now faced with a new democratic

[18] Baerwald, p. 79n.

revolution, a people's democratic revolution, against the two enemies, American imperialism and Japanese monopoly capitalism. The central task of the party is to form a racial united front against racial oppression, the revival of militarism and imperialism, political reaction, exploitation, and the war policy of traitorous reactionary forces led by American imperialism and Japanese monopoly capitalism. The united front would provide a basis for the establishment of a people's democracy and people's government, which would build an independent, democratic, peaceful, and neutral Japan. The democratic coalition dictatorship of the people led by the workers and farmers, would accomplish the goals of independence and democracy in alliance with the forces of world peace, democracy, and socialism, and would prevent the revival of political and economic rule by monopoly capitalism, abolish monarchy, establish a people's republic by fundamentally reforming the reactionary state structure, and firmly establish the regime of the people's democratic state with the Diet as its supreme authority. The present people's democratic revolution would clear the way for the transition to a socialist revolution and the complete abolition of capitalism.[19]

The Communists pointed out that whether or not the revolution is carried out peacefully depends on "the response of our enemies."[20] It would appear that the Japanese Communists have returned to their former united front tactics, with the idea of ultimately communizing Japan through participation in a transitional coalition regime which they would dominate. This line was followed successfully in the establishment of "people's democracies" in eastern Europe[21] and the People's Republic of China.[22]

The Sino-Soviet Dispute

The reaction of the Japanese Communists to the Cominform criticism in 1950 provided ample evidence of the subservience of Japanese Communism to foreign leadership, or the principle of "proletarian internationalism." At that time, however, the Japanese Communists refused to capitulate to the Cominform until the Chinese Communist Party called upon Nosaka to correct his errors. Thus, the influence of the Chinese Communists over the line followed by their fraternal party in Japan has unquestionably been great. At the twenty-second congress

[19] *Asahi Nenkan, 1962,* pp. 281–282.

[20] *Japan Times,* July 26, 1961.

[21] Cf. especially Jan Kozak, *How Parliament Can Play a Revolutionary Part in the Transition to Socialism and the Role of the Popular Masses* (London: Independent Information Centre, 1961).

[22] Cf. Mao Tse-tung, *On New Democracy* (Peking: Foreign Languages Press, 1954).

of the Communist Party of the Soviet Union in October, 1961, Peking delegates supported the Hoxha regime in Albania in opposition to Moscow. Most Asian Communists sympathized with Peking, but the Japanese representatives, Nosaka and Miyamoto, took a very guarded attitude. In December, 1961, the *Red Flag* carried an editorial entitled "In Order to Fight to the Last the Two Enemies in the Interest of the Unity of International Communist Movement," which read in part as follows:

> All the Marxist-Leninist parties are independent and equal. Each party decides its own policy according to the concrete situation of its own country on the basis of the principles of Marxism-Leninism. . . . If there should arise a problem for any party regarding the activities of its fraternal parties, its leadership should bring the matter to the attention of the leadership of the other. And if necessary, it should hold a conference to discuss it.[23]

Thus the Japanese Communists appear to support the Peking-Tirana line against the Moscow line. It would seem that the Japanese comrades are coming increasingly under the influence of Peking and that Moscow hopes to check this trend. The Japanese Communist leaders presumably do not wish to get caught in the crossfire of the Sino-Soviet dispute. The issue is one which could give rise to serious new factional disputes within the party.

Party Organization

The All-Japan Party Congress (Zenkoku Tōtaikai) constitutes the supreme authority within the Japan Communist Party.[24] Party congresses were convened in December, 1945, February, 1946, and December, 1947. No congresses were held during the eleven years between 1947 and 1958. At the seventh party congress, held in July, 1958, it was determined to convene the congress every two years, and the eighth congress met in July, 1961. Delegates are elected by party members through their local organizations. The congress formulates the party platform, discusses governing regulations, and lays down the principles of political action. In view of its size and the infrequency of its meetings, the congress is unable to initiate policy. The principle of "democratic centralism" applies.

The congress elects the members and candidates of the central committee (chūō iinkai). In 1961, the party congress elected 60 members and 35 candidates.[25] There is a central committee directorate of eight members. Nosaka Sanzō is chairman of both the central committee

---

[23] *Japan Times,* May 22, 1962.
[24] Swearingen and Langer, p. 90.
[25] *Asahi Nenkan, 1962,* p. 281.

and its directorate. The central committee meets at least once every three months.[26] It is aided by its secretariat, subcommittee on labor problems, the *Red Flag* editorial committee, the central organ publication policy committee, the parliamentary group, the *Vanguard* editorial committee, and the *Materials on World Politics* editorial committee. The secretariat of the central committee is made up of ten members, headed by the secretary-general, who is Miyamoto Kenji. There are the following sections, usually headed by members of the central committee: organization; personnel; propaganda, education and culture; labor unions; farmers and fishermen; youth and students; women; citizens; united front; rules policy; election policy; municipalities; economics investigation; publications; finance; and Diet policy.[27]

The party congress also elects a central control and supervision committee. The central committee, the directorate of the central committee, the secretariat of the central committee, and the various sections are together referred to as party headquarters (hombu). In 1959, there were 309 employees (including 114 party publication workers) in the headquarters, located in the Yoyogi district of Tokyo.

Following the seventh party congress, regional committees were abolished and in their place ten regional offices (chihōkyoku) representing the central committee have been established (in Kyushu, Shikoku, Chūgoku, Kansai, Tōkai, Hokuriku, Tokyo, Kantō, Tōhoku, and Hokkaido). Twelve members and four candidates of the central committee were assigned to the regional offices.[28]

In addition to its national organs, the party is organized with the following echelons: prefectural, district, and cell. In each of the forty-six prefectures, there is a prefectural party conference which meets at irregular intervals and a prefectural committee which it elects to conduct its affairs. Each prefectural committee is organized with specialized sections similar to those of the central committee, e.g., finance section, organization section, culture section, propaganda and education section, etc. The 294 district party organizations are analogous to those of the center and prefecture. The cell (saibō) is the basic unit or "home" of the party. In 1960, there were approximately 6,000 cells. Cells vary in size from three to over 100 members and are to be found in enterprises (16.2 per cent of all cells), government offices (8.6 per cent), mass organizations

[26] Kōan Chōsachō, *Nihon Kyōsantō no Genjō* [*Present Condition of the Japan Communist Party*] ([Tokyo?], 1960), pp. 77–78.

[27] *Asahi Nenkan, 1962,* p. 282.

[28] Kōan Chōsachō, pp. 78–79.

(4.9 per cent), schools (6.6 per cent), farm villages (21.9 per cent), and residential localities (34.7 per cent).[29] In July, 1961, the party claimed to have 80,000 members.[30] Its candidates received 1,159,649 votes (2.93 per cent) in the 1960 House of Representatives election, and Communists exercise great influence in the labor movement and among intellectuals.

The JCP gets its funds from party dues, party enterprises, and contributions. Article 56 of the party regulations provides that every member must pay one per cent of his monthly salary to the party as dues, and even the poorest members must pay a minimum of 30 yen monthly.[31] It has been estimated that the average member paid a sum of 120 yen as monthly dues in 1959.[32] It seems, however, that many members do not pay the required dues. The principal party enterprises are the headquarters publications: the *Red Flag* (*Akahata*), a daily newspaper, the Sunday edition of the *Red Flag*, the *Vanguard* (*Zen-ei*), a monthly theoretical journal, and *Materials on World Politics* (*Sekai Seiji Shiryō*). Other echelons of the party also have journalistic enterprises. Income is also derived from admissions to lectures, and motion pictures. It is said that yen earned by the Russian circus and Bolshoi Ballet in Japan found their way into the hands of the Communist Party. During the early Occupation when medicines were in short supply, Communists sold santonin, apparently smuggled from Russia, in order to raise money. More recently, Communists have been reportedly peddling heroin and other narcotic drugs illegally imported from Communist China.[33]

The "Rightists"

In contemporary Japan, the extreme right is remarkably similar in spirit to what it was in the prewar era. In the 1930's the military, supported by the ultranationalists, succeeded in establishing its political hegemony over the nation, but today the violent right is numerically small and has no significant political influence. Nevertheless, the "rightists" (uyokusha), by assuming a strongly patriotic and anti-Communist pose, may still be regarded as a potential threat to democratic institutions. In the event of a severe economic depression or a gross deterioration of Japan's international relations, it is conceivable that influential conservative elements in the country would be tempted to condone violent rightist attacks on socialist politicians

---

[29] *Ibid.,* p. 88.   [30] *Japan Times,* July 26, 1961.
[31] Kōan Chōsachō, p. 106.   [32] *Ibid.,* p. 107.
[33] Richard L-G. Deverall, *Red China's Dirty Drug War* (Tokyo, 1954).

and labor leaders. It has happened before, and many Japanese today are keenly aware that it could happen again.

The first important rightist incident after the war was the attack by members of the "New and Powerful Masses Party," a band of extortionists pretending devotion to democracy, on Kikunami Katsumi, in January, 1947. Kikunami was a Communist member of the Diet and Chairman of the Congress of Industrial Unions, which was planning a general strike. The stabbing of Kikunami was hailed by the rightists as a patriotic act and cited by the left as evidence of a revival of prewar fascism. In July, 1948, a member of the All Japan Anti-Communist League attempted to assassinate Tokuda Kyūichi, secretary-general of the Japan Communist Party. The terrorist threw a stick of dynamite at the speaker's platform during an address Tokuda was giving. Tokuda was hospitalized for a week. Another unsuccessful attempt on his life was made a year later.[34]

During the 1960 Security Pact struggle, a number of instances of rightist terrorism occurred. On April 2, ten members of the Matsubakai, a rightist organization, tore up the main office of the moderate *Mainichi Shimbun* and threw sand into the rotary presses. On June 15, right-wing thugs drove a truck into a line of leftist student demonstrators near the Diet and injured a number of the students. The excited students then attacked the police in protest against the failure of the police to protect them and stormed the gates of the Diet compound. Hundreds of students and police were ultimately hurt, and a coed was killed. As a consequence, the Kishi Government cancelled the Eisenhower visit. Although the left received most of the blame for the fracas, it is nevertheless true that the rightists had provoked the riot, probably deliberately. Two days after the June 15 incident, Kawakami Jōtarō, the Socialist leader, was stabbed while he was collecting signatures for a petition near the Diet.

At a party to celebrate the election of Ikeda Hayato as President of the Liberal-Democratic Party on July 14, Prime Minister Kishi was stabbed in the leg by a right-wing fanatic, who had had a long prewar record of affiliation with terrorist organizations.

The most notorious terrorist deed in the postwar era was the Asanuma stabbing. The NHK national television network, no doubt prompted by the example of Messrs. Kennedy and Nixon, sponsored a debate among the heads of the three major political parties in October, 1960, in Hibiya Public Hall in Tokyo. Ikeda, Asanuma, and Nishio were present. When Asanuma Inejirō, chairman of the

[34] Ivan Morris, *Nationalism and the Right Wing in Japan: A Study of Post-War Trends* (London: Oxford University Press, 1960), p. 91.

Socialist Party, rose to speak, a seventeen-year-old youth in a black student's uniform leaped onto the stage and before a terrified audience plunged a dagger into the speaker. The boy was immediately captured, and, while awaiting trial, hanged himself.

The assassin was Yamaguchi Otoya, son of a Ground Self-Defense Force colonel. He had been arrested more than ten times during the year for his fanatical anti-leftist rioting, but was each time released because of his youth. After being expelled from the Great Japan Patriotic Party, a rightist group led by Akao Bin, he joined the All-Asia Anti-Communist League, another group of rightist storm troopers.[35] He told police that he had perpetrated the assassination singlehandedly and without the help of collaborators. He said that he had been overwhelmed with a sense of danger concerning the future of his fatherland in light of the disturbances over the United States-Japan Security treaty. Since July he had planned to kill one of the three spokesmen of the leftist movement — Asanuma, Nosaka, and Kobayashi Takeshi, Chairman of the Japan Teachers Union. The boy was an admirer of Yoshida Shōin and Saigō Takamori, patriotic leaders of the Meiji era, and of Adolf Hitler.[36]

The Socialists, of course, made political capital of the incident. Mass demonstrations were held by Sōhyō and the Zengakuren. The left accused the Liberal-Democrats of condoning and encouraging right-wing terrorism. At a funeral ceremony held near the scene of the killing political leaders of all parties, including Premier Ikeda, spoke. Asanuma's widow ran for the Diet seat vacated by her martyred husband, and won. The Asanuma assassination was a principal issue of the 1960 election, at least as far as the Socialists were concerned.

Someone in the Government had to assume responsibility, and Yamazaki Iwao, Autonomy Minister, resigned. Yamazaki had a reactionary record and had been forced to resign as Home Minister in the Higashikuni Cabinet by order of MacArthur's Headquarters and later purged.

The postwar rightist movement in Japan came to a climax in December, 1961, when the police discovered an elaborate plot to assassinate the Ikeda Cabinet. One of the ringleaders of the intrigue was Mikami Taku, a former naval lieutenant who had served a thirteen-year prison term for his connection with the assassination of Prime Minister Inukai in 1932. Also involved were Sakurai Tokutarō, a former lieutenant general in the Imperial Army and Kawanami

[35] *Japan Times,* October 17, 1960.
[36] *Ibid.,* October 18, 1960.

Toyosaku, a businessman who had helped to finance the effort. This group of rightists hid their activities behind a study group known as the Society for Japanese History and had gathered together 300 helmets, 150 gas masks, and a substantial quantity of other equipment similar to that used by the Self-Defense Forces. They had attempted, apparently without success, to enlist the support of members of the Forces.

The plotters had reportedly planned to assassinate not only Premier Ikeda and the sixteen members of his Cabinet, but also to bomb police headquarters and the headquarters of the Sōhyō and the Communist Party. They were said to believe that the Ikeda Government was incapable of preventing a Communist revolution in Japan. It seems possible that the military coup d'état in Korea in May, 1961, may have encouraged the Japanese rightists.[37]

The political and ideological significance of "incidents" (jiken) in Japan should be noted. Both before and after the war incidents have been exploited by extremist parties, and find their way into political mythology. Some become great *causes célèbres*. An incident may be an assassination or attempted assassination, an attempted coup d'état, or a bombing. The authors of incidents are usually obscure and unbalanced individuals who have been highly agitated by rightist (or occasionally leftist) propaganda. Each conceives of his act as one which may save the nation or Emperor from political corruption, treason, or Communism. The public figures singled out for assassination are often little known personally to the assassins: the victim is a symbol. An assassination by a rightist is seized upon by the political left as evidence that the conservative government is indifferent to the threat of fascism and is willing to see its political opponents terrorized, beaten up, or killed. The political right, on the other hand, is prone to deplore the incident but at the same time point out leftist excesses which may have provoked the act. If the motives of the assassin are pure the deed seems less dreadful to the public.

The present-day ultranationalist groups are not generously financed as were some of the prewar groups. Furthermore, they have thus far failed to elicit sympathy among the masses, as they did before the war. A successful coup d'état by the extreme right would be impracticable under present circumstances, because it would be unwelcome to Japanese conservatives, who, through the Liberal-Democratic Party, already rule Japan. At the same time, the highly articulate and well-organized left could be counted upon to mobilize mass resistance to a rightist coup.

[37] Washington *Evening Star,* December 12, 1961.

Labor

The lot of the Japanese worker has never been an easy one. The oversupply of labor in Japan has made it easy for employers to hire workers at low wages, and Japan's need to export and compete in world markets has been a powerful argument to keep wages down. In the prewar era, labor unions and "proletarian" political parties were intermittently suppressed by the government, which normally sided with the employers. The labor movement has been and remains constantly rent with disputes over theoretical and practical questions. In 1936, the peak year of the labor movement in prewar Japan, labor unions included only 420,000 members, 6.9 per cent of the non-agricultural workers. A period of decline set in because of government interference and repression, and by the end of the Pacific War, labor unions were virtually nonexistent.

In the first year of the Occupation, MacArthur's Headquarters, especially the Labor Division of the Economic and Scientific Section, fostered the expansion of labor unions as part of its democratization program. The Trade Union Law of 1945 was patterned after the Wagner Act (1935) of the American New Deal, which gave labor the rights to organize, to strike, and to bargain collectively. By the end of 1946, there were in Japan two large national federations of labor: the Congress of Industrial Unions (Sambetsu) and the All-Japan Federation of Labor (Sōdōmei). To the American observer, these corresponded to the CIO and the AFL in the United States.

Almost from the very beginning, the Supreme Commander was seriously embarrassed by the Communist and pro-Communist leadership of some, though not of all, of the labor movement. A common tactic used by labor unions early in the Occupation was "production control," in which strike leaders took over the complete management of enterprises involved in labor disputes. The radical politics of the Japanese labor leaders should not have been surprising since many of them had been hounded by the police or imprisoned during the prewar period. The frequent political strikes to bring about the fall of the first Yoshida Cabinet showed that the labor movement in Japan was not politically "neutral" in the tradition of the American labor movement and that organized labor's commitment to parliamentarism was doubtful. The great general strike planned for February 1, 1947, was called off by a direct order of General MacArthur to the strike leaders. Toward the end of March, 1948, the Communications Workers Union organized a movement for a nation-wide strike for better wage standards for government workers, but the strike was banned by General Marquat, of the Economic and Scientific Section (ESS). In July, 1948, General MacArthur informed Prime Minister Ashida that strikes of government employees would henceforth be forbidden. The Chief of the Labor Division in ESS, James S. Killen, resigned in protest against the new attitude of SCAP towards labor.

In 1949, SCAP pressured the Japanese government into revising the Trade Union Law to follow more closely the restrictive provisions of the Taft-Hartley Act, enacted in the United States in 1947. By 1950, MacArthur's Headquarters had assumed a posture of hostility towards organized labor, which resulted in distrust and resentment of the Occupation and the United States.[38] Aside from measures of suppression, SCAP merely lectured the workers and infiltrated union organizations with "Democratization Leagues," "which were essentially SCAP-sponsored anti-Communist cells."[39]

In December, 1961, 5,969,860 workers were members of unions with affiliations as follows:[40]

Sōhyō (Nihon Rōdō Kumiai Sōhyō Gikai):	3,801,410
Zenrō (Zen Nihon Rōdō Kumiai Kaigi):	938,100
Shinsambetsu (Zenkoku Sangyōbetsu Rōdō Kumiai Rengō):	43,600
Neutral:	1,186,750
Total	5,969,860

The principal affiliates of Sōhyō are public workers unions such as the All-Japan Government and Public Workers Union, National Railways Workers Union, and Japan Teachers Union (Nikkyōso). The Sōhyō is closely affiliated with the Socialist Party. It nominates most of the Socialist candidates and provides the bulk of their campaign funds and votes.

The Sōhyō leadership throws its support to many leftist movements. As in the 1960 Security Pact struggle, it has called widespread strikes, even among the National Railway workers, who legally may not strike, and can pay small subsidies to its demonstrators. But notwithstanding the large numbers of people it can mobilize, the general level of ideological consciousness among the workers, even those demonstrating, is relatively low. The Sōhyō is under constant criticism for its frequent use of mass pressure against the government. Its most notable political successes have been the defeat of the Police Duties Revision Bill in 1958, and the cancellation of the Eisenhower visit and resignation of Kishi in 1960. The Anti-Violence Bill, spon-

[38] Kazuo Kawai, *Japan's American Interlude* (Chicago: University of Chicago Press, 1960), p. 165.
[39] *Ibid.*, p. 166.
[40] *Asahi Nenkan, 1962*, p. 331.

sored by the Democratic-Socialists and Liberal-Democrats in 1961, was largely aimed at preventing recurrences of Sōhyō-organized mob pressure on the Diet.

The Socialists, in 1961, supported the principle of "structural reform," which seems to imply the achievement of socialist aims by evolutionary means and without socialist revolution. The Sōhyō mainstream, on the other hand, has attacked structural reform as a form of "revisionism." Notwithstanding this doctrinal difference, in which Sōhyō stands slightly to the left of the Socialists, Sōhyō continues to support the Socialist Party rather than the Communist Party. Sōhyō also tends to oppose the rationalization of industry, no doubt because of the fear of technological unemployment.

The Zenrō federation supports the Democratic-Socialist Party and favors rationalization of industry in order to advance the welfare of the people. The Zenrō-backed Democratic-Socialists cooperated with the Liberal-Democrats in formulating the 1961 Anti-Violence Bill and gave it high priority in their legislative program. The defeat of the measure, largely as a result of Sōhyō and Socialist opposition, was a defeat for both Zenrō and the Democratic-Socialists.

Japanese unionism has a number of weaknesses. Most unions are "enterprise" unions, i.e., based upon single enterprises, although not company controlled. Unions often include a high proportion of white-collar workers, who have affiliations with management but whose organizational skill is needed by the workers. The great national labor federations are actually loosely articulated federations of federations. The relation of the top leadership to the rank and file is very tenuous. The labor federations, like the political parties, are plagued with rivalries among leaders and disputes over ideology and tactics. Workers in government industries, which include most of the railroads and communications, are not permitted legally to strike; when they do so they are subject to punishment. About one-third of organized labor is made up of government employees. Much energy which might be concentrated on obtaining concrete economic benefits for the workers is expended on political strikes.

In part these weaknesses are traceable to a bifurcation in the Japanese economy. On the one hand, the great zaibatsu enterprises are engaged in efficient, increasingly automated, mass production. In these modern industries, labor is concentrated and easily organized, and management can afford to pay relatively good wages. On the other hand, in the vast number of small enterprises, often little more than household shops, the ties between employer and employee are paternalistic, and because of undercapitalization and inefficiency, wages are necessarily low. Furthermore, there has been a labor excess in the country, which impels workers to accept low wages in industry and agriculture. For Japan to compete in world markets, it is necessary that the cost of labor be kept low, especially in those industries which are not adequately mechanized.

One source of the political influence of organized labor in America has been its lack of permanent commitment to a single political party. By making both political parties bid for its support, labor is in a strong bargaining position to get what it wants from the government. In Japan, on the other hand, labor is committed to the Socialist and Democratic-Socialist Parties. These parties are apt nearly always to do labor's bidding, but they cannot win control of any of the branches of the national government. The Liberal-Democratic Party controls the government and it can win elections without catering to organized labor, which is an electoral minority in Japan. As a consequence, the political influence of labor in Japan is weak except when it engages in extraparliamentary tactics. Labor will perhaps exercise more political influence only when the socialists reunite into a single party and broaden their appeal to agriculture and the middle class so as to win a parliamentary majority. This broadening of the socialist base would probably mean a lessening of union domination over the socialists, which the unions are reluctant to allow. Organized labor in Japan, therefore, seems to be caught in a vicious circle making for political impotence and frustration. This frustration helps to account for its propensity to political strikes and mob demonstrations.

Business and Agriculture

The close ties between the zaibatsu and the party politicians in the prewar era tended to discredit political parties and the Diet as organs representing the interests of the masses of the people. The Liberal-Democratic Party is, of course, the lineal descendant of both the Seiyūkai Party, which was subsidized by the Mitsui monopoly, and the Minseitō, which was affiliated with the Mitsubishi. Baron Shidehara, the Minseitō Foreign Minister, was married into the Iwasaki family, which controlled the Mitsubishi companies. Today, the ruling Liberal-Democratic Party is the party of business.

It is said that each of the Liberal-Democratic candidates in the 1960 election spent an average of 10,000,000 yen[41] on his campaign, and that the Socialist candidates spent an average of 2,500,000, Demo-

[41] At the official exchange rate of 360 yen to one dollar, this would amount to $27,777.00.

cratic-Socialists an average of 5,000,000, and Communists an average of 1,000,000. Possibly over three-fourths of the total funds spent by all parties on campaigns are disbursed by the Liberal-Democrats.[42] The candidates get money from their party headquarters, faction leaders, and personal supporters.

In 1955, in order to regularize contributions to political parties, big businesses established the "Conference of Economic Reconstruction" (Keizai Saiken Kondankai), whose primary function was to subsidize the Liberal-Democrats, although some aid was to be given other parties. The organization contributed 20,000,000 yen monthly to the Liberal-Democratic Party, and at election time granted a large sum, amounting in the 1960 election to about 800,000,000 yen. During the six years of its existence, the Kondankai contributed about 3,800,000,000 yen to the Liberal-Democratic Party.[43] In addition, business circles subsidized the various factions of the party. Obviously, since much government activity is concerned with business, it is sometimes difficult to differentiate between a bribe and a political contribution. The high cost of subsidizing the party and the adverse publicity resulting from this activity led to the abolition of the Kondankai in 1961. The Liberal-Democratic Party has recently organized a People's League which is intended to raise funds for conservative candidates. Most of the funds for the support of Socialist candidates come from labor unions.

Each of the great factions in the Liberal-Democratic Party has affiliated with it a fund-raising organization, which usually bears a more or less academic-sounding name. Thus, the Fujiyama faction is supported by the "International Political, Economic, and Cultural Research Association." The faction's funds are spent not only for election campaigns of its members to the Diet, but may be generously disbursed during a party convention in order to elect the faction leader as party president.

The Liberal-Democrats are supported by organizations of small business and agriculture as well as by big business. Thus, seven national mass organizations of barbers and cosmeticians, laundrymen and dry cleaners, hotel managers, innkeepers, public bath operators, theater owners, and culinary employees help the party. These groups, of course, expect and often get legislation favorable to them.

Nearly every Japanese farmer belongs to an Agricultural Cooperative Association, and these associations are vital to the fortunes of individual conservative politicians and the Liberal-Democratic Party

[42] Scalapino and Masumi, p. 86.
[43] *Asahi Nenkan, 1962,* p. 275.

as a whole.[45] The Agricultural Problems Research Association, operated by leaders of various agrarian organizations, collects and disburses campaign funds for the Liberal-Democrats. The government fixes the price of rice, determines support for agriculture research, and is able in many ways to determine policies affecting agriculture, so that the farmers have a real interest in the outcome of elections. Since the Liberal-Democrats are the more or less permanent ruling party, they are in a much stronger position than the opposition parties to solicit funds from interest groups.

Japan's Political Party System: An Evaluation

Every modern state, whether democratic or totalitarian, has one or more political parties. In democratic countries, although political parties are usually unmentioned in constitutions, parties provide the public with platforms and candidates to choose from. Without parties to define alternative policies and sponsor candidates for office, it would be virtually impossible for the population in a large nation to express a mandate for a given program or for a given candidate. Parties serve as the link between the voters and the government. Parties are necessary even in dictatorial regimes for the mobilization of mass support for governmental policies, because the government must have at least the tacit acquiescence if not the enthusiastic support of a large percentage of the population. Every government depends upon consent (at least the consent of the police and army) as well as on coercion to enforce its will.

Party systems in various countries may be classified in terms of the number of political parties which are active, i.e., as one-party, two-party, or multi-party. Since 1955, Japan like the United States and Great Britain has had an essentially two-party system. However, because of the importance of factions within the two major parties and because of the existence of the two minor parties (Democratic-Socialist and Communist), Japanese politics retains some of the characteristics of the multi-party system.

The Japanese party system differs in a number of important respects from the party system in the United States. First, since the Japanese parties function in the framework of the parliamentary-cabinet form of democracy, they concentrate their energy on the election of members of parliament and are not involved in nominating presidential candidates. Second, the Japanese parties do not have strong grass roots.

[45] Robert A. Scalapino, "The Foreign Policy of Modern Japan," in Roy C. Macridis, ed., *Foreign Policy in World Politics,* 2nd ed. (Englewood Cliffs: Prentice-Hall, 1962), p. 254.

They are thought of primarily as organizations of politicians rather than as organizations of ordinary citizens. The undemocratic character of party organization has made it feasible for politicians to switch from one party to another, taking their followers with them. Third, internal personal and ideological factionalism has been a constant threat to the unity and even to the continued existence of the political parties. Fourth, whereas the American parties become active on a national basis only once every four years for a presidential election, Japanese parties are perennially busy preparing either for a lower house election, which usually occurs every two or three years, or for an upper house election, which occurs regularly every third year. Fifth, the Japanese political parties are not organized on a federal and decentralized basis, as is the case in the United States, and the governorship of a political subdivision does not directly lead to the office of chief executive. Sixth, the democratic principle of rotation in office does not operate effectively because the Socialists have never had the parliamentary majority necessary to form a one-party Socialist Cabinet and they have little prospect of obtaining the necessary majority for some time to come. The Socialist Party and the other parties of the left tend to take impractical and doctrinaire, if not irresponsible, stands on many issues since they are not accustomed to governing and have no immediate prospect of assuming such a responsibility. Seventh, the Japanese parties are more sharply divided along ideological lines than are the American parties. In the United States, both parties include liberals and conservatives, although the Republican Party probably includes a greater proportion of conservatives than does the Democratic Party. In Japan, the Liberal-Democratic Party is the "conservative" party, and the Socialist, Democratic-Socialist, and Communist Parties are the "progressive" parties. Ideological issues project themselves into virtually every political conflict, and every issue is apt to be interpreted in terms of its implications for social stability or class struggle. The conservative fear of revolution and veneration for the Throne and the radical fear of a revival of fascism and militarism are extremely vivid, and color attitudes towards educational reform, rearmament, political demonstrations, labor struggles, constitutional revision, foreign relations, and parliamentary procedure. There appears to be little common ideological ground between right and left, and there are no "bipartisan" policies. Eighth, violence and the threat of violence are a conspicuous feature of the Japanese political process.

A popular attitude towards politicians is that they are corrupt, self-seeking, and uninterested in the welfare of the people. The notion that political parties can be effective vehicles for the expression of the

Table 3

House of Representatives Election Results

	April 10, 1946	April 25, 1947	January 23, 1949	October 1, 1952	April 19, 1953	February 27, 1955	May 22, 1958	November 20, 1960
Liberal-Democratic							287	296
Progressive (Democratic)	94	121	69	85	76	185		
Liberal (Democratic-Liberal)	140	131	264	240	199	112		
Hatoyama Liberal					35			
Cooperative (People's Cooperative)	14	29	14					
Socialist	92	143	48				166	145
Right-Wing Socialist				57	66	67		
Left-Wing Socialist				54	72	89		
Democratic-Socialist								17
Labor-Farmer			7	4	5	4		
Communist	5	4	35	0	1	2	1	3
Minor Parties	38	25	17	7	1	2	1	1
Independent	81	13	12	19	11	6	12	5
Total seats	464	466	466	466	466	467	467	467

Sources: Nakamura Kikuo, *Shōwa Seiji Shi* [*Shōwa Political History*] (Tokyo: Keiō Tsūshin, 1958), pp. 237, 242–243, 246, 265, 267, 270–271, *Asahi Nenkan, 1959*, p. 189, *Japan Times*, November 22, 1960.

Table 4

House of Councillors Election Results

(Figures in parentheses refer to the prefectural constituencies. Figures not in parentheses refer to the national constituency.)

Date	Total	Democratic Party	Liberal Party	Kokumin Kyōdō Party	Socialist Party	Democratic-Socialist Party	Laborers' and Farmers' Party	Communist Party	Ryokufukai	Miscellaneous	Independent
April 20, 1947	100 (150)	6 (22)	8 (30)	3 (6)	17 (30)			3 (1)		6 (7)	57 (54)
June 4, 1950	56 (76)	1[a] (8)[a]	18 (34)		15 (21)		1 (1)	2 (1)	6 (3)	1 (2)	12 (7)
April 24, 1953	53 (75)	3[b] (5)[b]	16 (30)		11 (17)				8 (8)	(1)	15 (14)
July 8, 1956	52 (75)	*Liberal-Democratic Party* 19 (42)			21 (28)			1 (1)	5	1	5 (4)
June 2, 1959	52 (75)	*Liberal-Democratic Party* 22 (49)			17 (21)			1	4 (2)	1	7 (3)
July 1, 1962	51 (76)	*Liberal-Democratic Party* 21 (48)			15 (22)	3 (1)		2 (1)	*Dōshikai* 2		8 (4)

[a] Progressive Party (Shimpotō) [b] Progressive Party (Kaishintō)

Sources: Japanese Government, Office of Prime Minister, Bureau of Statistics, *Japan Statistical Yearbook, 1961*, p. 452; *Japan Times*, July 4, 1962.

will of the people has not taken strong root. The failure of the politicians to gain the confidence of the people in the 1920's opened the way for militarism and fascism in the 1930's. Until the political parties have won the backing of the masses of the people, the prospects for democracy in Japan will remain uncertain.

Table 5

Results of July 1, 1962, House of Councillors Election

(The House of Councillors consists of 250 members, of which 125 are elected every three years.)

A. DISTRIBUTION OF SEATS

Party	Elected July 1, 1962	Hold-overs	Total seats	Total seats before election
Liberal-Democrat	69	73	142	137
Socialist	37	29	66	65
Democratic-Socialist	4	7	11	16
Sōka Gakkai	9	6	15	9
Communist	3	1	4	3
Independent and others	5	7	12	14
Totals	127	123	250	244

B. DISTRIBUTION OF VOTES

Party	Absolute number of votes	Percentage of total votes	Percentage of total votes in 1959 election
Liberal-Democrat	16,581,219	46.38%	41.2%
Socialist	8,666,438	24.24	26.5
Democratic-Socialist	1,899,717	5.31	—
Communist	1,123,902	3.14	1.9
Independent and others (including Sōka Gakkai)	7,484,496	20.93	30.4
Totals	35,755,770	100.00%	100.00%

Source: *Japan Report,* Vol. 8, No. 9, July 20, 1962, p. 2.

SUGGESTED READINGS

Battistini, Lawrence H. *The Postwar Student Struggle in Japan.* Tokyo: Charles E. Tuttle, 1956. An historical account.

Colbert, Evelyn S. *The Left Wing in Japanese Politics.* New York: Institute of Pacific Relations, 1952. On the labor and socialist movements during the Occupation.

Cole, Allan B. *Japanese Society and Politics: The Impact of Social*

Stratification and Mobility on Politics. Boston: Boston University, 1956. An analysis of the social infrastructure of Japanese politics.

Farley, Miriam S. *Aspects of Japan's Labor Problems.* New York: The John Day Co., 1950.

Gibney, Frank. *Five Gentlemen of Japan: The Portrait of a Nation's Character.* New York: Farrar, Straus and Young, 1953. A study of a newspaperman, an ex-Navy vice-admiral, a steel worker, a farmer, and the Japanese Emperor.

Ike, Nobutaka. *Japanese Politics: An Introductory Survey.* New York: Alfred A. Knopf, 1956. A study of Japanese political behavior.

Kurzman, Dan. *Kishi and Japan: The Search for the Sun.* New York: Ivan Obolensky, Inc., 1960. A very readable account.

Morris, Ivan. *Nationalism and the Right Wing in Japan: A Study of Post-War Trends.* London: Oxford University Press, 1960. A comprehensive analysis.

Okochi Kazuo. *Labor in Japan.* Tokyo: Government Printing Bureau, 1958. A short study.

Scalapino, Robert A. *Democracy and the Party Movement in Prewar Japan: The Failure of the First Attempt.* Berkeley and Los Angeles: University of California Press, 1953. A classic study.

Scalapino, Robert A., and Junnosuke Masumi. *Parties and Politics in Contemporary Japan.* Berkeley and Los Angeles: University of California Press, 1962. One of the best accounts in English of the Japanese political process.

Swearingen, Rodger, and Paul Langer. *Red Flag in Japan: International Communism in Action, 1919–1951.* Cambridge: Harvard University Press, 1952. A penetrating analysis relating Japanese Communism to the international movement.

Uyehara, Cecil H. *Leftwing Social Movements in Japan: An Annotated Bibliography.* Tokyo: Charles E. Tuttle, 1959. A very impressive review of the literature in Japanese.

Yoshida, Shigeru. *The Yoshida Memoirs: The Story of Japan in Crisis,* trans. Yoshida Kenichi. Boston: Houghton Mifflin Co., 1962. Gives the opinions of the former Prime Minister concerning the burning domestic and foreign issues of the postwar era.

7

Local Government and the Judicial System

Local Government

Local Government before the Pacific War

Japan is today divided into forty-six major political subdivisions known as prefectures. Prefectures were first established following the Meiji Restoration and the abolition of the feudal fiefs in the 1870's. The dispatch of a governor appointed by the Emperor to each of the prefectures symbolized the replacement of the authority of the daimyo by that of the Emperor. The Meiji reformers saw to it that none of the prefectures bore the names of the provinces of the feudal era. Provincial names, however, persist in common usage to refer to particular regions. In most instances the prefectures were given the names of the cities chosen as their capitals.

The reformers were determined to break down feudal particularism and establish a strong central government. The Meiji Constitution and the Law Concerning the Organization of Urban and Rural Prefectures (1890) established a unitary rather than a federal system of government such as Americans are familiar with. Consequently, the tradition of local autonomy is weak, and the constitutional theory of "states' rights" is virtually nonexistent in the Japanese political consciousness. The constitutional status of the prefectural governments is not to be compared with that of the state governments in the United States, and the governmental role of the Japanese prefecture is analogous to that of the *département* in France or the county in the United States.

A number of factors explain the persistence of the unitary tradition in Japan. The small area of the entire country (smaller than California) does not make necessary the establishment of semi-autonomous

154

subdivisions and facilitates control from Tokyo. Whereas dissimilarities of language and religion have necessitated federalism in Switzerland, the Japanese for centuries have all spoken the same language and have not been rent by serious religious differences. The agricultural, fishing, commercial, and industrial economy is widely dispersed throughout the whole country, so that regional economic differences are not sufficiently great to require a large measure of regional autonomy. Japanese nationalism and the Emperor system have traditionally exalted national unity and centralized government over provincialism which has usually been equated with feudalism. From the time of the adoption of Chinese political forms in the seventh century, the Emperor, until 1947, appointed territorial governors to rule in his behalf. Although the governors in many instances never left the court and allowed local military nobles to usurp their functions, the ideal of imperial rule has persisted for well over a millennium.

During the period of the Meiji Constitution, the governor (chiji) of each prefecture was appointed by the Emperor on recommendation of the Home Minister. As "imperial appointees" (chokunin), prefectural governors were officials of the national government of rank just below that of Vice-Ministers. The governor had the power to override decisions of the prefectural legislature, and could withhold approval of candidacies for village or town head. He had the prerogative of formulating the prefectural budget, which was difficult for the prefectural assembly to veto, and had considerable control over the budgets of villages, towns, and cities. The Cabinet Ministers of the central government had the authority to issue directives and instructions to governors and to suspend or cancel actions of the governors. The Ministries most concerned with prefectural affairs were the Home Ministry and the Ministry of Finance. Centralization and bureaucracy rather than local autonomy and democracy were the prevailing principles of local government in prewar Japan.

Postwar Local Government

The Occupation authorities did not attempt to introduce in Japan the American type of federal system; such an effort they felt would not have been successful. They were nevertheless determined to provide opportunity for more democracy and "home rule."[1] Chapter VIII of the new Constitution concerned local self-government, and provided that the organization and operations of local public entities

[1] Supreme Commander for the Allied Powers, Government Section, *Political Reorientation of Japan: September 1945 to September 1948*, 2 vols. (Washington: Government Printing Office, n.d. [1949?]), I, 260. These volumes will subsequently be cited as *Political Reorientation*.

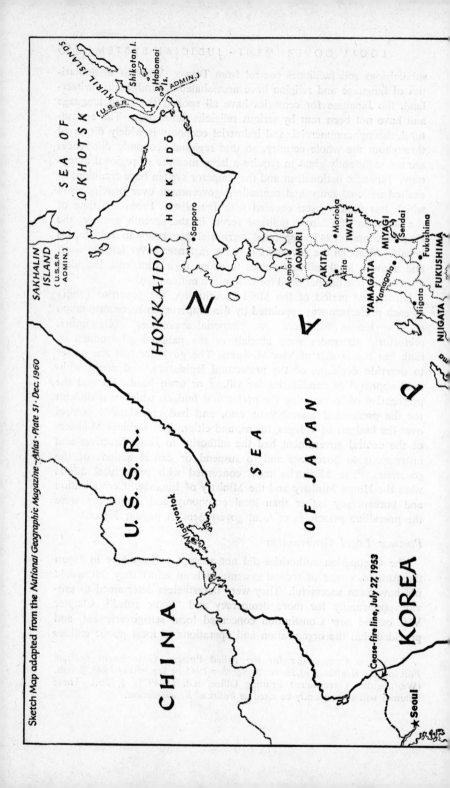

Sketch Map adapted from the *National Geographic Magazine – Atlas · Plate 51 · Dec. 1960*

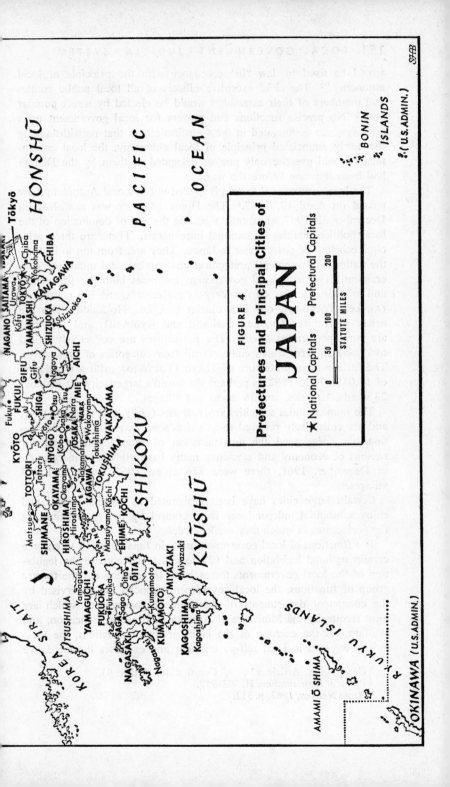

FIGURE 4

Prefectures and Principal Cities of

JAPAN

★ National Capitals • Prefectural Capitals

STATUTE MILES

0   50   100   200

would be fixed by law "in accordance with the principle of local autonomy."[2] The chief executive officers of all local public entities and members of their assemblies would be elected by direct popular vote.[3] No precise functions and powers for local government units are anywhere enumerated in the Constitution, so that notwithstanding the newly enunciated principle of local autonomy, the local governments would exercise only powers delegated to them by the Diet as had been the case before the war.

The local government system is spelled out in Local Autonomy Law passed on April 17, 1947.[4] The Home Ministry was abolished on December 31, 1947, apparently signaling the end of domination of the local political entities by national bureaucrats. There are three principal echelons of government in Japan. They are, from top to bottom, the national government, prefectural government, and municipal government. The term local government embraces both the prefectural and municipal levels. Of the forty-six prefectures, one is a metropolis (*to,* i.e., Tōkyō-to), one is a district (*dō,* i.e., Hokkaidō), two are urban prefectures (*fu,* i.e., Ōsaka-fu and Kyōto-fu), and forty-two are rural prefectures (*ken*). The prefectures are collectively called *todōfuken,* a term which embraces all four categories of prefectures. The metropolitan prefecture of Tokyo (Tōkyō-to), with a population of 10,019,296 in 1962, is perhaps the world's largest city. It includes 23 wards, 10 cities, and 36 towns and villages.

The municipalities are cities (*shi*), towns (*chō*), and villages (*son*), and are collectively referred to as *shichōson.* In recent years legislation has encouraged the amalgamation of municipalities, and for reasons of economy and efficiency many have chosen to merge. As of December, 1961, there were 556 cities, 1963 towns, and 947 villages.[5]

Certain large cities have been designated as "special cities" and enjoy substantial independence from control by the governments of the prefectures in which they are located.

The functions of local government units in Japan are (1) to enforce certain national legislation and (2) to enact and enforce the legislation of the local governments themselves. In carrying out the former group of functions, the local government agencies are supervised by the competent departments of the national government, which are most frequently the Ministries of Autonomy, Finance, Education, and Welfare. In the exercise of the latter group of functions, the local unit is engaged in local self-government and exercises the legislative

---

[2] Constitution, Article 92.   [3] Constitution, Article 93.
[4] *Political Reorientation,* II, 902–959.
[5] *Asahi Nenkan, 1962,* p. 312.

as well as the executive function. The local governments do not possess judicial branches; justice is a function of the national government, which maintains courts on various echelons throughout the country independently of prefectural and municipal governments. The powers of the local governments are delegated to them by "law," legislation passed by the Diet. Prefectural and municipal government in Japan is both organizationally and legally quite different from state and local government in the United States, where the federal principle prevails. Nevertheless, local bodies politic are not completely at the mercy of the central government. Article 94 of the Constitution provides that local public entities "have the right to manage their property, affairs, and administration and to enact their own regulations within the law." Article 95 lays down the principle that "A special law applicable only to one local entity, cannot be enacted by the Diet without the consent of the majority of the voters of the public entity concerned, obtained in accordance with law."

According to the Local Autonomy Law, the matters with which local governments may deal include maintenance of public order, protection of health and safety of the local inhabitants, establishment and management of parks, playgrounds, canals, irrigation and drainage waterways, water plants, sewerage systems, electric plants, gas plants, public transportation systems, docks, piers, warehouses, schools, libraries, museums, hospitals, asylums for the aged, jails, crematories, cemeteries, disaster relief, protection of minors, indigents and the infirm, land reclamation, identification and registration of inhabitants, zoning, coordination of activities with other local bodies, and levying and collection of local taxes. The national government, however, may also deal with these matters when it wishes. There is no enumeration of the specific powers of the local governments in the Constitution. Local public bodies may not deal with national affairs including judicial matters, penal punishment, national transportation and communication, post offices, and national institutions of learning and research. Local governments may not contravene the laws and Cabinet orders and ministerial regulations authorized by law. At the same time, a municipality may not contravene any of the by-laws of a prefecture. Unauthorized actions by a local entity are legally null and void.

Chief Executives

Governors of prefectures and mayors of municipalities are elected by the voters of their respective units for terms of four years, subject to recall by the voters and votes of nonconfidence by the relevant deliberative bodies. The Local Autonomy Law provides that when acting in his capacity as an organ of the national government, a governor is subject to the direction and supervision of the competent Cabinet Minister. When acting for the national government, a mayor is subject to the direction and supervision of both the competent Minister and the governor of the prefecture. If a governor refuses to enforce a national law or Cabinet order which he is required to carry out by the national government, the competent Cabinet Minister can request a court order requiring the governor to perform the function in question. In the event of continued recalcitrance by the governor, the competent Minister himself may enforce the law, and the Prime Minister may remove the governor from office. Likewise, if a mayor fails to enforce certain national or prefectural legislation, the prefectural governor may compel him to do so by means of a court order or may remove him from office.

Thus the local chief executives must serve two masters, since they function as agents of the national government in national matters and as officers of their local governments in local matters. A Japanese governor is very different from his American counterpart, who certainly does not regard himself as a functionary of the national administration. Eighty per cent of all the work handled by local government units consists of administrative affairs entrusted to them by agencies of the central government. Today the number of local government employees stands at about 1,400,000. The administrative structure of the prefectural and municipal offices is largely determined by laws enacted by the Diet.

Most governors are conservative independents rather than party men. In 1960, of the 46 governors, 31 were independents, while 14 were Liberal-Democrats and 1 was a Socialist. Mayors are likewise apt to be independents. In 1960, of 555 mayors of cities, 458 were independents, 71 were Liberal-Democrats, 25 were Socialists, and 1 was Democratic-Socialist. The 2,955 chief executives of towns and villages were divided among 2,829 independents, 105 Liberal-Democrats, 13 Socialists, 1 Democratic-Socialist, 1 of a minor party, and 6 vacancies.[6]

Local Assemblies

The size of prefectural assemblies is determined by law and varies from between 40 and 120 members, depending on the population of the prefecture. The size of municipal councils is likewise determined by national law and varies from 12 to 100 members, depending on the population of the municipality. Assemblymen and councilmen are elected for four-year terms subject to dissolution by the governor

[6] *Jiji Nenkan*, 1962, p. 902.

or mayor respectively. They may be recalled by the voters, who may also demand a dissolution of the entire body.

The local legislative bodies are empowered to enact "by-laws" (jōrei) on subjects enumerated in the Local Autonomy Law. Only the national Diet can pass laws (hōritsu). The subjects within the scope of the legislative authority of the local legislative bodies include the budget of the local government, the acquisition, management, and disposal of the entity's property, levying and collecting local taxes, and matters falling under the jurisdiction of the assembly in accordance with laws and Cabinet orders.

The governor or mayor may veto a measure passed by the relevant assembly, but the assembly may pass the measure over the veto by a two-thirds vote. The assembly may vote nonconfidence in the chief executive provided that there is a quorum of two-thirds of the membership and that three-fourths of the legislators vote for the non-confidence resolution. When a nonconfidence resolution is passed, the local chief executive, like the Prime Minister, must either resign or dissolve the legislative body. If after a dissolution the newly elected assembly immediately votes nonconfidence in the local chief executive he must resign. Nonconfidence votes occur very rarely in the local political entities. In the event that the local assembly persists in passing a resolution which the executive regards as *ultra vires* or in contravention of national laws and ordinances, he may bring a court action against the assembly.

Since the war, political parties have played an increasingly conspicuous role in prefectural assemblies. In 1961, the political composition of prefectural assemblies was as follows: Liberal-Democrats: 1520; Socialists: 337; Democratic-Socialists: 115; Communists: 6; Independents: 115; others: 595.[7] Prefectural politics are training grounds for those aspiring to higher offices in the national government.

In addition to the executive and legislative branches of the local government there are on the prefectural level and often on the municipal level, boards of education, public safety commissions, inspection (auditing) commissions, and personnel commissions, made up of members usually appointed by the governor or mayor with the approval of the deliberative organ. Local commission members, like local chief executives and assemblymen, are subject to recall by the voters.

The Local Autonomy Law provides for the exercise of initiative, recall, and referendum by the voters in local entities. If one-fiftieth of the registered voters of a locality sign a demand for the enactment of

[7] *Asahi Nenkan, 1962*, p. 311.

a by-law, the chief executive must present the demand together with his opinion thereon to the local assembly. Local chief executives, certain other executive officials, assemblymen, and members of the commissions may be removed from office by a recall vote held as a result of a petition signed by one-third of the voters of the relevant constituency.

Perhaps nowhere more than in the field of local government has the "reverse course" been more evident. Not only has national control over the police, education, and local finance been in large measure re-established, but in 1960, the Autonomy Agency became the Autonomy Ministry, concerned with the supervision of local governments. Conservatives have been advocating the restoration of national appointment of prefectural governors, but public opinion favors the retention of the present system of electing chief executives. A principal reason for the partial recentralization of government in Japan has been the inability of the local units to collect adequate taxes to fulfill the heavy demands placed on them.

Education

Educational Reform

In prewar times, the Minister of Education had used the educational system to instill nationalistic doctrines among the people. The Imperial Rescript on Education of 1890[8] established the philosophy of Japanese education. In it, the "Shinto ideology of Emperor worship was combined with the Confucian ethical concepts of loyalty, filial piety, and obedience to superiors. . . . Ancestor worship, loyalty to the Emperor, duty to State, and filial piety were crystallized as State morals and absolute virtues. The Rescript tied together religion, patriotism, and the family system."[9] In 1937, the principles of the Rescript were elaborated upon in the *Kokutai no Hongi*, which was required reading for all school teachers.[10] General Araki Sadao, a leading militarist, became Minister of Education in 1938.

During the Occupation, the Emperor renounced his divinity, State Shinto was disestablished, military men were forbidden to teach, ultranationalism and militarism were banned from the textbooks and the schools, and the goals of education were reformed to instill democratic attitudes, individualism, and practical citizenship. In 1947, the Diet enacted the Fundamental Law of Education,[11] which declared

[8] Text in Ronald S. Anderson, *Japan: Three Epochs of Modern Education* (Washington: Government Printing Office, 1959), p. 215.
[9] *Ibid.*, p. 13.   [10] Cf. Chapter III, *supra*.
[11] Text in *Political Reorientation*, II, 865.

the aims of education to be the "full development of personality," the "esteem of individual value," and "independent spirit." In 1948, the Diet passed a resolution rescinding the Imperial Rescript on Education.[12]

To break the grip of the bureaucracy on education, the administration of the school system was democratized and decentralized with the establishment of locally elected school boards patterned after those in the United States.[13] Parent-Teacher Associations were established even in the smallest communities. The new Constitution provided that all people would have the right to receive "an equal education corresponding to their ability" and that ordinary education would be free and compulsory.[14] On the urging of Occupation authorities, the American-type 6-3-3-4 (six years elementary, three years junior high, three years senior high, and four years college) system replaced the European structure of education. The prewar ethics (shūshin) course, which had indoctrinated the students with authoritarian, undemocratic attitudes was abolished, and history books were rewritten to make them less nationalistic. Students were taught to think for themselves rather than merely memorize what textbooks said. Textbooks were no longer compiled by the Ministry of Education, but were published by private companies and selected by local educators. The first nine years of school (elementary and lower secondary) were made compulsory.

In the first few years of the postwar era, the post of Minister of Education was held by distinguished educators, but in recent years appointment to the post is primarily based upon partisan political considerations. The Ministry was reorganized by the Ministry of Education Establishment Law of May, 1949, to harmonize its structure with the Occupation policies of democratization and decentralization. Since the administration of education would be primarily the responsibility of local and prefectural school boards, its functions were reduced to advising, coordination, and research.

The Reverse Course

The "reverse course," as the reactionary policies of the government from 1949 to 1960 were called, had as one of its aims the revision of the educational system to instill patriotism and love of country in the student body. It was felt that juvenile delinquency and pacifism were a reflection of the lack of adequate moral training in the school system. Furthermore, the powerful Japan Teachers Union (Nikkyōso),

---

[12] Text in *ibid.*, II, 585.
[13] Cf. The Board of Education Law in *ibid.*, II, 1207–1215.
[14] Constitution, Article 26.

under leftist leadership, threatened to use the school system to instill the youth of the country with Marxism. Socialists and school teachers were often able to get themselves elected to local school boards. In 1956, the Diet passed a bill making the school boards appointive rather than elective. Prefectural school boards are made up of five members, and local school boards of three members, appointed by the prefectural governor or mayor respectively. No single political party may command a majority in the board. The Minister of Education enjoys some right of veto over the acts of the boards of education. Appointments of superintendents by prefectural boards have to be approved by the Ministry, and appointment of local superintendents have to be approved by the prefectural board.

There are no specific local school taxes, and the national government collects nearly all taxes. From 1940 to 1945, the central government paid one-half the salaries of the teachers, but in 1949, the Local Finance Equalization Grant of the central government to prefectures and municipalities meant that teachers' salaries were subsidized less directly. In 1953, a more direct subsidy was provided for. Today, the teachers' salaries in elementary and lower secondary schools are paid half by the prefecture and half by the national government.

The restored centralization of the educational system has been described by Kiyose Ichirō, Minister of Education in 1956.[15] He has said that the Ministry of Education can now "positively advise, guide, and help Prefectures, and they in turn help municipalities. . . . The new legislation clarifies the lines of command in the educational structure."[16] The morals course was restored to the curriculum in 1958 over the bitter opposition of liberals and the political left, who, understandably, fear that such a course would, as in the past, spread anti-democratic and militaristic ideology.

Higher Education

There are in Japan 72 universities supported by the national government. These national universities include the famous prewar Imperial Universities. There are 33 "public" (i.e., prefectural or municipal) universities and 140 private universities, making a total of 245 institutions of higher learning.[17] A large number of these universities, national, public, and private, were established after World War II, and they are plagued in many instances with a lack of adequately trained staff. Salaries of professors are notoriously poor,

[15] Kiyose had served as defense counsel for General Tōjō in the war crimes trial.

[16] Anderson, p. 88.

[17] *Asahi Nenkan, 1962,* p. 583.

even in the best institutions, and the economic condition of many of the students is miserable. The competition to enter universities is extremely keen, and Japan is frequently referred to as "examination hell," where children and youths are constantly cramming for examinations to enter a university. Although it is difficult to get into a good university, once admitted as a student, life is easy because academic standards are not high, and almost anyone can graduate.

The Zengakuren, or All-Japan Federation of Student Self-Government Associations, has long been under leftist leadership.[18] In 1960, when it was distinguished for its great anti-government demonstrations, its mainstream faction was led by elements which had been expelled from the Japan Communist Party for their "left-wing adventurism." Consequently, the term "Trotskyism" is frequently applied to the ideology of this student movement.

The Police

Occupation Reforms

From the time of the Meiji Restoration, the police were an agency of the Imperial Government not only for the maintenance of law and order but also for the purpose of suppressing internal political opposition. The Home Ministry, which supervised the police, sometimes used the officers of the law for forcibly intervening in elections. The police, like other government officers, assumed dictatorial attitudes towards the people whom they seemed more concerned to oppress than to protect. The police were responsible for the extirpation of "dangerous thoughts," i.e., liberal, democratic, and socialistic ideas. The police system thus played an important role in enforcing authoritarianism and fascism in Japan.

A principal feature of Occupation reform was the partial decentralization of the police system, so that it could no longer be used by the national government for enforcing its will on the people. The Home Ministry was abolished in 1947, and a dual system of National Rural Police and Police of Autonomous Entities was established.[19] The National Rural Police of 30,000 men was placed under the administrative control of the National Public Safety Commission and under the operational control of Prefectural Public Safety Commissions. Each municipality of over 5,000 population was responsible for the maintenance of its own police (Police of Autonomous Entities) and the enforcement of law and order. These 1,600 munici-

---

[18] For the history of the Zengakuren see Lawrence H. Battistini, *The Postwar Student Struggle in Japan* (Tokyo: Tuttle, 1956).

[19] Cf. Police Law, *Political Reorientation*, II, 1062–1071.

palities each had an independent police force functioning under the operational and administrative control of a municipal Public Safety Commission.

The Reverse Course

Fears that the decentralized police system would be inadequate to cope with large-scale leftist-led demonstrations and riots inspired General MacArthur, in 1950, to direct the formation of a National Police Reserve of 75,000 men, when American forces moved to Korea. The Police Reserve was an embryo army and has since become the Self-Defense Force.

The expense and inefficiency of the Police of Autonomous Entities proved too much of a drain on the budgets of local governments, and an amendment to the Police Law, in 1951, made it possible for many local entities to relinquish the privilege of maintaining their own police and to rely on the National Rural Police.

Finally, in 1954, the Diet passed a new Police Law sponsored by the Yoshida Government.[20] Fearing a return of the prewar police state, the Socialists boycotted the deliberations. The new law abolished both the National Rural Police and the Police of Autonomous Entities and replaced them with Prefectural Police. In principle, the expense is borne by the prefecture. The police in each prefecture are under the operational control of a Prefectural Public Safety Commission composed of three or five members appointed by the governor with the approval of the prefectural assembly. The Chief of the Prefectural Police Headquarters is appointed by the National Public Safety Commission with the consent of the Prefectural Public Safety Commission.

The National Public Safety Commission is headed by a Cabinet Minister (in recent years the Autonomy Minister) and has five additional members, appointed by the Prime Minister with the consent of the Diet. The National Public Safety Commission administers police affairs relating to state security, exercises general control over such matters as police education, communication, criminal identification, and criminal statistics, and coordinates police administration on the whole. Under its jurisdiction, the National Police Agency is concerned with criminal investigation, scientific crime detection, and police communications.

The Prime Minister may, upon recommendation of the National Public Safety Commission, proclaim a state of national emergency

[20] The background of this legislation is discussed in Yoshida Shigeru, *The Yoshida Memoirs: The Story of Japan in Crisis,* trans. Yoshida Kenichi (Boston: Houghton Mifflin, 1962), pp. 176–181.

concerning part or all of the country. He may then assume control over the police in the areas involved. Such an emergency proclamation must be ratified by the Diet within twenty days. Actually there have been no instances — not even during the turbulent summer of 1960 — when the Prime Minister has availed himself of this power.[21]

In 1958, the Police Duties Act Revision Bill, sponsored by the Kishi Government, met with widespread popular opposition. It was doubtful whether the proposed legislation, which was of questionable constitutionality, was really necessary.[22] As a result of obstruction in the Diet and mass demonstrations, the measure was not submitted to a vote in the Diet, although the Government commanded sufficient votes to pass it.

The challenges faced by the police in Japan are much greater than in America. Communist-instigated riots, assassinations by rightists, the narcotics traffic, smuggling, and gangsterism are acute problems. It often seems that constitutional legal limitations on the police, intended to protect the democratic rights of the individual, benefit terrorists, Communists, and criminals more than law-abiding people. Thus, constitutional and legal revisions are constantly proposed to strengthen the hands of the police, but as in the case of the 1961 Anti-Violence Bill, it is virtually impossible to bring about agreement between the two major parties concerning the specific provisions of such legislation.

The Judicial System

Since the 1890's, Japan has enjoyed the Continental system of codified law as contrasted with the Anglo-Saxon system of common, or judge-made, law. The codes were drawn up after European models largely in order to hasten the end of extraterritoriality (exemption from Japanese law) enjoyed by foreigners in Japan. Extraterritoriality was a keenly felt limitation on Japanese sovereignty and a most unpopular feature of Japan's "unequal treaties" with Western states. Although in form the codes were similar to those of Europe, in content they embodied traditional Japanese Confucian morality. During the Occupation, sweeping revisions were made in the codes to bring them into conformity with the democratic provisions of the new Constitution.

Under the Meiji Constitution, the Minister of Justice exercised administrative supervision over the courts, and the government appointed and dismissed judges, so that the judicial branch was not independent from the executive. During the Occupation the judicial system was

[21] John M. Maki, *Government and Politics of Japan: The Road to Democracy* (New York: Praeger, 1962), p. 102.
[22] *Ibid.*, pp. 196–197.

thoroughly reformed.[23] The Court of Administrative Litigation, which had been inspired by the European example for trying of cases in administrative law, was abolished, and such cases are now handled by the regular courts. There is no system of state courts paralleling the national courts, as in the United States, since Japan is a unitary state. All courts are organs of the national government rather than of the local governments.

The relation of the courts to the rest of the government has been altered to ensure the rule of law and the independence of the judicial branch. In postwar Japan, as in the United States, the Constitution is the "supreme law of the land."[24] Japan's Supreme Court is "the court of the last resort with power to determine the constitutionality of any law, order, regulation, or official act."[25] The power of judicial review is explicitly granted the Japanese Supreme Court by the new Constitution; the Court does not derive this power merely from its own interpretation of the Constitution, as occurred in the United States. As in the United States, the Supreme Court rules on constitutionality only when there is a question whether the law or order concerned should be applied in an actual lawsuit. The Supreme Court, with the exception of certain laws passed to implement Occupation directives, has never held any law, order, regulation, or official act unconstitutional,[26] but has upheld a few as constitutional. In the famous Sunakawa case (1959) the Supreme Court ruled that the stationing of American forces in Japan did not violate Article 9 of the Constitution. The principle was also stated that unless a treaty is "obviously unconstitutional and void, it falls outside the purview of the power of judicial review granted to the court."

The hierarchy of courts includes, from top to bottom, one Supreme Court, 8 High Courts, 49 District Courts (with 235 branches), and 570 Summary Courts. There are also 49 Family Courts (with 235 branches).

The Chief Judge of the Supreme Court is designated by the Cabinet and appointed by the Emperor.[27] Imperial appointment supposedly endows the Chief Judge with prestige comparable to that of the Prime Minister. The fourteeen other Judges are appointed by the Cabinet subject to popular review. At the first House of Representatives election following the appointment and every ten years thereafter the voters review the appointment. If they disapprove, the Judge is dismissed.[28] Actually, no more than 11.05 per cent of the votes were cast against any Judge, so that no Judge has ever been voted out of

[23] Cf. Court Organization Law, of April 16, 1947, in *Political Reorientation*, II, 885–893.

[24] Constitution, Article 98. [25] Constitution, Article 81.

[26] Maki, p. 106. [27] Constitution, Article 6.

[28] Constitution, Article 79.

office.[29] The system of popular review could conceivably result in drawing the Court into the rough and tumble of partisan politics.

The judges of the inferior courts are appointed by the Cabinet from a list of persons nominated by the Supreme Court. All judges of inferior courts serve for ten years with the privilege of reappointment.[30] Judges may not be removed unless judicially declared mentally or physically incompetent to perform their official duties.[31] All judges retire at an age specified by law.[32] Judges may be impeached by a Court of Impeachment made up of members of both houses of the Diet.[33]

The Supreme Court is vested with a sweeping rule-making power under which it determines the rules of procedure and of practice, and of matters relating to attorneys, the internal discipline of the courts and the administration of judicial affairs. The Supreme Court may delegate some of its rule-making authority to lower courts. Public procurators (prosecutors) are subject to the rule-making power of the Supreme Court.[34] The present Constitution does not provide for a jury system.

Corresponding to each court at every level are public procurators who represent the state in criminal cases. Thus, there are a Supreme Public Procurator's Office, High Public Procurator's Offices, District Public Procurator's Offices, and Local Public Procurator's Offices. The procurators are civil servants under the supervision and control of the Minister of Justice. Less than one-half of one per cent (0.4 per cent) of all persons tried are acquitted, so that the procurators seem to be doing an effective job.

The "status-of-forces" agreement between the United States and Japan gives Japan the authority to try American soldiers for offenses committed while not on official duty. This agreement, which was applied in the Girard case, is important to the preservation of Japanese sovereignty and national prestige.

SUGGESTED READINGS

Anderson, Ronald S. *Japan: Three Epochs of Modern Education.* Washington: Government Printing Office, 1959. A well-rounded study of the Japanese educational system.

[29] Cf. *Asahi Nenkan, 1962,* p. 318, for relevant statistics.
[30] Constitution, Article 80. [31] Constitution, Article 78.
[32] Constitution, Article 79. [33] Constitution, Article 64.
[34] Constitution, Article 77.

Beardsley, Richard K., John W. Hall, and Robert E. Ward. *Village Japan*. Chicago: University of Chicago Press, 1959. A comprehensive anthropological, sociological, political, and geographic analysis of a Japanese village.

Dore, R. P. *City Life in Japan: A Study of a Tokyo Ward*. Berkeley and Los Angeles: University of California Press, 1958. A penetrating sociological description.

Dull, Paul S. "Maeda Shoichi: A Case Study of a Japanese Political Boss," in Ward, Robert E., ed. *Five Studies in Japanese Politics* (Center for Japanese Studies, Occasional Papers No. 7). Ann Arbor: University of Michigan Press, 1957. On local politics.

Eells, Walter Crosby, comp. *The Literature of Japanese Education, 1945–1954*. Hamden, Connecticut: The Shoe String Press, 1955. A comprehensive annotated bibliography of periodical and book materials in English, much of it of interest to the general student of Japanese affairs.

Gokijō Kakiwa. "The Judicial System of Japan," *The Annals of the American Academy of Political and Social Science,* Vol. 308 (November, 1956), pp. 28–39.

Hall, Robert King. *Education for a New Japan*. New Haven: Yale University Press, 1949. A study of the education policies of the Occupation by a former SCAP official.

Japanese National Commission for UNESCO. *Japan: Its Land, People and Culture*. Tokyo: Printing Bureau, Ministry of Finance, 1958. An imposing study of nearly every aspect of Japanese life.

Ministry of Justice. *Criminal Justice in Japan*. Tokyo: Government Printing Bureau, 1958.

Ministry of Justice. *The Constitution of Japan and Criminal Statutes*. Tokyo: Government Printing Bureau, 1958.

8

Foreign Relations and National Defense

The Rise and Fall of the Japanese Empire

One hundred years ago the Japanese were confined principally to the four islands of Honshu (or Hondo), Kyushu, Shikoku, and Ezo (present Hokkaido). The Russian Empire was uncomfortably close. For some decades Russia and Japan exercised condominium over Sakhalin (Karafuto) Island and the Kurile Islands, but as the frontier regions became more populous complications arose. In 1875 Russia and Japan came to an amicable agreement to partition the region between them; Japan received the Kuriles while Russia retained Sakhalin.

In 1871, Formosan aborigines murdered some Okinawan fishermen. The Kingdom of Okinawa, in the Ryukyu (Liuchiu) Islands, was at that time a tributary of both China and Japan. The Japanese government sent a punitive expedition to Formosa (Taiwan) in 1875 and obtained an indemnity from the Chinese government. The king of the Ryukyus was taken to Tokyo, and in 1879 the islands were annexed to Japan as Okinawa Prefecture.

In 1895, as the result of her victory in the first Sino-Japanese War, Japan gained from China Taiwan and the Penghu (Pescadores) Islands and assurances concerning the independence of Korea. Ten years later, Japan conquered from the Czar the Kwantung Leasehold, including the Port Arthur naval base, in southern Manchuria, control of the South Manchurian Railway, and the southern half of Sakhalin. With the diplomatic support of Britain and Russia and the acquiescence of the United States, Japan formally annexed Korea to the Empire in 1910. The Japanese language supplanted the Korean

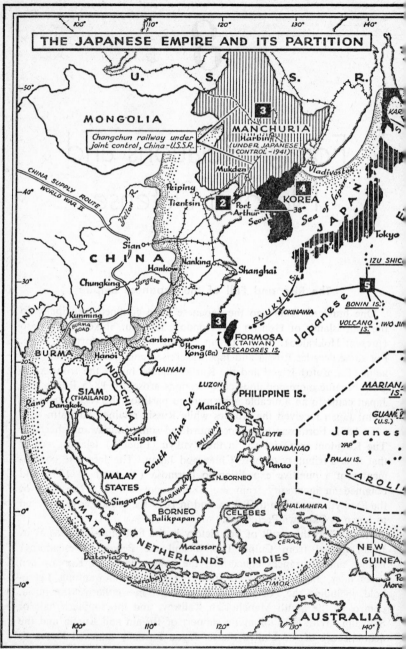

THE JAPANESE EMPIRE AND ITS PARTITION

U. S. S. R.

MONGOLIA

Changchun railway under
joint control, China-U.S.S.R.

3

MANCHURIA
Harbin
(UNDER JAPANESE
CONTROL - 1941)
Mukden

Vladivostok

Peiping
Tientsin

2

Port
Arthur

4

KOREA

Seoul
38°

Sea of Japan

JAPAN

Tokyo

Sian

C H I N A

Nanking

Hankow

Yellow R.

Shanghai

IZU SHIC

Chungking

Yangtze
R.

Kunming

BURMA ROAD

Canton

Hong
Kong (Br.)

3

FORMOSA
(TAIWAN)
PESCADORES IS.

RYUKYU IS.

OKINAWA

Japanese

BONIN IS.

5

VOLCANO
IS.

IWO JIM

INDIA

CHINA SUPPLY ROUTE
WORLD WAR II

HAINAN

LUZON

PHILIPPINE IS.

MARIAN
IS.

Rang

Bangkok

SIAM
(THAILAND)

Saigon

INDO-CHINA

Hanoi

Manila

PALAWAN

LEYTE

MINDANAO

Davao

GUAM
(U.S.)

J a p a n e s

YAP

PALAU IS.

CAROLI

MALAY
STATES

Singapore

SARAWAK

N. BORNEO

BORNEO
Balikpapan

CELEBES

HALMAHERA

South China Sea

SUMATRA

NETHERLANDS

Macassar

CERAM

INDIES

NEW
GUINEA

Batavia

JAVA

Soerabaja

TIMOR

AUSTRALIA

Po
More

Appearing in JAPAN'S MODERN CENTURY by Hugh Borton.
Copyright 1955 The Ronald Press Company.

Figure 5

JAPAN IN WO

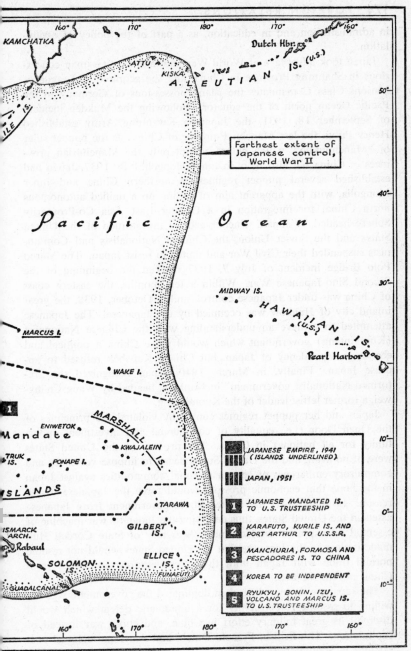

Farthest extent of
Japanese control,
World War II

KAMCHATKA

ATTU
KISKA
Dutch Hbr.
ALEUTIAN IS. (U.S.)

Pacific Ocean

MIDWAY IS.

HAWAIIAN IS. (U.S.)

MARCUS I.

WAKE I.

Pearl Harbor

MARSHALL IS.

Mandate

ENIWETOK

KWAJALEIN

TRUK IS.

PONAPE I.

ISLANDS

TARAWA

GILBERT IS.

ELLICE IS.

FUNAFUTI

ISMARCK ARCH.

Rabaul

SOLOMON IS.

GUADALCANAL

▓	JAPANESE EMPIRE, 1941 (ISLANDS UNDERLINED)
▥	JAPAN, 1951
1	JAPANESE MANDATED IS. TO U.S. TRUSTEESHIP
2	KARAFUTO, KURILE IS. AND PORT ARTHUR TO U.S.S.R.
3	MANCHURIA, FORMOSA AND PESCADORES IS. TO CHINA
4	KOREA TO BE INDEPENDENT
5	RYUKYU, BONIN, IZU, VOLCANO AND MARCUS IS. TO U.S. TRUSTEESHIP

After a map in M.I.T. Series Strategic Area Maps.
Copyright by Massachusetts Institute of Technology.

WAR II AND AFTER

in administration and in education, as a part of the policy of assimilation.

Japan took advantage of World War I to take over German concessions in Shantung Province in China, and she acquired as League of Nations Class C mandates the island possessions of Germany in the Pacific Ocean north of the equator. Following the Mukden incident of September 18, 1931, the Japanese Kwantung Army established Henry Pu-yi, the last Manchu Emperor of China, as the puppet ruler of "Manchoukuo," which embraced not only the Manchurian provinces of China but also Jehol in Inner Mongolia. By 1937, Japan had established several puppet regimes in northern China and Inner Mongolia, with the apparent aim of setting up a unified autonomous north China, for integration in a Greater East Asia Co-Prosperity Sphere headed by Japan. Encouraged by the attitude of the United States and the Soviet Union, the Chinese Nationalists and Communists suspended their Civil War and united to resist Japan. The Marco Polo Bridge incident of July 7, 1937 marked the beginning of the Second Sino-Japanese War. Within a few months, the eastern coast of China was under Japanese control, and in October, 1938, the great inland city of Hankow was occupied by the Japanese. The Japanese attempted to achieve an understanding with the Chinese Nationalist (Kuomintang) government which would make China a political and economic dependency of Japan, but Chiang Kai-shek refused to appease Japan. Finally, in March, 1940, Japan recognized the "reformed Nationalist government" in Nanking, headed by Wang Ch'ing-wei, a former leftist leader of the Kuomintang.

Japan and her puppet regimes constantly violated the principles of the Open Door (i.e., equality of commercial and investment opportunity for all nations) in China. The protests of the United States were of no avail, and the United States began to impose voluntary and compulsory embargoes of certain essential commodities against Japan in the hope that economic pressure would force the Japanese to see reason. In July, 1941, the United States government froze Japanese assets in the United States, thus depriving the Japanese war machine of essential oil supplies. In November, Secretary of State Cordell Hull made it clear to the Japanese that the United States would not resume normal trade with Japan until the latter withdrew its forces from China and Indo-China.

The Japanese Army, which then dominated the government, was not willing to assume responsibility for a diplomatic defeat which would discredit its great military effort in China, and chose war instead of capitulation. The British, French, Dutch, and American colonial possessions in Southeast Asia were quickly overrun by Japanese forces in the winter of 1941–1942, but the Battle of Midway (June, 1942) brought the westward advance of Japan to a halt. For three years, however, the demands of the European war deprived the Allies of the manpower and material needed to roll back the Japanese. After the surrender of German forces on May 7, 1945, the Allies stepped up their diplomatic and military effort to force Japan to surrender. The reader is already familiar with the story of the Potsdam Declaration and the Japanese capitulation.

The Cairo Declaration of Roosevelt, Chiang, and Churchill of December 1, 1943, had provided that Japan would be stripped of all the islands in the Pacific which she had "seized or occupied" since the beginning of the first World War in 1914, and that "all the territories which Japan had stolen from the Chinese, such as Manchuria, Formosa, and the Pescadores," would be restored to the Republic of China. Japan would be expelled from "all other territories which she had taken by violence and greed." Korea "in due course" would become free and independent. The Potsdam Declaration reasserted the Cairo provisions and stated the Japanese sovereignty would be limited to the islands of Honshu, Hokkaido, Kyushu, and Shikoku, and such minor islands as determined by the Allied Powers.

In view of Japan's surrender and acceptance of the Potsdam Declaration and her immediate demilitarization, there should not have been any difficulty about the liquidation of the Japanese Empire at the close of the hostilities. However, the outbreak of the Civil War in China and the rise of nationalist movements in the Southeast Asian possessions of France, the Netherlands, and Great Britain meant that a return to the *status quo ante bellum* would not be a simple matter.

The present international tension in East Asia in a sense represents a quarrel among the victors over the division of the spoils of war. The vacuums left by the extinction of the German and Japanese Empires have become the theaters of the Cold War. SCAP's General Order Number 1, of September 1, 1945, provided that Soviet troops rather than Chinese Nationalists would accept the Japanese military capitulation in Manchuria, and Soviet and American forces would accept the Japanese surrender in northern and southern Korea respectively. Chinese Nationalist and British forces would accept the surrender of the Japanese in northern and southern French Indo-China, pending the arrival of the French, and the British would accept the surrender in the Dutch East Indies, pending the arrival of the Dutch. The British, not the Chinese, occupied Hongkong. The Chinese Nationalists, the French, and the Dutch did not have the military wherewithal to halt the rise of revolutionary nationalism and Communism in the territories which they hoped to see returned to them.

The Alliance with America

The Korean War and the San Francisco Treaty

As early as March, 1947, General MacArthur told American news-men that it was time for a peace treaty with Japan. The inability of the Americans and Russians to achieve the unification of Korea and the Civil War in China, however, raised serious questions concerning the security of a disarmed Japan, and military planners in the Pentagon were unwilling to give up American bases in Japan. In June, 1950, North Korean forces, armed and trained by the Soviet Union, invaded South Korea, where they were met by American-trained South Korean troops. American air and naval units based in Japan immediately went to the aid of the South Koreans and within a few days, United States army units, with the sanction of the United Nations Security Council, moved to Korea. A United Nations force made up mostly of Ameri-cans and the Republic of Korea (South Korea) forces were combined under the United Nations Command headed by General Douglas MacArthur.

To maintain internal order in Japan in the absence of the Americans who had gone to fight in Korea, Premier Yoshida, acting on the in-structions of MacArthur, established by Cabinet order a 75,000-man Japanese Police Reserve, which was organized along military lines.[1] Through no choice of their own, the Japanese people suddenly found themselves involved in a war. Japan, only five years before at war with the United States, was now providing the American-led U.N. forces with air and naval bases for attacks against the Korean Com-munists and later the Chinese Communist "volunteers." U.N. head-quarters were located in Tokyo, and Japanese industry was caught up in a war boom supplying U.N. forces with all kinds of materiel. If General MacArthur was impatient to bomb the "privileged sanctuary" of Manchuria, where Communists mounted their air attacks on his forces, it seemed equally possible that the Chinese Communists might attack MacArthur's air bases in Japan, some of which were uncom-fortably near large cities, including Tokyo.

The Americans were distressed to note that a large segment of the Japanese public seemed to be indifferent if not unsympathetic towards the American effort to fend off Communism. The American policy of demilitarizing Japan psychologically and constitutionally as well as materially had perhaps been too successful. The pacifism and neutral-

[1] Cabinet Order No. 260, August 10, 1950, English translation in Harold S. Quigley and John E. Turner, *The New Japan: Government and Politics* (Minneapolis: University of Minnesota Press, 1956), pp. 435–437.

ism of the Japanese people were being exploited by Communists to stir up political difficulties for the United States in Japan. The feeling grew among American policy-makers that the Japanese would become more aware of their stake in the struggle against Communist imperialism if they were given their national independence. The United States proposed a formula whereby Japan would regain her sovereignty but American forces would remain in Japan. Such an arrangement would presumably satisfy both the Japanese who wished to see the Occupation ended and the American military. John Foster Dulles, a leading Republican who was expected to be Secretary of State if the Republicans won the presidential election of 1952, was assigned the responsibility for negotiating an Allied peace with Japan on behalf of the Truman Administration. In late 1950, the Soviet Union indicated that a peace treaty with Japan should first be approved by the four chief Allied Powers, China, the United Kingdom, the Soviet Union, and the United States, and that China should be represented by the Communist government in Peking rather than the Chiang Kai-shek regime in Taiwan. The Soviets further insisted on continuing controls to prevent the future rearmament of Japan. The Soviet views were not accepted by the United States, which refused to concede that the Soviet Union had a right to veto the conclusion by others of a peace with Japan. The entrance of Chinese Communist "volunteers" in the Korean War and the dismissal of General MacArthur did not halt Dulles' peace efforts.

The Western Allies were not in complete accord concerning the Dulles proposals, and compromises had to be worked out. Dulles had hoped to bring into existence a Pacific Mutual Security Pact, similar to the North Atlantic Defense Treaty of 1949. Australia, New Zealand, and the Philippine Republic, however, were still fearful of Japanese aggression. Three separate defense treaties were therefore devised: (1) a bilateral defense arrangement between the United States and Japan, (2) a defense treaty between Australia, New Zealand, and the United States (ANZUS), and (3) a defense agreement between the United States and the Philippines. By midsummer of 1951, the main differences among the Allies, save for the Communist states, had been ironed out, and the United States and the United Kingdom jointly invited fifty-five of the Allied Powers at war with Japan to a peace conference to be held in September for the signing of the peace with Japan. No changes were to be made in the proposed treaty after August 13.

The Peace Conference in San Francisco was attended by representatives of all of the fifty-five governments invited, except Burma, India, and Yugoslavia. China was not invited because of American objections to the Communist regime and British objections to the Nationalist regime. The Soviet delegate demanded that Communist China be invited to the conference and objected that the draft treaty did not restrict the rearmament of Japan or adequately guarantee democratic freedom. Instead, he asserted, it permitted Japan to join regional security pacts, which threatened the peace of the Far East, and its territorial provisions violated the rights of the Soviet Union and China. The Soviet proposals for changes in the treaty were defeated, and the Soviet Union, Poland, and Czechoslovakia refused to sign it.

On September 8, 1951, forty-eight Allied nations and Japan signed the Dulles treaty.[2] The conference was popularly regarded as a diplomatic victory over the Soviet Union. Nevertheless, the shooting war in Korea and the technical state of war between the Soviet Union and Communist China on the one hand and Japan on the other had not been brought to an end. Distrust of Japan was widespread even among those countries whose representatives had signed the treaty.

The San Francisco treaty required Japan to recognize the independence of Korea and to renounce all right, title, and claim to Formosa, the Pescadores, the Kurile Islands, Sakhalin, League of Nations-mandated islands (Caroline, Mariana, and Marshall Islands), Antarctica, and the Spratly and Paracel Islands. It is significant that the treaty did not indicate to what states Formosa, the Pescadores, the Kuriles, South Sakhalin, and the Spratly and Paracel Islands were being transferred. The ultimate disposition of these territories was to await post-treaty developments. Japan also accepted the establishment of the United Nations Strategic Trusteeship administered by the United States over the Pacific Islands formerly mandated to Japan by the League of Nations. She agreed to concur with any proposal of the United States to the United Nations to place under American-administered trusteeship the Nansei Shotō, which included the Ryukyu and Daitō Islands, and the Nanpō Shotō south of Sofu Gan, which included the Bonin (Ogasawara) Islands, Rosario Island, the Volcano (Iwo) Islands, and Parece Vela and Marcus Island. In the meantime the United States would exercise all powers of administration over these areas. The Allied Powers recognized that "Japan as a sovereign nation possesses the inherent right of individual or collective self-defense referred to in Article 51 of the Charter of the United Nations and that Japan may voluntarily enter into collective security arrangements." Japan declared her intention to apply for membership in the U.N. and to conform to the principles of the Charter of the U.N. It was

[2] Text of the Japanese Peace Treaty is given in Edwin O. Reischauer, *The United States and Japan,* rev. ed. (Cambridge: Harvard University Press, 1957), pp. 362–378.

provided that Japan should pay reparations to the Allied Powers for the damage and suffering she had caused during the war. "Nevertheless it is also recognized that the resources of Japan are not presently sufficient, if it is to maintain a viable economy, to make complete reparation for all such damage and suffering and at the same time meet its other obligations." Japan would enter into negotiations with those Allied Powers who so desired to arrange for reparations.

The 1951 Security Pact

Although the Peace Treaty recognized Japan's right of self-defense, Article 9 of the Constitution had renounced war and arms, and Japan had been completely disarmed by the Allied Powers. The Korean War was still raging, and on the same day that the Peace Treaty was signed, Japan and the United States also contracted a Security Treaty, in which Japan indicated her desire that, as a provisional arrangement for its defense, the United States maintain armed forces of its own in and about Japan so as to deter armed attack on the latter.[3] The United States expressed its willingness to maintain armed forces in Japan "in the expectation, however, that Japan will itself increasingly assume responsibility for its own defense against direct and indirect aggression."

The Security Pact went beyond simply allowing American forces to remain in Japan after the Occupation. It apparently looked forward to Japanese rearmament. Neither the Peace Treaty nor the Security Treaty mentioned the Japanese Constitution. The signing of the Security Treaty meant that Japan became an ally of the United States on the very same day that she had ceased to be an enemy. The American forces in Japan would be used to maintain "international peace and security in the Far East" as well as to protect Japan from armed attack from without. Japanese bases could presumably be employed in the pursuit of almost any policy the United States might follow with respect to Korea, Formosa, and mainland China. Furthermore, American forces might assist, upon the express request of the Japanese government, in putting down large-scale internal riots and disturbances in Japan, "caused through the instigation or intervention by an outside power or powers." Thus the United States acquired a conditional right of armed intervention in Japanese internal affairs. The conditions governing the disposition of armed forces of the United States in Japan were determined by an administrative agreement between the two governments concluded in February, 1952.

When the Peace and Security Treaties went into effect and the Occupation officially ended on April 28, 1952, there was little visible evi-

[3] Text is given in Reischauer, pp. 379–380.

dence of change in Japan. The American forces remained and enjoyed, under the terms of the administrative agreement, essentially the same extensive extraterritorial privileges that they had enjoyed during the Occupation. Before the dismissal of MacArthur, the Allied Headquarters had virtually ceased issuing directives to the Japanese Government, but the continued presence of the American troops gave the appearance that Japan was still an occupied country. The political opposition on both right and left made political capital of the alleged subservience of the Yoshida regime to the American military.

In 1954, as a result of an American hydrogen bomb test in the Bikini area, men aboard the Japanese fishing vessel *Fukuryū Maru* were showered with radioactive ashes. Their catch of fish had already been partly sold and distributed throughout Japan before it was condemned as unsafe. As a consequence, there was a widespread fear that ocean fish, a staple of the Japanese diet, were unsafe to eat. The failure of American authorities to express their sympathy for the victims of the test until the facts were all in aroused widespread resentment throughout Japan. Further indignation was aroused at reports that Admiral Strauss of the Atomic Energy Commission had said that the fishing boat might have been within the advertised danger area for purposes of espionage. Finally, the Americans belatedly admitted that the fallout from the Bikini bomb had been on a scale and in a direction not expected by the scientists in charge, found that the fishing boat had been outside the danger zone, and paid a compensation to the injured fishermen. The apparent American indifference to human values shown in this episode could not be excused on the basis of military necessity as had the atomic bombings of Hiroshima and Nagasaki.[4]

After the termination of the Occupation, Japanese magazines and newspapers were full of more or less sensational articles concerning the moral and economic effects of American military bases. The land occupied by the bases, it was held, was sorely needed by the peasants for raising crops. The Americans had left behind large numbers of illegitimate children with marked negroid or caucasoid features, such as blond or crinkly black hair, blue eyes, or long noses. These unfortunate "mixed bloods" (konketsu) would suffer from discrimination and lack of opportunity throughout their lives. The disreputable bars and other establishments pandering to the vices of free-spending American G.I.'s often created difficulties. Of course, leftist agitators made great capital of the "base problem," in order to hasten the withdrawal of the foreign troops. In 1957 the apparently thoughtless killing by an American soldier of a Japanese peasant woman salvaging shell cases

[4] Richard Storry, *A History of Modern Japan* (London: Penguin Books, 1960), pp. 260–262.

at an American firing range aroused much indignation. A controversy over whether Army Specialist William Girard should be tried by a Japanese court or a United States military court aroused much ill will on both sides of the Pacific Ocean. A visit by Prime Minister Kishi to President Eisenhower was followed by the announcement in June, 1957, that within a year the United States would withdraw its ground forces from Japan, with the exception of supply and administrative elements. American air and naval units in Japan, however, would remain.

The 1960 Security Pact

The Socialists and others criticized the 1951 Security Treaty because it gave the right to the Americans to maintain bases in Japan without obligating the United States to defend Japan. It permitted the United States to "put down large-scale riots and disturbances in Japan" on the request of the Japanese government, and to utilize the Japanese bases for the maintenance of international peace "in the Far East," so that there was a danger that the United States might draw Japan into a war (e.g., a war arising from United States-Communist Chinese hostilities in the Formosa Strait). The Security Treaty, with all of its disadvantages for Japan, had been signed by the Yoshida Administration in part as compensation to the United States for the Peace Treaty which restored Japan's independence.

The Kishi Government negotiated a new security pact with the United States which would commit the United States to defend Japan and require "previous consultation" — interpreted to mean Japanese consent — before the Americans could use their Japanese bases for military operations outside Japan or introduce nuclear weapons into Japan. The new treaty would not give the United States forces the right to put down internal riots. Kishi and the Liberal-Democrats believed that the new pact would usher in an era of greater independence and international prestige for Japan.

Notwithstanding the advantages from a Japanese point of view of the new treaty over the old, the neutralists and Socialists were dissatisfied. They were determined that the alliance with the United States should be ended and attacked the new treaty in order to accomplish this purpose. They held that the treaty would increase international tension in the Far East and might drag Japan into American military adventures in which she had no interest. In March, 1959, the Socialist Party, Sōhyō, the Council Against Hydrogen Bombs, and the People's League to Protect the Constitution banded together to form the People's Council Against the Revision of the Security Pact. In the same month, the Tokyo District Court ruled that the stationing of American forces in Japan, as provided in the 1951 Security Pact, violated Article 9 of the Japanese Constitution. This decision, which was not reversed by the Supreme Court until the following December, raised grave doubts concerning not only the status of American forces then in Japan but also concerning the constitutionality of the new treaty. In January, 1960, Zengakuren student demonstrators attempted to prevent Kishi and his party from taking off at Haneda Airport to sign the new treaty in the United States. Kishi's party managed to evade the students, who rioted and tore up the airport restaurant, and signed the Treaty of Mutual Cooperation and Security, in Washington on January 19, 1960.

In February, a special committee on the new security treaty was organized in the Japanese House of Representatives, and debated a total of 150 hours on the pact. The Socialists evidently hoped to filibuster until the Diet session ended, thus preventing the passage of the treaty. On May 19, the House of Representatives Steering Committee voted in favor of a 50-day extension of the session, but this recommendation was not considered valid by the opposition parties, which had been boycotting the committee. At 10:25 P.M. a bell in the Diet building announced a plenary meeting of the lower house. The committee on the security pact broke up in a riot, in the course of which, the Liberal-Democrats claimed, the committee had voted its approval of the treaty. The Socialists had locked from the outside and barricaded with furniture the office of the aged Speaker of the house and staged a sit-down in the corridor of the building to prevent him from going to the chamber to call the meeting to order. Finally, after giving a warning, he telephoned for the police, who forcibly removed the angry, kicking Socialists from the corridor. Diet guards escorted the Speaker to his rostrum, where he called the House of Representatives to order. Although Socialists, Democratic-Socialists, and some factions of the Liberal-Democratic Party were absent, the house immediately voted a fifty-day extension of the session. The meeting adjourned at 11:52 and reopened at midnight. Again, with only Liberal-Democrats present, at 0:18 the house, without forewarning and without debate, suddenly voted to approve the security pact. The crisis of the afternoon and most of the evening had concerned only the proposed extension of the Diet session. There had been no suggestion even to many members of the Government party that the treaty would be voted on.

Newspaper accounts of the night of May 19–20 emphasized the introduction of the police into the Diet and the absence of the opposition parties when the vote was taken on the pact. The press, as ever hostile to the Government, played down the refusal of the Socialists to allow the house to convene peacefully.[5] The vote was referred to as a "forcible passage." The Government defended its procedure on the ground that this was the only way in which the parliamentary majority could pass the treaty in the face of the violent obstruction of the Socialists. The Socialists asserted that "the way the Government party forced the treaty through the Diet apparently indicates the war-criminal Kishi and his Cabinet have started to conduct their power politics openly and have trampled on the basic authority of the National Diet."

The Democratic-Socialists announced:

> The nation's parliamentarism was negated by the violence of the majority and the introduction of police into the Diet by the Government and the Liberal-Democratic Party. The Democratic-Socialist Party, for the protection of the nation's democracy, demands the dissolution of the Lower House and the holding of general elections as a means of measuring the nation's will.[6]

The May 20 coup was referred to among intellectuals as fascistic and Hitlerite, even though it might have been legal in view of the majority which voted for the treaty. Most of the writers for mass media seemed to believe that public opinion was against Kishi and the Security Pact and that the passage of the treaty was in violation of the popular will and democracy. In the heat of partisan maneuver and agitation, the controversy over the terms of the Security Treaty became inextricably confused with the controversy over parliamentary procedure. Many people who had not felt strongly about the Security Pact now became highly indignant towards the Government for its role in the events of May 19–20. Beginning on May 20, a wave of mass demonstrations and strikes calling for Kishi's resignation, the dissolution of the Diet, and the blocking of the Security Pact broke out in Tokyo.[7] The demonstrators were for the most part students, labor unionists, professors, business employees, and government employees. Although the parades were orderly, they tied up automobile traffic and in some instances penetrated the Ginza shopping district, where a

[5] For a comprehensive account of the role of the press in the 1960 crisis, see Edward P. Whittemore, *The Press in Japan Today: A Case Study* (Columbia: University of South Carolina Press, 1961).

[6] *Japan Times,* June 8, 1960.

[7] The author was fortunate to be in Tokyo during the summer of 1960 to witness some of the events here described. For a more complete account in English, see Whittemore, *op. cit.,* and Robert A. Scalapino and Junnosuke Masumi, *Parties and Politics in Contemporary Japan* (Berkeley and Los Angeles: University of California Press, 1962), pp. 125–153.

municipal ordinance forbade demonstrations. Especially moving were night processions of white collar workers carrying paper lanterns. Over 10,000,000 people signed petitions denouncing the new Security Treaty.

Zengakuren students had a number of violent clashes with police at the official residence of the Prime Minister. On June 4, the Sōhyō labor federation sponsored an illegal two-hour railway strike against the Kishi regime and the Security Pact. Normally, such strikes antagonized the public; however, in this instance, students posted at railroad stations explained the political motive of the movement to delayed commuters and won widespread support from the public. On the same day, tens of thousands of people, including 6,000 university professors, demonstrated near the Diet demanding the resignation of Kishi and new elections. A million college students went on strike, and Sōhyō estimated the total number of strikers in Japan at 5,600,000. Plans were then made for similar "united movements" on June 17 and June 19, when President Eisenhower was scheduled to arrive in Japan, and Sōhyō leaders added the prevention of the Eisenhower visit as one of their objectives. The Socialist members of the Diet signed formal resignations of their seats, but in the face of adverse public opinion, did not submit them.

Three former Prime Ministers, Higashikuni, Katayama, and Ishibashi, published a message to the nation calling for Kishi's resignation and the dissolution of the Diet. They notified the premier that the only solution for the crisis was his resignation and the establishment of a caretaker Cabinet to supervise a general election. Yoshida Shigeru was then traveling abroad.

The Abortive Eisenhower Visit

The Constitution provides that treaties are approved by the Diet thirty days after their passage by the lower house irrespective of the action of the upper house, unless the lower house recesses or is dissolved in the meantime. The visit of President Eisenhower, which was scheduled for June 19, would coincide with the final Diet approval of the Security Pact. It was widely asserted that Kishi had deliberately chosen May 20 as the date for the "forcible passage" of the treaty in order to provide Mr. Eisenhower with a "souvenir" (o-miyage) of his Japan trip. The "Ike visit" was thus inextricably connected with the fate of the Security Pact, the Diet crisis, and the anti-Kishi movement. The Socialists feared that the Eisenhower visit would be used by the Prime Minister to save his regime at the very time that it was in its most serious difficulty. The opposition parties were in a good position to exact concessions from the government in exchange for their support in welcoming Eisenhower — concessions such as the resignation of the Cabinet and the dissolution of the Diet. The Eisenhower visit could not have come at a worse time. The anti-Kishi movement began to develop into an "anti-Ike visit" movement. Demonstrations before the American Embassy in Tokyo became a daily occurrence.

When the President's press secretary, James Hagerty, arrived at Tokyo airport on June 7, he was met by a demonstration organized by the People's Council Against the Security Pact. The demonstration began to get out of hand, reportedly as a result of a Communist intrigue of which the Council leaders were unaware. Demonstrators climbed over the Cadillac carrying Mr. Hagerty and Ambassador Douglas MacArthur II, broke some windows and cut the tires. They threw stones at a United States Marine helicopter as it maneuvered a landing to rescue the trapped Americans. After police reinforcements arrived, "Ambassador MacArthur dashed from the car and was the first to climb into the helicopter, followed by Hagerty and Appointments Secretary Thomas E. Stephens."[8] The Ambassador's party flew to Hardy Barracks in mid-Tokyo, and from there drove to the rear entrance of the embassy to avoid the 5,000 demonstrators gathered in front.

The Communist press throughout the world had a field day celebrating this great demonstration of the wrath of the Japanese masses against the American imperialists. The American and Japanese governments now made belated efforts to assure the Japanese people that the Ike visit was intended to celebrate the one hundredth anniversary of American-Japanese friendship and that it was not intended to lend support to a particular regime or treaty.[9]

Business leaders, university professors and leading Christians[10] friendly to the United States urged that in view of the circumstances it would be advisable for the President to postpone his visit. However, as it became clear that Eisenhower was personally determined to come, efforts were made by the press and labor leaders to improve the atmosphere for him. Unfortunately, on June 15, an attack by rightist terrorists on student demonstrators around the Diet touched off a clash between students and police resulting in the hospitalization of 341 police and 459 students and the death of a coed by crushing. The students insisted that police brutality was the cause of Miss Kamba's

[8] *Japan Times,* June 11, 1960.

[9] Nevertheless, an AP dispatch of June 10 reported that U.S. officials in Washington believed that cancellation of the Eisenhower visit "would be a smashing blow to the friendly Kishi government and to prospects for Japanese ratification of the pending U.S.-Japan security treaty." (*San Francisco Examiner,* June 11, 1960.)

[10] A small minority of the Japanese middle-class and intelligentsia are Christians.

death. College students and professors throughout the country held memorial ceremonies, mourning parades, and protest meetings, and went on strike. Apparently fearing that the Emperor himself might become the victim of a Hagerty-type incident, imperial chamberlains urged that His Majesty, who had been scheduled to ride in an automobile from the airport to Tokyo with President Eisenhower, should not be put in a position where he might be involved in politics.[11] On June 16, Kishi requested the American Ambassador for a "postponement" of the Eisenhower visit.

With the Eisenhower visit called off, the question remained whether Kishi could remain in office long enough to exchange ratifications of the treaty with the United States. On the night that the treaty would receive its automatic approval by the Diet two or three hundred thousand demonstrators surrounded the Diet building, but there was no violence. The Japanese press followed with close interest the debate on the pact in the United States Senate. At one point it appeared that Secretary of State Herter's definition of "the Far East" used in the treaty varied from that which the Japanese government had given the Diet. The State Department then issued a clarifying statement to the effect that the Far East defense zone did *not* include Soviet Siberia and Communist China. On June 23, the day following the United States Senate approval of the treaty, ratification documents were exchanged at the official residence of the Foreign Minister in Tokyo. For fear of hostile demonstrations which might interrupt the proceedings, the time and place of the exchange was not made public in advance. President Eisenhower had signed the American ratification document and sent it to Ambassador MacArthur even before the United States Senate had approved the treaty. As was to be expected, the Socialists denounced the government for its secretiveness and underhandedness. After the ratifications had been exchanged, Premier Kishi announced his decision to resign. It is possible that had he resigned sooner, the Eisenhower visit would have been feasible. Since, from an American point of view, the new treaty was inferior to the one which it superseded it is questionable whether Kishi did the American allies a favor by provoking a political crisis simply in order to ratify the pact.

The Socialist Party declared that the new treaty was not binding on the Japanese people:

> We absolutely cannot permit this fascistic, dictatorial act by the government, which has trampled underfoot democratic parliamentarism and, heaping absurdity upon absurdity, has imposed upon the people a long series of accomplished facts. As we have already

[11] *Time Magazine,* June 27, 1960, p. 18.

made clear in our declaration of nonrecognition, it is beyond doubt that the substance of the new treaty violates the peace Constitution and the United Nations Charter, and that the manner in which the treaty was deliberated upon was illegal and improper, so that legally the treaty is completely invalid. Firmly convinced that such a pact has no binding force whatsoever upon the Japanese people, we swear to fight to the last ditch to make a dead letter of the treaty made in complete disregard of the will of the people and to destroy the Japanese-American military alliance.[12]

In the subsequent November 1960 lower house election campaign, the new Security Treaty figured as a principal issue. The comfortable victory of the Liberal-Democrats, who easily won more votes and seats than all of the opposition parties combined, was interpreted by some observers as an indication that the Japanese people favored the American alliance. However, many Japanese who opposed the treaty voted for the Liberal-Democrats on the basis of other issues or personalities. American bases are not popular in Japan; they are at best regarded as necessary evils. Even so ardent an advocate of the American alliance as Kishi prided himself on persuading the Americans to give up their army bases in Japan in 1957. The American naval and air bases, which remain, are no more popular than the army bases.[13]

Okinawa

The battle of Okinawa (April 1–June 21, 1945) had been one of the bitterest phases of the Pacific War for both the Americans and the Japanese. Tens of thousands of civilians as well as soldiers lost their lives in the struggle. Okinawa was not a mere colony of Japan; it had been a prefecture since 1879. The indigenous population had originally spoken the Okinawan language, which was closely related to Japanese, and readily adopted the latter language. Unlike the Koreans, the Okinawans came to regard themselves as Japanese, although the mainland Japanese often regarded them with condescension. Many Japanese families had settled permanently in Okinawa and become integrated with the local population.

During the war Chiang Kai-shek had hoped that the Ryukyu (Liuchiu) Islands, of which Okinawa is the most important, would be "returned" to China under his interpretation of the terms of the Cairo Declaration, which did not mention the Ryukyus by name. When the

[12] *Tokyo Shimbun,* June 23, 1960. Translation by the present author.

[13] Douglas H. Mendel, *The Japanese People and Foreign Policy: A Study of Public Opinion in Post-Treaty Japan* (Berkeley and Los Angeles: University of California Press, 1961), pp. 102–108.

war ended, Okinawa was occupied by American troops. The Civil War in China, Chinese maladministration in Formosa, and the strategic importance of the Ryukyu Islands influenced the United States to maintain its position in Okinawa notwithstanding Chinese claims. From the very beginning of the Occupation of Japan, the Ryukyus were removed from Japanese jurisdiction and placed directly under United States military government. The Japanese Peace Treaty provided that Japan would concur in any United States proposals to the United Nations to place the Ryukyu and the Bonin Islands and other specified islands under its trusteeship system. In the meantime, the areas involved would be administered by the United States.

The conflicts and tension in Korea, Southeast Asia, and the Formosan straits have made necessary the maintenance of strong United States bases in East Asia. At the same time, the usefulness of American bases in Japan is limited by the terms of the 1960 American-Japanese Security Treaty and by political developments in Japan. The Okinawa bases, on the other hand, are located in territory under the *de facto* jurisdiction of the United States and their use is less dependent upon local political uncertainties. In his State of the Union Message in January, 1954, President Eisenhower said that United States forces would have to remain "indefinitely" because of the Communist menace in Asia.[14]

The population of the Ryukyus consists of about 852,000 Japanese[15] (Okinawans) and about 90,000 Americans, military and civilian. The Americans live in a colonial atmosphere with a standard of living incomparably higher than that of the native population. The local economy has become largely dependent upon the military bases. At the same time, the bases have taken up much of the necessary farmland. For a number of years, the terms of the American leases on Okinawan land were a source of much dissatisfaction, and in 1956, the outspoken anti-American Senaga Kamejirō was elected mayor of Naha. The demand for the return of Okinawa to Japan became so strong that it appeared to some observers that Okinawa might become an American Cyprus. In 1959, the land problem was settled fairly satisfactorily and extremist agitation tapered off. Occasionally Okinawan leaders chide the Japanese government for giving the Ryukyuan people less typhoon relief than the Americans. Nevertheless, the Okinawans look forward to the return of Japanese rule, and all Okinawan politicians proclaim their devotion to this patriotic principle.

[14] William J. Jordan, "Japan's Diplomacy between East and West," in Hugh Borton, *et al., Japan Between East and West* (New York: Harper, 1957), p. 143.

[15] *Asahi Nenkan, 1961*, p. 230.

Under the terms of a presidential directive of 1957, the Government of Okinawa is under the authority of a High Commissioner appointed from the American military by the Secretary of Defense. A Civil Administrator serves below the High Commissioner. In 1962, Dr. Shannon McCune, Korean-born American educator and Far East expert, became the first civilian to be appointed Civil Administrator. The 29 members of the Okinawan Legislative Assembly (Rippō-in) are popularly elected in single-member districts. Shortly before the 1960 election, the High Commissioner announced that the post of Chief Executive (Shuseki) would be held by a member of whichever political party won the most seats. As a consequence of the election, Ōta Seisaku of the Liberal-Democratic Party was reappointed Chief Executive.

The Liberal-Democratic Party and Social Mass Party (Shakai Taishutō) both advocate social and economic reforms in cooperation with the United States. The Socialist Party (Shakaitō) and People's Party (Jinmintō) advocate the abolition of the military occupation and the immediate return of Okinawa to Japan. The results of the 1960 Assembly election were as follows (seats held in previous Assembly are indicated in parentheses):

Liberal-Democrats:	22	(14)	People's:	1	(5)
Socialist Mass:	5	(9)	Independent:	1	(1)

The Chief Executive has proposed the establishment of a tripartite agency to promote greater cooperation between the Japanese, United States, and Okinawan Governments in the solution of Okinawan problems.[16]

Americans assisted in the establishment of the University of the Ryukyus in Shuri (near Naha), the site of the Okinawan royal palace which had been destroyed during the Battle of Okinawa. In principle, the university was to be bilingual (Japanese and English), but English is still a foreign language in the university and in Okinawa generally. The culture of Okinawa today is thoroughly Japanese: Okinawan news broadcasts emphasize news of Japan, Japanese motion pictures are vastly more popular than American films, and Japanese textbooks are used in all of the schools. The Americans in Okinawa do not learn Japanese, and the Okinawans, on the whole, speak a broken pidgin English at best. It is sometimes said that the Okinawans are better off under the Americans than they ever were under the Japanese, and economically speaking, this may be true. However, Okinawa's present prosperity, dependent as it is upon the military establishments, is largely

16 *Ibid.*, pp. 230–231.

artificial. Okinawans continue to regard Americans as foreigners and look forward to the return of Japanese rule.[17]

Economic Ties with America

During the Occupation, the United States extended very substantial economic aid to Japan. Japan's yearly imports amounted to about one-half a billion dollars more than her exports, and American assistance made good the trade deficit. The Korean war created a boom for the Japanese economy, which was mobilized in support of the United Nations military effort.

Today, the United States buys 29.82 per cent of Japan's exports and supplies Japan with 35.92 per cent of Japan's imports.[18] Thus one-third of Japan's foreign trade is with North America. The United States is Japan's best customer, and Japan, after Canada, is the United States' best customer. There can be no question that Japan's close economic ties with the United States since World War II have been a decisive factor in Japan's remarkable industrial revival.

There is, unfortunately, a negative side to the picture. Because Japan's prosperity is so closely linked with that of America, a recession in the United States or a change in American tariff policies could prove disastrous for the Japanese. As one Japanese diplomat has commented to an American, "When your economy catches cold, ours is likely to develop pneumonia."[19] Japan, then, is in somewhat the same position with respect to the United States as are Latin American states whose economies are heavily dependent upon the North American market. In order to lessen Japan's excessive economic dependence on the United States, the government has made strong efforts to increase trade with mainland China and Southeast Asia. Leftist critics have asserted that the alliance with the United States is the only thing which stands in the way of normalization of trade with mainland China, and that if Japan were to assume a neutral position in the Cold War, she would enjoy more prosperity than she does today.

It should be noted that notwithstanding the many issues which have contributed to unpleasant feeling in Japan towards Americans, polls indicate that the Japanese have normally rated the United States as their most liked foreign nation, with India and other non-Communist nations far behind. Russia, on the other hand, seems to be the most disliked country.[20]

[17] The author lived in Okinawa in the fall of 1959 and gave several lectures at the University of the Ryukyus. These comments stem in part from his observations at that time. See also Mendel, pp. 141–146.

[18] In 1959. Japan, Ministry of Foreign Affairs, *The Japan of Today* (Tokyo: Toppan, 1961), inside back cover.

[19] Mendel, p. 49.   [20] *Ibid.*, p. 50.

Japan and Asia

Japan and Nationalist China

It was anticipated at the end of the Pacific War that Nationalist China would play a leading role in the maintenance of peace and security in the Far East. China was one of the four veto-holding powers in the Far Eastern Commission and was represented in the four-power Allied Council for Japan. The prestige of the Nationalist regime, nevertheless, was enormously damaged by its retreat to Formosa and the loss of mainland China to the Communists in 1949. The United States and Great Britain were unable to agree on which of the rival Chinese regimes, Nationalist or Communist, should be invited to the Japanese Peace Conference, and, as a result, China was not represented at all.

The Cairo Declaration of November 1943 had promised the return of Formosa to China. In September 1945, the Allies' General Order No. 1 specifically directed that Japanese forces in Formosa, as well as in China (excluding Manchuria) and northern French Indo-China, surrender to "Generalissimo Chiang Kai-shek." In the San Francisco Peace Treaty, the Japanese renounced all claim to Formosa and the Pescadores, but the treaty did not indicate to whom sovereignty over the islands would be assigned. From the time of the Japanese surrender through the signing of the San Francisco Treaty, the claim of the Chinese Nationalists to Formosa was not officially recognized by Japan. Nationalist maladministration in Taiwan, which provoked a rebellion there in 1947, gave rise to suggestions that Taiwan be placed under some kind of U.N. trusteeship or that a plebiscite be held to determine its status. More recently, the "two-Chinas" policy has been urged. The weak legal claim of the Nationalists to Formosa and the Pescadores provided an opening for proposals to remove the islands from Nationalist control. If today the Nationalists were forced to leave Formosa and the Pescadores, they would be left without a territorial base.

The Yoshida Government, acting under strong United States pressure,[21] signed a peace treaty with the Nationalist regime on April 28, 1952, the day that Japan became sovereign.[22] This treaty, which recognizes Nationalist sovereignty over Taiwan and the Penghus, and Japanese diplomatic recognition are both of great importance to the

[21] Sir Esler Dening, *Japan* (New York: Praeger, 1961), pp. 207–208. Mr. Dening was British Ambassador in Tokyo from 1952–1957.

[22] The text of the treaty between the Republic of China and Japan is given in *The Japan Yearbook, 1949–1952* (Tokyo: The Foreign Affairs Association of Japan, 1952), pp. 485–488.

Nationalists in maintaining their claim to be the *de jure* government in Taiwan. It must, however, be noted that the Japanese government has been encouraging trade between Japanese firms and Communist China and seems to be moving in the direction of a two-Chinas policy. Furthermore, Japanese recognition of the Nationalist government is largely dependent upon United States policy.

The Formosan people, as distinguished from the Nationalist officials, were under Japanese rule for fifty years. Many speak Japanese in addition to the Fukienese dialect and are prone to compare their lot under the Nationalists with that under the Japanese. After the 1947 revolt, a number of Formosans in Japan organized a Formosa independence movement, which would give the Taiwanese self-government free of Nationalist or Communist domination. The movement has its headquarters in Tokyo and is, of course, illegal in Formosa itself. It is said by some Nationalists to be Japanese-inspired.

Relations with Communist China

The Peking regime (Central People's Government of the People's Republic of China) was scarcely four months old when, on February 14, 1950, it and the Soviet Union contracted their famous Treaty of Friendship, Alliance and Mutual Assistance.[23] The two parties agreed to adopt all necessary measures at their disposal to prevent the resumption of aggression and violation of peace on the part of Japan or any other state that might collaborate with Japan directly or indirectly in acts of aggression. "In the event of one of the Contracting Parties being attacked by Japan or any state allied with her and thus being involved in a state of war, the other Contracting Party shall immediately render military and other assistance by all means at its disposal." This Sino-Soviet alliance was aimed specifically at Japan and implicitly at the United States.[24]

In the same year, the North Korean government launched its invasion of South Korea. Although occupied Japan was not a belligerent, the United States Air Force flew sorties from bases in Japan. After United Nations forces repelled the invasion and moved north of the 38th parallel towards Chinese territory, the Chinese Communists sent "volunteers" into the war. U.N. Commander Douglas MacArthur urged that the Chinese Communist coast be blockaded, that Chiang Kai-shek be "unleashed" to invade the mainland, and that U.N. forces be authorized to bomb Communists bases in Manchuria, i.e., in China.

[23] Text in Chinese People's Institute of Foreign Affairs, ed., *Oppose the Revival of Japanese Militarism: A Selection of Important Documents and Commentaries* (Peking: Foreign Languages Press, 1960), pp. 1–4.

[24] A. Doak Barnett, *Communist China and Asia: A Challenge to American Policy* (New York: Random House, 1960), p. 258.

MacArthur was dismissed from his command purportedly in order to keep the war limited, and in 1953 a truce brought an end to the Korean hostilities.

The Soviet Union and Communist China have not yet negotiated peace treaties with Japan to settle World War II. So long as Japan permits the United States to maintain bases on Japanese territory from which an attack upon China may be launched, and so long as the Chinese Communists retain their anti-Japanese alliance with the Soviet Union and encourage internal subversion in Japan, a substantial improvement in the relations between the Peking regime and the Tokyo government will be impossible.

The attitude of the Japanese generally towards Communist China has differed from the prevailing American attitude. Japanese intellectuals tend to feel a sense of remorse for Japan's aggression against China in the 1920's and 1930's and are prone to forgive Chinese expressions of distrust for Japan. Furthermore, many Japanese share with the Chinese their fear of a revival of Japanese militarism and fascism. All Japanese, of no matter what political coloration, are keenly conscious of Japan's cultural indebtedness to China, which provided Japan with her Buddhist and Confucian heritage and her ideographic system of writing.[25]

Many Japanese merchants, especially those in the Osaka area, have kept up a constant clamor for increased trade with Communist China. In many respects, the Japanese and Chinese economies are complementary: China needs Japanese heavy machinery, ships, telecommunications equipment, and steel; Japan needs Chinese coal, iron ore, and soy beans. Many Chinese leaders were educated in Japan and speak Japanese and millions of Japanese have served at one time or another as soldiers, officials, businessmen, or technicians in China and Manchuria. On the whole, the Japanese do not fear the Chinese, but are conscious of Japanese superiority in technology, administrative skill,

[25] Of course, Japanese views differ from individual to individual. When I visited with former Prime Minister Katayama in the summer of 1960, he kindly gave me a copy of his recently published book of Japanese translations of the poems of Po Chü-i (772–846), one of China's best known poets (Katayama Tetsu, *Hakuraku Ten: Tōyō no Shi to Kokoro* [Tokyo: Shakai Shisō Kenkyūkai Shuppanbu, 1960]). The foreword is written in Chinese calligraphy by Kuo Mo-jo, Minister of Culture of the People's Republic of China, and the frontispiece pictures Kuo Mo-jo and Mr. Katayama in friendly conference in Peking in 1959. Mr. Katayama, a devout Presbyterian, pointed out that he had given the poetry a Christian interpretation. For all of his fondness for Chinese literature, Mr. Katayama does not feel that more active cultural exchange with China should begin until Japanese living standards have been improved to the point where Japan can resist Communist infiltration.

and living standards. Renewed trade and cultural exchange with mainland China are desired by most Japanese, and the present lack of official relations between the two countries is widely regarded as abnormal and undesirable.

The Peking government has fostered the development of "people's diplomacy" in order to capitalize on the desire of many Japanese for more contacts and to increase internal pressure on the Japanese government for official recognition. Since Japan obtained her independence in 1952, many delegations of Japanese, including leading conservative politicians and businessmen, have visited Communist China in an unofficial capacity and have made unofficial and quasi-official "trade agreements" with Communist officials.[26] Although Japan, as a member of the U.N. and a loyal ally of the United States, conforms with the rules of the U.N. embargo on strategic goods for China, some trade has grown up between China and Japan. The Peking regime has increasingly sought to make diplomatic recognition a condition for trade, while the Japanese government has insisted that economic questions should be kept separate from political.

Peking's trade relations and "people's diplomacy" with Japan since 1952 have of course been very disturbing to the Nationalist regime in Formosa. If they led to Japanese diplomatic recognition of the Peking government, the Nationalist hold on Taiwan would be seriously undermined. The fourth private trade agreement of March, 1958, between some private Japanese groups and the Chinese Communists provided that the consent of the Japanese government would be obtained for the right of the Chinese Communist trade agency in Japan to enjoy diplomatic immunities and fly the flag of the Peking government. As a result of vigorous Nationalist protests and a brief suspension of Nationalist trade with Japan, Japanese officials announced that they would not recognize the right of the Chinese Communists to fly their flag or enjoy official status in Japan.[27] It was now the turn of the Peking government to protest furiously. Following an incident in which a Japanese rightist tore down the flag which the Peking trade agency was flying without authorization in Nagasaki, the Chinese Communists, after demanding an apology without success, denounced the Kishi Government, completely halted all trade with Japan, and canceled existing trade contracts.[28]

---

[26] English translations of some of the agreements are given in James William Morley, *Soviet and Communist Chinese Policies Toward Japan, 1950–1957: A Comparison* (New York: Institute of Pacific Relations, 1958).

[27] *China Yearbook, 1958–1959,* pp. 195–196, 758–759.

[28] Peter S. H. Tang, *Communist China Today: Domestic and Foreign Policies* (Washington: Research Institute on the Sino-Soviet Bloc, 1961), p. 665.

On March 17, 1959, Asanuma Inejirō, Secretary-General of the Japan Socialist Party, and Chang Hsi-jo, President of the Chinese People's Institute of Foreign Affairs, issued a joint statement in Peking which summarized the common attitude of the Chinese Communist government and of the opposition party in Japan towards Sino-Japanese relations.[29] Both sides held that the forces against imperialism and colonialism were growing stronger and that these developments were favorable to Japan in her efforts to defeat the Japan-United States security system and regain Okinawa and the Ogasawara Islands, and to China in her efforts to liberate Taiwan. "Both countries should join hands to oppose the cold war and atomic war, implement the five principles of peaceful co-existence and the ten principles of Bandung, and safeguard peace in Asia and the world." The statement further declared that the Japanese Socialists were determined to defend the peace Constitution of Japan, and prohibit the manufacture, stockpiling, use, and importation of any nuclear weapons by Japan. Both the Japanese Socialists and the Chinese Communists agreed on the need to set up an area free from nuclear weapons in Asia and the Pacific. Premier Kishi's unfriendly attitude towards Communist China was blamed for the failure of efforts to establish diplomatic relations between Peking and Tokyo. The Japanese Socialists denounced the two-Chinas policy and demanded the abolition of the Japan-Nationalist China peace treaty and the representation of Communist China in the U.N.

The Socialist alternative to the Japanese-American alliance was stated:

After Japan puts an end to the Japan-U.S. "security" system, achieves complete independence and concludes mutual non-aggression agreements with China and the Soviet Union, then, it can be expected that the military clauses concerning Japan in the Sino-Soviet Treaty of Friendship, Alliance and Mutual Assistance directed against Japanese militarism will naturally become null and void. Following the conclusion of a collective security treaty between the Asian and Pacific countries, first of all between China, Japan, the Soviet Union and the United States, the neutrality of Japan will be further guaranteed. Both sides have reached a unanimity of views in these matters.

In 1960 and 1961, trade on a very limited scale was resumed between Japan and Communist China. In light of the favorable attitude of the Japanese government towards trade with China, not-

[29] Full text in Chinese People's Institute of Foreign Affairs, ed., *op. cit.*, pp. 59–65.

withstanding its alliance with the United States and recognition of the Taipei government, it would perhaps be correct to say that Japan has been pursuing what appears to be a kind of "two-Chinas" policy. This policy has been plagued with many diplomatic difficulties, but there are indications that the government intends to continue this line of action. Nevertheless, it appears that Peking, Taipei, and Washington will continue to place many obstacles in the path of a full-fledged two-Chinas policy.

Relations with the Soviet Union

The Soviet Union honored its Neutrality Pact of April 13, 1941, with Japan until August 9, 1945, when it declared war on the island empire only five days before the final Japanese offer to surrender. The Yalta Agreement of February, 1945, had provided that the Soviet Union would enter the war against Japan two to three months after the war in Europe ended. In return for this help, Churchill, Roosevelt, and Stalin agreed that Japan would have to return to the Soviet Union the Manchurian ports and railroads and the southern half of Sakhalin Island which she had conquered from Russia in the Russo-Japanese War. In addition, the Kurile Islands, which reached from the Eastern tip of Hokkaido northward to the Kamchatka peninsula of Siberia, were to be turned over to the Soviets.[30] General Order Number 1, of September 2, 1945, assigned the southern Sakhalin and the Kuriles to Soviet military occupation. By terms of the San Francisco Peace Treaty, Japan renounced all claims to these northern territories, without, however, stipulating that they were being transferred to Russian control.

The Kurile Islands (Chishima Rettō) had long stood as a Japanese barrier between much of Soviet Siberia and the Pacific Ocean. They were used as a base for launching the attack on Pearl Harbor in 1941. Their strategic relation to Japan, the Soviet Union, the Aleutian Islands, the northern sea and air route from Japan to the United States, and the polar route from Japan to Europe is readily evident from a glance at a polar map. Possession of the Kurile Islands is important to the Soviet Union today not only strategically but also diplomatically. The Soviets could make their partial or complete return to Japan dependent upon the removal of American bases from Japan, or upon the American evacuation from Okinawa, or upon some other valuable diplomatic *quid pro quo*. The Japanese

[30] The text of the now famous, but once top secret, Yalta agreement regarding the entry of the Soviet Union into the war against Japan is published in U.S. Department of State, *Foreign Relations of the United States Diplomatic Papers: The Conferences of Malta and Yalta 1945* (Washington: Government Printing Office, 1955), p. 984.

eagerly desire the return of the Kurile Islands, although they are less concerned with them than with Okinawa, where many of their fellow countrymen reside. A particularly touchy problem has been that of Shikotan and the Habomai Islands, which the Soviet occupies notwithstanding Japanese assertions that these are not actually part of the Kuriles.

The Soviet Union refused to sign the San Francisco Treaty and bitterly protested the termination without her consent of the Occupation and the demise of the Far Eastern Commission and the Allied Council for Japan, where Russia could influence Occupation policies. The Soviet Mission in Tokyo, housed in the former Soviet Embassy, continued to reside in the capital. The Soviet Union persistently vetoed Japanese entrance into the United Nations. Following the death of Stalin and the termination of the Korean hostilities, there were indications of a less unfriendly Russian attitude.

Formal talks to prepare a Soviet-Japanese peace settlement began in London in 1955. Among their more extreme demands, the Russians insisted that the Sea of Japan be closed to warships of all countries except the Soviet Union, Korea, and Japan. The discussions continued sporadically for ten months, but broke down primarily because of the failure of the two sides to agree on the future of the Kurile Islands. Immediately the Soviet Union announced stringent restrictions on fishing by the Japanese in northern waters. Kōno Ichirō, Minister of Agriculture and Forestry, obtained a ten-year fishing agreement with Russia which would go into effect either when a peace treaty was signed or diplomatic relations were resumed. As a result, the fishing industry in Japan put great pressure on the Japanese government to arrive at an understanding with Russia.

Foreign Minister Shigemitsu Mamoru renewed peace negotiations in Moscow, but again was unable to get the Russians to renounce their claim to the Kuriles. Finally, Prime Minister Hatoyama went to Moscow. He too was unable to achieve a settlement of the territorial dispute, and no peace treaty emerged from the talks. On October 19, 1956, Hatoyama signed a declaration which restored formal diplomatic relations between Japan and the Soviet Union and brought the fisheries agreement into force. The Soviet government stated its willingness to return Shikotan and the Habomais on condition that Japan agree to a peace treaty confirming Soviet sovereignty over all of the Kuriles. The Soviet Union stopped vetoing Japan's admission to the United Nations, and in December, 1956, Japan entered the world organization.

Japan and the Soviet Union have still failed to sign a peace treaty largely because of the dispute over the Kuriles. The Japanese assert that their renunciation of the island chain in the San Francisco Peace Treaty in no way affects their dispute with the Russians, because the Soviet Union did not sign the Peace Treaty. In any case, they argue, Shikotan, the Habomais, and the Southern Kuriles are not part of the Kurile Islands which Japan gave up at San Francisco.

Unquestionably a most important factor in Japanese-Soviet relations is the alliance between Japan and the United States and the presence of American bases in Japan which may be used against the Soviet Union. At the same time, the great cities of Japan are extremely vulnerable to air attack from the Soviet Union. The Russians will no doubt continue to exploit the fisheries and the territorial issues in the hope of weakening the Japanese-American alliance.

A principal source of Japanese dissatisfaction with the Soviet Union has been the prolonged detention by the latter of Japanese prisoners of war. In 1956, the Soviet Union agreed to return to Japan 1,400 "war criminals," although the Japanese held that some 10,000 Japanese prisoners were in the Soviet Union. In comparison with her trade with other parts of the world, Japan's commercial relations with the Soviet Union are not extensive. She has, however, sold ships to the Soviet.

On the whole, the attitude of the Japanese towards Russia is antipathetic. The two nations have for decades been rivals for power in northeast Asia and have been at war twice within this century. Many Japanese leftists (especially the "Trotskyite" students) hold that the Soviet Union has become bureaucratic and betrayed the principles of Karl Marx. The resumption by the Soviet Union of nuclear tests in October, 1961, came as a great shock to the Japanese, including the leftist leadership of the Gensuikyō.

Japan and Korea

Japan has always been much interested in Korea. According to a hoary Japanese tradition, in A.D. 200, the three kingdoms of ancient Korea were subdued by the Japanese Empress Regent Jingō, who put a stone in her sash to delay the birth of her child in order to make the expedition. The god Sumiyoshi was the pilot of her fleet, and when a storm arose, big fishes came to the surface of the sea to prevent her boats from floundering. When Jingō returned to Japan, she gave birth to the Emperor Ōjin, who later was deified as Hachiman, the Shinto god of war and tutelary deity of the Minamoto. The Japanese fought wars and made alliances with Korean states in the fifth, sixth, and seventh centuries, until expelled by the T'ang dynasty of China. Korea was a staging platform for the attempted Mongol invasion of Japan in the thirteenth century. In the 1590's, the Japanese invaded

Korea in preparation for the conquest of China, which was not accomplished. In 1895, Japan defeated China in a war fought primarily over Korea, and in 1904–1905 Japan fought with Russia for dominance in Korea. Korea was the "dagger pointed at the heart of Japan." The Japanese annexation of the peninsula in 1910 was impelled by strategic and commercial, as well as political, motives. At the close of World War II, the Soviet Union and the United States occupied north and south Korea respectively. When the Soviet Union supported the North Korean invasion of South Korea, United States forces charged with the defense of Japan fought first North Koreans and then Chinese Communist "volunteers" to beat off the Communist offensive which, if unchecked, would have imperiled the security of Japan.

Since the Pacific War, relations between Japan and Korea have been notoriously bad. Many Koreans still resent Japanese imperialism. After Korea was liberated from Japan in 1945, the South Korean government confiscated Japanese industrial and agricultural holdings in Korea and sold them to Korean private enterprisers and farmers. The Syngman Rhee regime also demanded, without success, reparations from Japan. About 930,000 Koreans living in Japan at the end of the war chose to return to Korea with what few possessions they could carry and a very limited amount of money. Thousands of returnees soon found life in Korea so difficult that they managed to re-enter Japan illegally. The Japanese are prone to regard the some 600,000 Koreans living in their midst with a measure of contempt, and the proportion of Korean residents who are in jail or on relief or making a living by illegal methods is much higher than that of the Japanese.

Since the Occupation, the principal sources of contention between Japan and Korea have been the "Rhee Line" and the repatriation of the North Koreans. In 1952, Republic of Korea (ROK) President Syngman Rhee announced an extension of South Korean control over large parts of the Sea of Japan, the Korean Straits, and the Yellow Sea, averaging some sixty miles from the Korean coast. The purposes of this "Peace Line" were to prevent the entry of Communist agents and smugglers and to conserve fishery resources from "rapacious Japanese exploitation." A truce halted the Korean hostilities in 1953, but in that year, the Rhee administration undertook to enforce the ban on Japanese fishing in the area by capturing Japanese vessels, confiscating the boats and their catches, and imprisoning the crew members. From 1953 to 1960, over two thousand Japanese fishermen were captured by the South Koreans on the charge of crossing what had become known as the Rhee Line. Often the fishermen were detained beyond the period of their sentences. Lawyers were not permitted to enter Korea in order to defend the Japanese. It was hoped that the overthrow of Syngman Rhee, which occurred in 1960, would result in more friendly policies towards Japan; however, the Korean National Assembly reaffirmed its strong support of the Rhee Line in February, 1961.[31] Occasionally Koreans detained in Japan for illegal entry have been exchanged for the return of the Japanese fishermen. On the whole, the Japanese, although highly indignant, were reluctant to use force to prevent the Korean seizures of Japanese fishermen.[32] The prevailing view is that the United States, which disarmed Japan and armed Korea, is obligated to intervene to prevent further Korean infringements on Japanese rights.

The Japanese depend upon fish as the principal source of protein in their diet. The policies of South Korea, the Soviet Union, the two Chinas and Australia exclude them from valuable fishing grounds. United States nuclear tests in the Pacific have also limited fishing possibilities.

About half of the Koreans living in Japan are affiliated with a political organization sympathetic to North Korea while about one-fifth of the Korean residents are in a political group favorable to South Korea. The government of the Republic of [South] Korea claims to be the protector of *all* Koreans both in Korea and abroad. In 1959, arrangements were made between the Japanese and North Korean Red Cross organizations for the repatriation of Koreans wishing to return to North Korea. The ROK government, the only Korean regime formally recognized by Japan, protested the "shipment into slavery" of its nationals, even though the repatriation was voluntary. Seoul cut off trade and diplomatic talks with Tokyo, but did not carry out its threat to intercept the chartered Soviet repatriation ships.[33] By December, 1961, 76,655 Koreans had returned to North Korea, and some 10,000 awaited repatriation.[34]

The overthrow of the unpopular Rhee regime in 1960 was generally welcomed in Japan and provided a model for Japanese student demonstrators who hoped to accomplish a similar revolution in their own country. The 1961 military revolution in Korea was the source of disillusionment to the Japanese as well as the Americans. The South Korean junta, however, seems determined to effect an improvement in Korean-Japanese relations. The United States, which has security

[31] Mendel, p. 191.

[32] *Ibid.*, pp. 178–192. One representative of a large Japanese fishing firm told the present author that the Koreans could understand nothing but force.

[33] *Ibid.*, p. 177.   [34] Washington *Evening Star*, December 9, 1961.

treaties with both Japan and South Korea, has been much embarrassed by the tensions between the two countries which have made difficult a unified resistance against Communism in Northeast Asia.

The Japanese cultural influence in Korea remains strong. Japanese textbooks are in some demand in Korea, where there is a shortage of good books in Korean, and Japanese remains the most widely understood foreign language. Japanese popular music may be heard in the coffee shops, even though anti-Japanese regulations may ban the playing of the Japanese lyrics. Notwithstanding their hatred of Japanese imperialism, the Koreans have a grudging respect for the Japanese for their industry and skill. The Japanese are still regarded as superior to the Chinese, who are thought of as lazy and ignorant.[35]

National Defense

Civil-Military Relations Before the Surrender

In prewar Japan, the Army was the virtual basis of state authority. The political importance of the Imperial Army was dramatically demonstrated in Satsuma in 1877, when samurai rebels under the leadership of Saigō Takamori were subdued by conscript troops loyal to the Imperial Government. In 1882, the Emperor Meiji issued his famous "Rescript to Soldiers and Sailors," in which he proclaimed:

> Our relations with you will be most intimate when We rely upon you as our limbs and you look up to Us as your head. Whether We are able to guard the Empire, and so prove Ourself worthy of Heaven's blessings and repay the benevolence of Our Ancestors, depends upon the faithful discharge of your duties as soldiers and sailors.[36]

The Emperor also pointed out, "The supreme command of Our forces is in Our hands, and though We may entrust subordinate commands to Our subjects, yet the ultimate authority We Ourself shall hold and never delegate to any subject." Articles XI and XII of the 1889 Constitution provided that the Emperor had the supreme command of the Army and Navy and determined the organization and peace standing of the Army and Navy. The imperial command prerogative was interpreted to mean that the military was independent of control by the Diet or the Cabinet. Military policies were formulated by the Board of Field Marshals and Fleet Admirals and the Supreme War Council, rather than by the Prime Minister and his Cabinet.

[35] These observations stem from the author's residence in Korea in 1958.
[36] Text in *The Japan Yearbook, 1936*, pp. 226–229.

The Ministers of War and Navy had to be generals or admirals respectively. When one of the services disagreed with the policies of the Prime Minister, the service Minister could resign or threaten to resign, bringing about a Cabinet crisis. Furthermore, the service Ministers, unlike other members of the Cabinet under the premier, had direct access to the throne. Not only was the military branch largely independent of the civilian branch of the government, it could and often did dominate the civilian branch.

The abolition of armed forces provided for in the new Constitution stands in striking contrast to the militaristic philosophy of the Imperial Rescript to Soldiers and Sailors. The new basic law further ensures civilian supremacy by providing that only civilians may become Ministers of State.

Rearmament

The present Constitution outlaws war and arms, but is now interpreted by the government to mean that defensive armament is permissible. Article 9 reads:

> Aspiring sincerely to an international peace based on justice and order, the Japanese people forever renounce war as a sovereign right of the nation and the threat or use of force as means of settling international disputes.
>
> In order to accomplish the aim of the preceding paragraph, land, sea, and air forces, as well as other war potential, will never be maintained. The right of belligerency of the state will not be recognized.

The first paragraph apparently does not renounce all kinds of war, only war and threat or use of force *as means of settling international disputes*. It has been very plausibly argued that war and the threat or use of force *as means of self-defense* are permissible. Similarly, the abolition of arms, in the second paragraph, may not be absolute. In 1951 Ashida Hitoshi, who had formerly served as chairman of the House of Representatives subcommittee on the revision of the Constitution, pointed out that he had inserted the phrase "in order to accomplish the aim of the preceding paragraph" to qualify the prohibition on armament, so that armaments for certain purposes, such as self-defense, might be permitted.[37] Nevertheless, when the Diet was

[37] Ashida Hitoshi, "Japan: Communists' Temptation," *Contemporary Japan*, Vol. XX, Nos. 1–3 (January–March, 1951), 15–24. For accounts in English of the history and interpretation of the disarmament clause see David Sissons, "The Pacifist Clause of the Japanese Constitution: Legal and Political Problems of Rearmament," *International Affairs*, XXXVII

deliberating on the draft Constitution in 1946, Premier Yoshida asserted that although Article 9 did not renounce the right of self-defense, armaments, even for purposes of self-defense, would be illegal. The full implications of the Ashida amendment were not made evident to the public until after the outbreak of the Korean war.

In 1950, when American troops in Japan were transferred to Korea, General MacArthur suggested to Prime Minister Yoshida the creation of a National Police Reserve. Yoshida created the Reserve by means of a Cabinet order (i.e., without the authorization of the Diet) in the fall of 1950 "for the purpose of supplementing the strength of the National Rural Police and the Local Autonomous Police Forces to the extent necessary to maintain peace and order within the country and to guarantee the public welfare."[38] Many Japanese regarded the establishment of the Police Reserve as a move to further centralize and strengthen the police for the purpose of suppressing left-wing violence. American policy-makers regarded the Reserve as the nucleus for an army.

The San Francisco Peace Treaty recognized Japan's "inherent right of individual or collective self-defense," and the accompanying Security Treaty stated the "expectation" that Japan would itself increasingly assume responsibility for its own defense against direct and indirect aggression.

The National Police Reserve received equipment and training from American forces in Japan. In August, 1952, the Police Reserve was reorganized as the National Safety Force (Hoan-tai) under the supervision of the National Safety Agency (Hoanchō). The signing of the MSA agreements with the United States in March, 1954, was intended to make the Safety Force a more effective military organization. In the following July, the Security Agency and Security Force became the Defense Agency and Self-Defense Force respectively. Each step in the conversion of the Police Reserve into a military force was accompanied by bitter political disputes centering on Article 9 of the Constitution and the alleged dangers of the military alliance with the United States. As one astute observer noted in 1957, "The ban on armed forces has already been turned by sheer casuistry into an open fraud."[39]

(January, 1961), 45–59, Grant Jiro Hirabayashi, "Renunciation of War and the Japanese Constitution" (unpublished Master's thesis, University of Southern California, 1957), and Theodore McNelly, "The Renunciation of War in the Japanese Constitution," *Political Science Quarterly*, LXXVII, No. 3, (September, 1962), pp. 350–378.

[38] Text of Cabinet Order 260, in Quigley and Turner, pp. 435–437.

[39] Reischauer, p. 251.

The Self-Defense Forces

As now organized, the Ground Self-Defense Force is made up of six divisions and four brigades, which, if full strength, would include a total of 171,500 men. The present shortage of 23,000 is accounted for by the economic boom which discourages enlistment. Numerically, the present Ground Self-Defense Force is not greatly inferior to the Japanese Army in 1931, the year of the Manchurian invasion, when the latter numbered 220,000. The force is equipped with 1,900 mortars, 300 recoilless guns, 200 antiaircraft guns, 10,700 machine guns, 180,000 rifles, 900 medium tanks, 300 armored cars, and 450 antiaircraft artillery, self-propelled. Most of this equipment was acquired from U.S. forces. In number of men, the Japanese "army" ranks about twelfth in the world after the Soviet Union, Communist China, the United States, France, Republic of Korea, India, North Korea, Nationalist China, Italy, Great Britain, and West Germany.

The Maritime Self-Defense Force has 250 vessels with a total tonnage of somewhat over 100,000, plus 230 freighters and other vessels totaling 20,000 tons. Many of these were leased or given by the United States to Japan. Plans are afoot to strengthen the antisubmarine power of the Force and to develop a fleet of eleven submarines by 1966. The present Japanese "navy" is believed to be the most powerful in Asia, although it cannot compare with the navies of the United States, Britain, or the Soviet Union.

The Air Self-Defense Force has a total of 1,130 airplanes. The Japanese air force is therefore comparable to those of West Germany, Italy, and Sweden. The present plans for modernization are intended to make the Japanese air force the strongest in Asia after that of Communist China.[40]

A principal problem faced by the Self-Defense Forces is that of morale. The defeat of Japan in 1945 was so overwhelming as utterly to discredit militarism and the military. Furthermore, the Self-Defense Forces are of very doubtful constitutionality and their personnel have been popularly referred to as tax-robbers (zeikin dorobō). There is a widespread feeling that the morale of the troops would be greatly enhanced by reviews by the Emperor. At the same time, it is widely suspected that the officer corps, which includes officers of the former Imperial Army and Navy, is attempting to indoctrinate the troops with fascist and militarist ideas. In this connection, the assassin of Asanuma Inejirō was the seventeen-year-old son of an officer in the Self-Defense Forces.

[40] *Japan Times Weekly*, November 11, 1961, p. 5.

The Defense Agency

The Defense Agency is headed by a civilian Director-General who is a member of the Cabinet and, as such, responsible to the Diet. Thus whereas under the pre-surrender Constitution the "prerogative of high command" was in the Emperor, the supreme control over the new defense forces is vested in the Prime Minister. The Prime Minister has the power to appoint and dismiss the Director-General of the Defense Agency, who is a Minister of State and therefore a civilian. In 1956, the National Defense Council was established, which included the Prime Minister, Deputy Prime Minister, Ministers of Foreign Affairs and Finance, Director-General of the Defense Agency, and the Head of the Economic Planning Board. All of these are members of the Cabinet. The Council's duties are to discuss and decide the following: (1) formulation of a basic plan for national defense, (2) adjustment of defense plans with related industries, (3) activation of national defense, and (4) all other matters that the Prime Minister considers necessary from the standpoint of defense.[41]

SUGGESTED READINGS

Butow, Robert J. C. *Japan's Decision to Surrender*. Stanford: Stanford University Press, 1954.

Chinese People's Institute of Foreign Affairs, ed. *Oppose the Revival of Japanese Militarism: A Selection of Important Documents and Commentaries*. Peking: Foreign Languages Press, 1960.

Feis, Herbert. *Japan Subdued: The Atomic Bomb and the End of the War in the Pacific*. Princeton: Princeton University Press, 1961.

Feis, Herbert. *The Road to Pearl Harbor: The Coming of the War between the United States and Japan*. Princeton: Princeton University Press, 1950.

Hersey, John. *Hiroshima*. New York: Alfred A. Knopf, Inc., 1946.

Jones, F. C., Hugh Borton, and B. R. Pearn. *Survey of International Affairs, 1939–1946: The Far East, 1942–1946*. London: Oxford University Press, 1955.

Maki, John M. *Conflict and Tension in the Far East: Key Documents, 1894–1960*. Seattle: University of Washington Press, 1961.

[41] Ivan Morris, *Nationalism and the Right Wing in Japan: A Study in Postwar Trends* (London: Oxford University Press, 1960), p. 233.

Maxon, Yale. *Control of Japanese Foreign Policy: A Study of Civil-Military Rivalry, 1930–1945.* Berkeley and Los Angeles: University of California Press, 1957.

Mendel, Douglas H. *The Japanese People and Foreign Policy: A Study of Public Opinion in Post-Treaty Japan.* Berkeley and Los Angeles: University of California Press, 1961.

Morley, James William. *Soviet and Communist Chinese Policies Toward Japan, 1950–1957: A Comparison.* New York: Institute of Pacific Relations, 1958.

Reischauer, Edwin O. *The United States and Japan,* rev. ed. Cambridge: Harvard University Press, 1957.

Scalapino, Robert A. "The Foreign Policy of Modern Japan," in Macridis, Roy C., ed. *Foreign Policy in World Politics.* 2nd ed. Englewood Cliffs, N.J.: Prentice-Hall, 1962.

Schwantes, Robert S. *Japanese and Americans: A Century of Cultural Relations.* New York: Harper and Brothers, 1955.

Shigemitsu, Mamoru. *Japan and Her Destiny: My Struggle for Peace.* New York: E. P. Dutton and Co., 1958.

Takeuchi, Tatsuji, *War and Diplomacy in the Japanese Empire.* Garden City: Doubleday, Doran and Company, Inc., 1935.

Thorp, Willard L., ed. *The United States and the Far East,* 2nd ed. Englewood Cliffs: Prentice-Hall, 1962.

Van Adouard, Baron E. J. Lewe. *Japan: From Surrender to Peace.* New York: Frederick A. Praeger, 1954.

✾ 9 ✾

Democracy in Japan:
An Assessment

To the foreign observer, democracy appears to flourish in Japan today. Advocates of totalitarianism, either of the left or of the right, are unable to generate mass support for the establishment of a dictatorship. The parliamentary-cabinet system of government, in which the executive branch is formally responsible to the legislative branch and indirectly to the people — the form of government which prevails in Great Britain and many other democratic countries — is operating effectively in Japan. All classes of society are enjoying unprecedented material prosperity. Freedom of speech and freedom to organize mass demonstrations are permitted to a degree which startles Americans.

During the 1960 crisis, in which the Kishi Cabinet was forced to resign primarily as the result of mass demonstrations, it appeared to many as if the country was being ruled by the mob rather than by a legitimate government. The demonstrations seemed to be under the control of leftist extremists who were manipulating people for the purpose of destroying democratic government. Nevertheless, public opinion overwhelmingly supported parliamentary government even though it deserted Kishi. The demonstrators and the government both emphatically proclaimed their loyalty to parliamentarism; a principal demand of the demonstrators was new parliamentary elections. The mobs dispersed after Kishi resigned and was replaced by another conservative premier; the movement was not fundamentally revolutionary notwithstanding the radicalism of some (but not all) of its leadership. Furthermore, if conservative government in Japan had really been threatened by the mob, the Self-Defense Force, well armed and loyal to the government, could have suppressed the demonstrators in short order. The conservative "Establishment" preferred to avoid bloodshed by letting Kishi, whose ill-advised parliamentary tactics had provoked the demonstrations in the first place, resign. Analysis seems to disclose that the situation was not as completely out of control as it appeared to be at the time.

As powerful as the left appears to be in Japan, it is much weaker than the right.[1] The left is divided into three political parties: Socialist, Democratic-Socialist, and Communist. These parties are internally divided and in violent mutual disagreement with each other on both the means and the ends of socialist transformation. Their relative lack of administrative experience in government and their political irresponsibility mean that their programs lack appeal to most voters, who are more concerned with bread-and-butter issues than socialist ideals.

The right has never seriously tried to mobilize mass demonstrations in support of its cause. But this is partly because the right is supported by responsible people who do not have time to make demonstrations, but do find the time to vote for the conservative candidates. About half of the voters are farmers and villagers. As a result of the land reform, ninety per cent of the farmers are landowners and are suspicious of socialism. Never in history has the left obtained a majority in the Diet. In the event of a very unlikely showdown between leftist rebels and the government, presumably the government could count on the decisive support of the Self-Defense Force.

Of course, it is possible that the left might gradually whittle away the props of the established order by well-organized obstructionism and by the indoctrination of the youth with socialist doctrine. However, these efforts must necessarily yield limited results unless or until a majority is obtained in the houses of the Diet, which is the key to political power in Japan. The Democratic-Socialists and Socialists are both making efforts to expand the basis of their support in other classes of society besides labor, which is a minority in Japan. In order to get multi-class support, the socialist parties must abandon or dilute their Marxism. This is what they have apparently begun to do. Thus, it would seem that if a socialist party were to obtain a parliamentary majority in Japan, it would not be an extremist socialist party but a moderate one. A reunification of the socialist movement as well as a substantial moderation of the doctrine appears to be the prerequisite for a socialist electoral success. Once the left had a parliamentary majority it might be possible, especially in the event of an economic depression, for the extreme left, especially the Communists, to use their influence on the government (as well as on mass movements)

---

[1] In Japan, the term "right wing" (uyoku) usually refers to extreme rightists and rightist terrorists. In the present chapter, however, the author uses the terms right and left to refer to conservatives of all shades and progressives of all shades, respectively.

to push the country leftward by isolating conservative and moderate groups and eliminating them one after another, as proved possible in Czechoslovakia. It seems very doubtful, however, that the Socialists would permit the Communists to seize the initiative from them.

The right in Japan, of course, is keenly aware of these varied possibilities. Curbs on the political activities of the radical Teachers Union and reforms in the public school curriculum are designed to check the spread of Marxism and enhance patriotism among youth. Municipal ordinances in principal cities limit the scope of political demonstrations. Government employees do not have the legal right to strike. If in time of depression the left greatly increased its influence, the conservatives might be expected to use their majority in parliament to enact legislation which would further narrow the political influence of the left. Such "emergency" legislation might include bans on political demonstrations and strikes, the dissolution of subversive political parties and labor unions, and some form of censorship. The conservative Diet might also reform the electoral system to provide for a single-member-district system, which would make it more difficult for the Socialists and Communists to elect men to the Diet. No doubt the opposition would, as they have in the past, mount political strikes and demonstrations against the proposed repressive legislation. The best conservative weapon would be constructive legislation that would deprive the Socialists of their campaign slogans. The Liberal-Democrats' promise of higher living standards and expanded welfare legislation together with Mr. Ikeda's program to double the national income by 1970 have already proven their political effectiveness.

As the Japanese have more experience with democracy and as the rules of parliamentary politics become established, it seems reasonable to expect more widespread popular support for freedom and democratic government. Also, as more of the population becomes urbanized and politically conscious, the political preferences of the population may drift to the left. On the other hand, the left, in order to acquire power, would have to broaden its appeal by moderating its platform. Since the conservative party is already committed to the welfare state and may be expected to enact more welfare legislation, the differences between the socialist and conservative camps in Japan may ultimately prove to be more apparent than real. Japan may then have a two-party system not greatly different from that of Great Britain and the United States, in which both parties are committed to the democratic form of government and to welfare policies.

The human rights provisions of the new Constitution have made a great impression in Japan. Students and intellectuals especially praise the rights guaranteed by the third chapter of the basic law. Notwithstanding its irregular origin and disputes over its interpretation, the new Constitution is almost universally recognized as legitimate. There appears to be a widening dedication to and understanding of democratic values. Since 1945, labor, the universities, the press, and the political parties have enjoyed and come to cherish their new rights and freedoms. It seems doubtful that they would give them up as readily as they did in the 1930's. At the same time, the expansion of the Japanese economy makes for greater social stability and strengthens the commitment of all major groups to the present liberal democratic system.

THE CONSTITUTION OF JAPAN

We, the Japanese people, acting through our duly elected representatives in the National Diet, determined that we shall secure for ourselves and our posterity the fruits of peaceful cooperation with all nations and the blessings of liberty throughout this land, and resolved that never again shall we be visited with the horrors of war through the action of government, do proclaim that sovereign power resides with the people and do firmly establish this Constitution. Government is a sacred trust of the people, the authority for which is derived from the people, the powers of which are exercised by the representatives of the people, and the benefits of which are enjoyed by the people. This is a universal principle of mankind upon which this Constitution is founded. We reject and revoke all constitutions, laws, ordinances, and rescripts in conflict herewith.

We, the Japanese people, desire peace for all time and are deeply conscious of the high ideals controlling human relationship, and we have determined to preserve our security and existence, trusting in the justice and faith of the peace-loving peoples of the world. We desire to occupy an honored place in an international society striving for the preservation of peace, and the banishment of tyranny and slavery, oppression and intolerance for all time from the earth. We recognize that all peoples of the world have the right to live in peace, free from fear and want.

We believe that no nation is responsible to itself alone, but that laws of political morality are universal; and that obedience to such laws is incumbent upon all nations who would sustain their own sovereignty and justify their sovereign relationship with other nations.

We, the Japanese people, pledge our national honor to accomplish these high ideals and purposes with all our resources.

CHAPTER I. THE EMPEROR

Article 1. The Emperor shall be the symbol of the State and of the unity of the people, deriving his position from the will of the people with whom resides sovereign power.

Article 2. The Imperial Throne shall be dynastic and succeeded to in accordance with the Imperial House Law passed by the Diet.

Article 3. The advice and approval of the Cabinet shall be required for all acts of the Emperor in matters of state, and the Cabinet shall be responsible therefor.

Article 4. The Emperor shall perform only such acts in matters of state as are provided for in this Constitution and he shall not have powers related to government.

The Emperor may delegate the performance of his acts in matters of state as may be provided by law.

Article 5. When, in accordance with the Imperial House Law, a Regency is established, the Regent shall perform his acts in matters of state in the Emperor's name. In this case, paragraph one of the preceding article will be applicable.

Article 6. The Emperor shall appoint the Prime Minister as designated by the Diet.

The Emperor shall appoint the Chief Judge of the Supreme Court as designated by the Cabinet.

Article 7. The Emperor, with the advice and approval of the Cabinet, shall perform the following acts in matters of state on behalf of the people:

Promulgation of amendments of the constitution, laws, cabinet orders and treaties.

Convocation of the Diet.

Dissolution of the House of Representatives.

Proclamation of general election of members of the Diet.

Attestation of the appointment and dismissal of Ministers of State and other officials as provided for by law, and of full powers and credentials of Ambassadors and Ministers.

Attestation of general and special amnesty, commutation of punishment, reprieve, and restoration of rights.

Awarding of honors.

Attestation of instruments of ratification and other diplomatic documents as provided for by law.

Receiving foreign ambassadors and ministers.

Performance of ceremonial functions.

Article 8. No property can be given to, or received by, the Imperial House, nor can any gifts be made therefrom, without the authorization of the Diet.

CHAPTER II. RENUNCIATION OF WAR

Article 9. Aspiring sincerely to an international peace based on justice and order, the Japanese people forever renounce war as a sovereign right of the nation and the threat or use of force as means of settling international disputes.

In order to accomplish the aim of the preceding paragraph, land, sea, and air forces, as well as other war potential, will never be maintained. The right of belligerency of the state will not be recognized.

CHAPTER III. RIGHTS AND DUTIES OF THE PEOPLE

Article 10. The conditions necessary for being a Japanese national shall be determined by law.

Article 11. The people shall not be prevented from enjoying any of the fundamental human rights. These fundamental human rights guaranteed to the people by this Constitution shall be conferred upon the people of this and future generations as eternal and inviolate rights.

Article 12. The freedoms and rights guaranteed to the people by this Constitution shall be maintained by the constant endeavor of the people, who shall refrain from any abuse of these freedoms and rights and shall always be responsible for utilizing them for the public welfare.

Article 13. All of the people shall be respected as individuals. Their right to life, liberty, and the pursuit of happiness shall, to the extent that it does not interfere with the public welfare, be the supreme consideration in legislation and in other governmental affairs.

Article 14. All of the people are equal under the law and there shall be no discrimination in political, economic or social relations because of race, creed, sex, social status or family origin.

Peers and peerage shall not be recognized.

No privilege shall accompany any award of honor, decoration or any distinction, nor shall any such award be valid beyond the lifetime of the individual who now holds or hereafter may receive it.

Article 15. The people have the inalienable right to choose their public officials and to dismiss them.

All public officials are servants of the whole community and not of any group thereof.

Universal adult suffrage is guaranteed with regard to the election of public officials.

In all elections, secrecy of the ballot shall not be violated. A voter shall not be answerable, publicly or privately, for the choice he has made.

Article 16. Every person shall have the right of peaceful petition for the redress of damage, for the removal of public officials, for the enactment, repeal or amendment of laws, ordinances or regulations and for other matters; nor shall any person be in any way discriminated against for sponsoring such a petition.

Article 17. Every person may sue for redress as provided by law from the State or a public entity, in case he has suffered damage through illegal act of any public official.

Article 18. No person shall be held in bondage of any kind. Involuntary servitude, except as punishment for crime, is prohibited.

Article 19. Freedom of thought and conscience shall not be violated.

Article 20. Freedom of religion is guaranteed to all. No religious organization shall receive any privileges from the State, nor exercise any political authority.

No person shall be compelled to take part in any religious act, celebration, rite or practice.

The State and its organs shall refrain from religious education or any other religious activity.

Article 21. Freedom of assembly and association as well as speech, press and all other forms of expression are guaranteed.

No censorship shall be maintained, nor shall the secrecy of any means of communication be violated.

Article 22. Every person shall have freedom to choose and change his residence and to choose his occupation to the extent that it does not interfere with the public welfare.

Freedom of all persons to move to a foreign country and to divest themselves of their nationality shall be inviolate.

Article 23. Academic freedom is guaranteed.

Article 24. Marriage shall be based only on the mutual consent of both sexes and it shall be maintained through mutual cooperation with the equal rights of husband and wife as a basis.

With regard to choice of spouse, property rights, inheritance, choice of domicile, divorce and other matters pertaining to marriage and the family, laws shall be enacted from the standpoint of individual dignity and the essential equality of the sexes.

Article 25. All people shall have the right to maintain the minimum standards of wholesome and cultured living.

In all spheres of life, the State shall use its endeavors for the promotion and extension of social welfare and security, and of public health.

Article 26. All people shall have the right to receive an equal education correspondent to their ability, as provided by law.

All people shall be obligated to have all boys and girls under their protection receive ordinary education as provided for by law. Such compulsory education shall be free.

Article 27. All people shall have the right and the obligation to work.

Standards for wages, hours, rest and other working conditions shall be fixed by law.

Children shall not be exploited.

Article 28. The right of workers to organize and bargain and act collectively is guaranteed.

Article 29. The right to own or to hold property is inviolable.

Property rights shall be defined by law, in conformity with the public welfare.

Private property may be taken for public use upon just compensation therefor.

Article 30. The people shall be liable to taxation as provided by law.

Article 31. No person shall be deprived of life or liberty, nor shall any other criminal penalty be imposed, except according to procedure established by law.

Article 32. No person shall be denied the right of access to the courts.

Article 33. No person shall be apprehended except upon warrant issued by a competent judicial officer which specifies the offense with which the person is charged, unless he is apprehended, the offense being committed.

Article 34. No person shall be arrested or detained without being at once informed of the charges against him or without the immediate privilege of counsel; nor shall he be detained without adequate cause; and upon demand of any person such cause must be immediately shown in open court in his presence and the presence of his counsel.

Article 35. The right of all persons to be secure in their homes, papers and effects against entries, searches and seizures shall not be impaired except upon warrant issued for adequate cause and particularly describing the place to be searched and things to be seized, or except as provided by Article 33.

Each search or seizure shall be made upon separate warrant issued by a competent judicial officer.

Article 36. The infliction of torture by any public officer and cruel punishments are absolutely forbidden.

Article 37. In all criminal cases the accused shall enjoy the right to a speedy and public trial by an impartial tribunal.

He shall be permitted full opportunity to examine all witnesses, and he shall have the right of compulsory process for obtaining witnesses on his behalf at public expense.

At all times the accused shall have the assistance of competent counsel who shall, if the accused is unable to secure the same by his own efforts, be assigned to his use by the State.

Article 38. No person shall be compelled to testify against himself.

Confession made under compulsion, torture or threat, or after prolonged arrest or detention shall not be admitted in evidence.

No person shall be convicted or punished in cases where the only proof against him is his own confession.

Article 39. No person shall be held criminally liable for an act which was lawful at the time it was committed, or of which he has been acquitted, nor shall he be placed in double jeopardy.

Article 40. Any person, in case he is acquitted after he has been arrested or detained, may sue the State for redress as provided by law.

CHAPTER IV. THE DIET

Article 41. The Diet shall be the highest organ of state power, and shall be the sole law-making organ of the State.

Article 42. The Diet shall consist of two Houses, namely the House of Representatives and the House of Councillors.

Article 43. Both Houses shall consist of elected members, representative of all the people.

The number of the members of each House shall be fixed by law.

Article 44. The qualifications of members of both Houses and their electors shall be fixed by law. However, there shall be no discrimination because of race, creed, sex, social status, family origin, education, property or income.

Article 45. The term of office of members of the House of Representatives shall be four years. However, the term shall be terminated before the full term is up in case the House of Representatives is dissolved.

Article 46. The term of office of members of the House of Councillors shall be six years, and election for half the members shall take place every three years.

Article 47. Electoral districts, method of voting and other matters pertaining to the method of election of members of both Houses shall be fixed by law.

Article 48. No person shall be permitted to be a member of both Houses simultaneously.

Article 49. Members of both Houses shall receive appropriate annual payment from the national treasury in accordance with law.

Article 50. Except in cases provided by law, members of both Houses shall be exempt from apprehension while the Diet is in session, and any members apprehended before the opening of the session shall be freed during the term of the session upon demand of the House.

Article 51. Members of both Houses shall not be held liable outside the House for speeches, debates or votes cast inside the House.

Article 52. An ordinary session of the Diet shall be convoked once per year.

Article 53. The Cabinet may determine to convoke extraordinary sessions of the Diet. When a quarter or more of the total members of either House makes the demand, the Cabinet must determine on such convocation.

Article 54. When the House of Representatives is dissolved, there must be a general election of members of the House of Representatives within forty (40) days from the date of dissolution, and the Diet must be convoked within thirty (30) days from the date of the election.

When the House of Representatives is dissolved, the House of Councillors is closed at the same time. However, the Cabinet may in time of national emergency convoke the House of Councillors in emergency session.

Measures taken at such session as mentioned in the proviso of the preceding paragraph shall be provisional and shall become null and void unless agreed to by the House of Representatives within a period of ten (10) days after the opening of the next session of the Diet.

Article 55. Each House shall judge disputes related to qualifications of its members. However, in order to deny a seat to any member, it is necessary to pass a resolution by a majority of two-thirds or more of the members present.

Article 56. Business cannot be transacted in either House unless one-third or more of total membership is present.

All matters shall be decided, in each House, by a majority of those present, except as elsewhere provided in the Constitution, and in case of a tie, the presiding officer shall decide the issue.

Article 57. Deliberation in each House shall be public. However, a secret meeting may be held where a majority of two-thirds or more of those members present passes a resolution therefor.

Each House shall keep a record of proceedings. This record shall be published and given general circulation, excepting such parts of proceedings of secret session as may be deemed to require secrecy.

Upon demand of one-fifth or more of the members present, votes of the members on any matter shall be recorded in the minutes.

Article 58. Each House shall select its own president and other officials.

Each House shall establish its rules pertaining to meetings, proceedings and internal discipline, and may punish members for disorderly conduct. However, in order to expel a member, a majority of two-thirds or more of those members present must pass a resolution thereon.

Article 59. A bill becomes a law on passage by both Houses, except as otherwise provided by the Constitution.

A bill which is passed by the House of Representatives, and upon which the House of Councillors makes a decision different from that of the House of Representatives, becomes a law when passed a second time by the House of Representatives by a majority of two-thirds or more of the members present.

The provision of the preceding paragraph does not preclude the House of Representatives from calling for the meeting of a joint committee of both Houses, provided for by law.

Failure by the House of Councillors to take final action within sixty (60) days after receipt of a bill passed by the House of Representatives, time in recess excepted, may by determined by the House of Representatives to constitute a rejection of the said bill by the House of Councillors.

Article 60. The budget must first be submitted to the House of Representatives.

Upon consideration of the budget, when the House of Councillors makes a decision different from that of the House of Representatives, and when no agreement can be reached even through a joint committee of both Houses, provided for by law, or in the case of failure by the House of Councillors to take final action within thirty (30) days, the period of recess excluded, after the receipt of the budget passed by the House of Representatives, the decision of the House of Representatives shall be the decision of the Diet.

Article 61. The second paragraph of the preceding article applies also to the Diet approval required for the conclusion of treaties.

Article 62. Each House may conduct investigations in relation to government, and may demand the presence and testimony of witnesses, and the production of records.

Article 63. The Prime Minister and other Ministers of State may, at any time, appear in either House for the purpose of speaking on bills, regardless of whether they are members of the House or not. They must appear when their presence is required in order to give answers or explanations.

Article 64. The Diet shall set up an impeachment court from among the members of both Houses for the purpose of trying those judges against whom removal proceedings have been instituted.

Matters relating to impeachment shall be provided by law.

CHAPTER V. THE CABINET

Article 65. Executive power shall be vested in the Cabinet.

Article 66. The Cabinet shall consist of the Prime Minister, who shall be its head, and other Ministers of State, as provided for by law.

The Prime Minister and other Ministers of State must be civilians.

The Cabinet, in the exercise of executive power, shall be collectively responsible to the Diet.

Article 67. The Prime Minister shall be designated from among the members of the Diet by a resolution of the Diet. This designation shall precede all other business.

If the House of Representatives and the House of Councillors disagree and if no agreement can be reached even through a joint committee of both Houses, provided for by law, or the House of Councillors fails to make designation within ten (10) days, exclusive of the period of recess, after the House of Representatives has made designation, the decision of the House of Representatives shall be the decision of the Diet.

Article 68. The Prime Minister shall appoint the Ministers of State. However, a majority of their number must be chosen from among the members of the Diet.

The Prime Minister may remove the Ministers of State as he chooses.

Article 69. If the House of Representatives passes a non-confidence resolution, or rejects a confidence resolution, the Cabinet shall resign en masse, unless the House of Representatives is dissolved within ten (10) days.

Article 70. When there is a vacancy in the post of Prime Minister, or upon the first convocation of the Diet after a general election of members of the House of Representatives, the Cabinet shall resign en masse.

Article 71. In the cases mentioned in the two preceding Articles, the Cabinet shall continue its functions until the time when a new Prime Minister is appointed.

Article 72. The Prime Minister, representing the Cabinet, submits bills, reports on general national affairs and foreign relations to the Diet and exercises control and supervision over various administrative branches.

Article 73. The Cabinet, in addition to other general administrative functions, shall perform the following functions:

Administer the law faithfully; conduct affairs of state.

Manage foreign affairs.

Conclude treaties. However, it shall obtain prior or, depending on circumstances, subsequent approval of the Diet.

Administer the civil service, in accordance with standards established by law.

Prepare the budget, and present it to the Diet.

Enact cabinet orders in order to execute the provisions of this Constitution and of the law. However, it cannot include penal provisions in such cabinet orders unless authorized by such law.

Decide on general amnesty, special amnesty, commutation of punishment, reprieve, and restoration of rights.

Article 74. All laws and cabinet orders shall be signed by the competent Minister of State and countersigned by the Prime Minister.

Article 75. The Ministers of State, during their tenure of office, shall not be subject to legal action without the consent of the Prime Minister. However, the right to take that action is not impaired hereby.

Chapter VI. Judiciary

Article 76. The whole judicial power is vested in a Supreme Court and in such inferior courts as are established by law.

No extraordinary tribunal shall be established, nor shall any organ or agency of the Executive be given final judicial power.

All judges shall be independent in the exercise of their conscience and shall be bound only by this Constitution and the laws.

Article 77. The Supreme Court is vested with the rule-making power under which it determines the rules of procedure and of practice, and of matters relating to attorneys, the internal discipline of the courts and the administration of judicial affairs.

Public procurators shall be subject to the rule-making power of the Supreme Court.

The Supreme Court may delegate the power to make rules for inferior courts to such courts.

Article 78. Judges shall not be removed except by public impeachment unless judicially declared mentally or physically incompetent to perform official duties. No disciplinary action against judges shall be administered by any executive organ or agency.

Article 79. The Supreme Court shall consist of a Chief Judge and such number of judges as may be determined by law; all such judges excepting the Chief Judge shall be appointed by the Cabinet.

The appointment of the judges of the Supreme Court shall be reviewed by the people at the first general election of members of the House of Representatives following their appointment, and shall be reviewed again at the first general election of members of the House of Representatives after a lapse of ten (10) years, and in the same manner thereafter.

In cases mentioned in the foregoing paragraph, when the majority of the voters favors the dismissal of a judge, he shall be dismissed.

Matters pertaining to review shall be prescribed by law.

The judges of the Supreme Court shall be retired upon the attainment of the age as fixed by law.

All such judges shall receive, at regular stated intervals, adequate compensation which shall not be decreased during their terms of office.

Article 80. The judges of the inferior courts shall be appointed by the Cabinet from a list of persons nominated by the Supreme Court. All such judges shall hold office for a term of ten (10) years with privilege of reappointment, provided that they shall be retired upon the attainment of the age as fixed by law.

The judges of the inferior courts shall receive, at regular stated intervals, adequate compensation which shall not be decreased during their terms of office.

Article 81. The Supreme Court is the court of last resort with power to determine the constitutionality of any law, order, regulation or official act.

Article 82. Trials shall be conducted and judgment declared publicly.

Where a court unanimously determines publicity to be dangerous to public order or morals, a trial may be conducted privately, but trials of political offenses, offenses involving the press or cases wherein the rights of people as guaranteed in Chapter III of this Constitution are in question shall always be conducted publicly.

CHAPTER VII. FINANCE

Article 83. The power to administer national finances shall be exercised as the Diet shall determine.

Article 84. No new taxes shall be imposed or existing ones modified except by law or under such conditions as law may prescribe.

Article 85. No money shall be expended, nor shall the State obligate itself, except as authorized by the Diet.

Article 86. The Cabinet shall prepare and submit to the Diet for its consideration and decision a budget for each fiscal year.

Article 87. In order to provide for unforeseen deficiencies in the budget, a reserve fund may be authorized by the Diet to be expended upon the responsibility of the Cabinet.

The Cabinet must get subsequent approval of the Diet for all payments from the reserve fund.

Article 88. All property of the Imperial Household shall belong to the State. All expenses of the Imperial Household shall be appropriated by the Diet in the budget.

Article 89. No public money or other property shall be expended or appropriated for the use, benefit or maintenance of any religious institution or association, or for any charitable, educational or benevolent enterprises not under the control of public authority.

Article 90. Final accounts of the expenditures and revenues of the State shall be audited annually by a Board of Audit and submitted by the Cabinet to the Diet, together with the statement of audit, during the fiscal year immediately following the period covered.

The organization and competency of the Board of Audit shall be determined by law.

Article 91. At regular intervals and at least annually the Cabinet shall report to the Diet and the people on the state of national finances.

CHAPTER VIII. LOCAL SELF-GOVERNMENT

Article 92. Regulations concerning organization and operations of local public entities shall be fixed by law in accordance with the principle of local autonomy.

Article 93. The local public entities shall establish assemblies as their deliberative organs, in accordance with law.

The chief executive officers of all local public entities, the members of their assemblies, and such other local officials as may be determined by law shall be elected by direct popular vote within their several communities.

Article 94. Local public entities shall have the right to manage their property, affairs and administration and to enact their own regulations within law.

Article 95. A special law, applicable only to one local public entity, cannot be enacted by the Diet without the consent of the majority of the voters of the local public entity concerned, obtained in accordance with law.

CHAPTER IX. AMENDMENTS

Article 96. Amendments to this Constitution shall be initiated by the Diet, through a concurring vote of two-thirds or more of all the members of each House and shall thereupon be submitted to the people for ratification, which shall require the affirmative vote of a majority of all votes cast thereon, at a special referendum or at such election as the Diet shall specify.

Amendments when so ratified shall immediately be promulgated by the Emperor in the name of the people, as an integral part of this Constitution.

CHAPTER X. SUPREME LAW

Article 97. The fundamental human rights by this Constitution guaranteed to the people of Japan are fruits of the age-old struggle of man to be free; they have survived the many exacting tests for durability and are conferred upon this and future generations in trust, to be held for all time inviolate.

Article 98. This Constitution shall be the supreme law of the nation and no law, ordinance, imperial rescript or other act of government, or part thereof, contrary to the provisions hereof, shall have legal force or validity.

The treaties concluded by Japan and established laws of nations shall be faithfully observed.

Article 99. The Emperor or the Regent as well as Ministers of State, members of the Diet, judges, and all other public officials have the obligation to respect and uphold this Constitution.

CHAPTER XI. SUPPLEMENTARY PROVISIONS

Article 100. This Constitution shall be enforced as from the day when the period of six months will have elapsed counting from the day of its promulgation.

The enactment of laws necessary for the enforcement of this Constitution, the election of members of the House of Councillors and the procedure for the convocation of the Diet and other preparatory procedures necessary for the enforcement of this Constitution may be executed before the day prescribed in the preceding paragraph.

Article 101. If the House of Councillors is not constituted before the effective date of this Constitution, the House of Representatives shall function as the Diet until such time as the House of Councillors shall be constituted.

Article 102. The term of office for half the members of the House of Councillors serving in the first term under this Constitution shall be three years. Members falling under this category shall be determined in accordance with law.

Article 103. The Ministers of State, members of the House of Representatives and judges in office on the effective date of this Constitution, and all other public officials who occupy positions corresponding to such positions as are recognized by this Constitution shall not forfeit their positions automatically on account of the enforcement of this Constitution unless otherwise specified by law. When, however, successors are elected or appointed under the provisions of this Constitution, they shall forfeit their positions as a matter of course.

INDEX

Abdication, 8–9, 55, 61
Abe Isoo, 81, 123
Administrative law, 168
Administrative Management Agency, 75
Agriculture, 125, 147–148
Ainu, 2, 4
Air Self-Defense Force, 204
Akao Bin, 141
Akihito, Crown Prince, 64
Aleutian Islands, 196
All-Japan Federation of Labor (Sō-dōmei), 130, 143
Allied Council for Japan, 29
Amami Ōshima, 93
Amaterasu, see Sun Goddess
Anami Korechika, 53
Ancestor worship, 162
Antarctica, 178
Anti-Violence Bill, 109–111, 131, 145
Araki Masuo, 85
Araki Sadao, General, 34, 162
Army, 21–22, 204
Asanuma Inejirō, 89, 99, 125, 195, 204; stabbing of, 140
Ashida Cabinet, 81, 83, 89, 124, 130, 133
Ashida Hitoshi, 36, 79, 81, 94, 117, 118, 131, 202–203
Assassination, 89, 111, 142, 167; of Asanuma, 140
Atcheson, George C., Jr., 36–39, 41
Atomic Energy Commission, 75, 84, 180
Audit, Board of, 63, 76
Australia, 28, 42, 45, 177
Autonomy Agency, 162
Ayabe Kentarō, 85

Ball, W. Macmahon, 46
Bandung, ten principles of, 195
Barons, military, 9, 12–13
Bicameral system, 110
"Bill of Rights," Japanese, 29–31, 80
Bonin (Ogasawara) Islands, 120, 178, 188, 195
Boycotts, 104–105, 166, 182
Brines, Russell, 46, 55n.18

British Commonwealth, 27, 29, 59
Buddhism, 2, 5–8, 11, 65, 193
Budget, 107
Bureaucracy, 90–95, 155
Burma, 28, 177
Business, 146–147
Byrnes, James, 37, 44, 51, 54

Cabinet (Naikaku), 16–18, 73–90, 113; prewar, 82; coalition, 82, 100; orders (seirei), 74; one-party, 83; stop-gap, 83; transcendental, 82; party, 82; "reconstructed," 85; resignation of, 88–89; list of, 95–96
Cairo Declaration, 175, 187, 191
Canada, 28, 190
Caroline Islands, 178
Carr, Sir Arthur Comyns, 55
Central Liaison Office (CLO), 28
Centralization, 155
Chancellor (Dajō-Daijin), 5
Chang Hsi-jo, 195
Chang Tso-lin, 20
Checks and balances, 68–70
Chiang Kai-shek, 20, 22, 25, 174, 177, 187, 191
China, 1, 3, 8, 12, 17–22, 28–29, 90, 117, 139, 171, 174, 177, 179; Communist, 176, 178, 186, 192–196, 204; Nationalist, 191–192, 204
Chōshū clan, 14, 15, 18
Christianity, 12, 65, 185
Churchill, 25, 54, 196
Civil Dictator (Kampaku), 8, 11
Civil Service, 90–95, 125
Clan oligarchs (hambatsu), 14, 18
Clans (uji), 2, 6, 8
Cloister Government (Insei), 9
Cominform criticism, 133–135
Commission on the Constitution (Kempō Chōsakai), 38, 76
Communism, 46, 52–53, 65, 68, 176
Communist China, 174, 176, 178, 186, 192–196, 204
Communist Party, 32–36, 40, 46, 48, 99, 110, 132–139, 208; or-

221

ganization of, 137; and Zen-gakuren, 165; and 1960 Security Pact, 185–187
Confucianism, 2–6, 10, 13, 18, 65–66, 90, 93, 167, 193; in education, 162
Congress of Industrial Unions (Sambetsu), 143
Constituent power, 57–58
Constitution Day, 66
Constitution of the Empire of Japan (1889), 15–17, 20, 56–60, 73, 78
Constitution of Japan (1947), 36–47, 168; Article 9, 168, 182, 202–203; legal and judicial system, 167–169; local government, 158–159
Constitution, "Seventeen-Article," 2–3
Constitutionality, 168
Court of Cassation, 62
Courts, 159, 167–169
Crown Prince, 64
Czechoslovakia, 178, 209

Daimyo, 9, 12–14
Daitō Islands, 178
Dajō-Daijin (Chancellor), 5
Dajō-kan (Great Council of State), 5
Defense, 201–205
Defense Agency, 75–76, 203, 205
Democracy in Japan, 207–210
Democratic-Liberal Party, 81, 83, 87, 117–118
Democratic Party (Minshutō), 117
Democratic (Progressive) Party, 80, 81, 83, 117–120, 123, 133
Democratic-Socialist Party, 99, 100, 104, 125, 129–132, 145, 208; and 1960 Security Pact, 182–184
Demonstrations, 89, 110, 144, 167
Depurge, 114
Diet: prewar, 16–19; and Cabinet, 74–75, 78–79, 81–90; contemporary, 97–113; Library, 105; powers of, 111–113; and local government, 158–162; see also House of Councillors, House of Representatives
Dissolution: of the House of Representatives, 86–90; of local assemblies, 161

Divine Clans, 2
Divine right, 56, 59, 60
Dodge Plan, 121
Dōkyō, 7
Dual government (diarchy), 10, 20
Dulles, John Foster, 177
Dutch East Indies, 175

Economic Planning Agency, 75–76
Economic and Scientific Section (ESS), 144
Eda Saburō, 125
Education, 162–165; boards of, 161, 163; Shinto in, 162
Eisenhower, Dwight D., 67, 120; visit of, 144, 184–187; and Okinawa, 188
Elder statesmen (genro), 18, 19, 78, 82
Elders (Rōjū), 12
Elections: for House of Representatives, 150; for House of Councillors, 151, 152
Electoral system, 97–103
Emergency, 108
Emergency proclamation, 166
Emperor, Japanese, 2–21; list, 70–71
Emperor system (Tennōsei), 48–72
England, see Great Britain
Ethics (shūshin), 163
Executive branch, 73–90
Extraparliamentary methods, 127, 146
Extraterritoriality, 17, 167

Factions, 83, 104, 119, 122–123, 147, 149; in Socialist Party, 125
Family system, 162
Far Eastern Advisory Commission, 26, 39
Far Eastern Commission, 28–29, 39, 42, 45–46, 191
Farmers, 125, 147
Federal system, 70; 155
Feudalism, 10–14
Filibusters, 105, 109, 182
Finance, local, 162
"Five-Article Charter Oath," 14
Foreign relations, 171–205; see also separate country headings
Former Prime Ministers (jūshin), 18, 52
Formosa, see Taiwan
Foundation Day (Kigensetsu), 15, 66–67

Fujii Shinichi, 5n, 7n, 23, 72
Fujiwara, 8–12, 21, 61
Fujiyama Aiichirō, 122
Fujiyama faction, 85, 122, 147
Fukuda Hajime, 85
Fusion of powers, 68–70

G–2 (Military Intelligence) Section, 81
General Order No. 1, 26, 175, 191, 196
General strike, planned for February 1, 1947, 132, 143
Genro (elder statesmen), 18, 19, 78, 82
Germany, 19, 27, 28, 32, 204; German concessions, 174
Gerrymander, 100, 103
Girard incident, 120, 169, 181
Go-Daigo, Emperor, 11
Gokijō Kakiwa, 170
Go-Sanjō, Emperor, 9
Government Section (GS), 81; and new Constitution, 40–47
Governors, 4, 6, 14, 155, 159–160
Gozen Kaigi (Imperial Conference), 53, 55
Great Britain, 28, 58–59, 105, 106, 113, 177, 204, 209
Great Council of State (Dajō-kan), 5
Great Japan Political Society (Dai Nippon Seiji Kai), 117
"Great Reform" (Taika), 4
Greater East Co-Prosperity Sphere, 174
Grew, Joseph C., 50–51
Ground Self-Defense Force, 204

Habomai Islands, 197
Hagerty, James, 185, 186
Hamaguchi Cabinet, 89, 117
Hamaguchi Osachi, 20, 81, 89
Hambatsu (clan oligarchs), 14, 18
Hara Cabinet, 89
Hara Takashi, 19, 78, 81, 89
Harriman, A., 26
Harris, Townsend, 13
Harris treaty, 13, 17
Hata, 34
Hatoyama Cabinet, 88–90, 107
Hatoyama Ichirō, 32–33, 66, 80–81, 88, 100, 111, 114–120, 197
Hatoyama Liberal Party, 117
Hayashi Senjūrō, General, 21, 81
Herter, 186

Hideyoshi (Toyotomi), 11, 12
Higai Senzō, 104
Higashikuni, Prince, 29, 30, 81, 184
Higashikuni Cabinet, 36, 80
Hirabayashi, Grant Jiro, 203n
Hirano Rikizō, 33, 124
Hiranuma Kiichirō, 34, 53, 81
Hirohito, Emperor, 55, 64
Hirota Kōki, 21, 34, 81
Hizen clan, 14, 15, 18
Hōjō clan, 11
Hokkaido, 26, 75, 158, 171
Home Ministry, 30, 158, 165
House of Councillors, 61, 74, 79, 101–113, 107, 108; election results, 151–152
House of Lords, 112
House of Peers (Kizoku-in), 16, 37, 64, 101, 112
House of Representatives (Shūgiin), 16, 20, 22, 61, 79, 81, 86, 90, 97–101, 107; dissolution of, 86–90; election results, 150
Hozumi Nobushige, 72
Hozumi Yatsuka, 49
Hull, Cordell, 51, 174

Ichimada Hisato group, 122
Ieyasu (Tokugawa), 12
Ikeda Hayato, 75, 80–81, 85–86, 94–95, 104, 121–122, 140–141, 209; faction, 85–86, 122; Cabinet, 84, 88, 90, 111, 141
Impeachment, 169
Imperial Clan, 2
Imperial Conference (Gozen Kaigi), 53, 55
Imperial Diet (Teikoku Gikai), 16
Imperial Family, 60, 64–65, 101
Imperial House, 59–63
Imperial House Law (Kōshitsu Tempan), 15–16, 43, 59–63
Imperial Party (Teiseitō), 15
Imperial Regalia, 7
Imperial Rescript on Education of 1890, 162–163
Imperial Rule Assistance Association (IRAA, Taisei Yokusan Kai), 22, 114, 128, 130
Imperial Rule Assistance Political Society (IRAPS, Taisei Yokusan Seijikai), 22, 117, 128, 130
"Imperial Way" (Kōdō), 50
India, 17, 28, 65, 177, 190, 204
Indo-China, 174, 175, 191

Initiative, 161
Inner Mongolia, 19, 174
Insei (Cloister Government), 9
Instrument of Surrender, 58, 118
Intellectuals, 125
International Military Tribunal for the Far East (IMTFE), 33
Inukai Cabinet, 89
Inukai Ken, 118
Inukai Tsuyoshi, 20, 21, 81, 89, 141
Ishibashi Tanzan, 32, 81, 89, 120, 122, 184
Ishida Hirohide faction, 122
Ishii Mitsujirō, 104, 121, 122; faction, 85, 122
Itagaki Taisuke, 15, 17
Itō Cabinet, 90
Itō Hirobumi, 15–18, 24, 56n, 57, 59n, 64, 72, 75, 89–90
Itō N., 46
Iwasaki, 146

James I, 67
Japan Teachers Union (Nikkyōso), 141, 144, 163, 209
"Japanese Bill of Rights," 29–31, 80
Japanese Empire, 171–175
Japanese language, 201
Japanese Peace Treaty, 116, 121, 176–179, 188, 191, 202; and Soviet-Japanese relations, 196–198
Jehol, 174
Jih-pen, 3
Jimmu Tennō (Emperor), 7, 66
Jingi-kan (Department of Religion), 5
Jingō, Empress Regent, 198
Jiyū-Minshutō, see Liberal-Democratic Party
Jiyūtō, see Liberal Party
Jōei, Formulary of, 11
Judicial system, 167–169
Junior Elders (Wakadoshiyori), 12
Jūshin (senior statesmen, former Prime Ministers), 18, 52

Kagawa Toyohiko, 123
Kaishintō (Progressive Party), 15, 39, 66, 116
Kamikaze ("Wind of the Gods"), 11
Kampaku (Civil Dictator), 8, 11
Kanamori Tokujirō, 32, 56n

Karafuto (Sakhalin Island), 26, 171, 178, 196
Katayama Cabinet, 89, 118, 130, 133
Katayama Tetsu, 79, 81, 105, 124–125, 130–131, 184; and Communist China, 193n
Katō Takaaki, 81, 117
Katō Tomosaburō, 82
Katsura Tarō, 18, 81; Cabinet, 89–90
Kawai, Kazuo, 33n, 47, 144n
Kawakami Jōtarō, 127–128, 140
Kawanami Toyosaku, 141–142
Kawashima Shōjirō, 86
Kaya group, 122
Keenan, Joseph B., 55
Kenseikai, 117
Kigensetsu (Foundation Day), 15, 66–67
Kikunami Katsumi, 140
Killen, James S., 144
Kishi Cabinet, 87, 90, 167
Kishi Nobusuke, 32, 66–67, 80–81, 85, 88–89, 94, 99, 111, 119, 120–122, 181; and 1960 Security Pact, 181; and Communist China, 194–196; faction, 85–86; Cabinet, 87, 90, 167
Kiyose Ichirō, 104, 164, 164n
Kobayashi Takeshi, 141
Koiso Cabinet, 118
Kokutai (national polity), 49–50, 55–56, 65, 162
Kondo Tsuruyo, Miss, 84, 86
Kōno Ichirō, 85, 86, 120, 122, 197; faction, 85, 122
Konoye Fumimaro, Prince, 21, 22, 36–38, 40, 52, 53, 114
Korea, 1, 2, 3, 12, 15, 27, 29, 171, 175, 176, 179, 188, 204; coup d'état, 142; relations with Japan, 198–201; war in, 135, 176, 203
Kubota Tsurumatsu, 104
Kurile Islands (Chishima Rettō), 171, 178, 196–198
Kwantung, 20, 171; Army, 174

Labor, 35–36, 143–146
Laborers and Farmers Party (Rō-nōtō), 123
Land reform, 34–35
Laws, enactment of, 106–113
Leahy, William D., 52–54

Legislative process, 75–76, 84, 106–113

Liberal-Democratic Party (Jiyū-Minshutō), 15, 58, 80, 85, 99–104, 107, 109, 110, 113, 114, 117, 119–123, 131, 146, 147, 209; Nishio's criticism of, 131; and 1960 Security Pact, 182–184; of Okinawa, 189

Liberal Party (Jiyūtō), 15, 39, 66, 80, 114–117, 123

Liuchiu, see Ryukyu Islands

Local government, 70, 92; before the Pacific War, 154–155; post-war, 155–167

MacArthur, General Douglas, 26–29, 32–39, 89, 98, 101, 116, 176; draft Constitution, 39–47; and Prime Minister, 80–82; attitude towards labor, 144; and Korean War, 192–193

MacArthur II, Ambassador Douglas, 185–186

MacLeish, Archibald, 51n

Maki, John M., 167n.21, 168n, 205

Manchoukuo, 120, 174

Manchuria, 19, 20, 29, 171, 175–176, 196

Manors, tax-exempt, 8–9

Mao Tse-tung, 13n

Marcus Island, 178

Mariana Islands, 178

Marquat, General, 144

Marshall Islands, 178

Marxism, 66, 125, 129, 164

Masumi, Junnosuke, 128n, 147n, 183n

Matsubakai, 140

Matsumoto Jōji, 38, 102n; and new Constitution, 40–44

Matsuoka, 33–34

McCune, Shannon, 189

McLaren, W. W., 16n, 24

Meiji Constitution (1889), 15–17, 20, 56–60, 73, 78

Meiji Restoration, 14

Mikami Taku, 141

Mikasa, 64, 66

Miki faction, 85–86

Miki Takeo-Matsumura Kenzō faction, 122

Minamoto clan, 9–12

Ministerial Council (Kakuryō Shingikai), 75

Ministry: of Autonomy, 158, 162, 166; of Education, 158, 162–163, 164; of Finance, 158; of Foreign Affairs, 82; of the Imperial Household, 5, 62; of Justice, 5, 62, 167, 169, 170; of the Navy, 21, 82; of War, 5, 21

Minobe Tatsukichi, 49–50

Minseitō, 21, 114, 117, 146

Minshu-Jiyūtō, see Democratic-Liberal Party

Mitsubishi, 35, 146

Mitsui, 35, 146

Miyamoto Kenji, 137–138

Miyazawa Kiichi, 86

Miyazawa Toshiyoshi, 66n

Mizutani Chōsaburō, 130

Mob rule, 111, 145

Mongolia, Inner, 19, 174

Motoori Norinaga, 13

Municipalities (shichōson), 158, 160–162

Murakami Kanji, 133n

Nagasaki, 53, 180; flag incident, 194

Nakagaki Kunio, 85

Nanpō Shotō, 178

Nansei Shotō, 178

Narcotics traffic, 139, 167

Nasu Ryosuke, 94, 126

National Defense Council (Kokubō Kaigi), 76, 205

National Democratic Party (Kokumin Minshutō), 118

National Personnel Authority (Jinji-in), 76, 91

National Police Reserve, 166, 203

National polity, see Kokutai

National Public Safety Commission, 75, 165, 166

National Rural Police, 165–166, 202

National Safety Force (Hoan-tai), 203

Nationalization, of coal industry, 118, 124

Netherlands, 28

Neutralism, 176–177, 181

New Deal, 143

New Zealand, 18, 177

Nikkyōso, see Japan Teachers Union

Nishimura, Eiichi, 85

Nishio Suehiro, 125, 129–131, 140

Nitobe, Inazo, 24

No confidence, 87–88, 95, 104, 121, 159; local government, 161
Nosaka Sanzō (Okano Susumu), 132–137
Nuclear tests, 200

Obstructionism, 109–113
Occupation of Japan, 25–47
Ogasawara (Bonin) Islands, 120, 178, 188, 195
Ogata Taketora, 117, 119, 120
Ōhashi Takeo, 85
Ōhira Masayoshi, 85
Oka Yoshitake, 35n
Okada, 82, 89; Cabinet, 21, 89
Ōkawa, 33
Okinawa, 171, 187–190, 195, 197
Okochi Kazuo, 153
Ōkuma Shigenobu, 15, 17, 18, 81
Ōmura Seiichi, 32
Ōno Bamboku, 121; faction, 85, 86, 122
Ōta Seisaku, 189

Pakistan, 28
Paracel Islands, 178
Parece Vela, 178
Parliament, British, 58; Japanese, see Diet
Parliamentarism, 207
Parliamentary procedure, 183
Parliamentary supremacy, 68–70
Party systems, 148–149
Patriotism, 67, 163
Peace Preservation Law, 19, 49, 98, 123
Peace treaty, see Japanese Peace Treaty
Peaceful coexistence, 135–136, 195
Peaceful revolution, 127, 132–133, 135
Peerage, 16, 64
Penghu (Pescadores) Islands, 171, 175, 178, 191
People's Cooperatives, 83
People's Council Against the Revision of the Security Pact, 181, 185
People's League for the Protection of the Constitution, 66, 181
Perry, Commodore Matthew Galbraith, 13, 17
Pescadores Islands, see Penghu Islands
Petitions, 184
Philippine Islands, 12, 17, 28, 177

Police, 109–111, 144, 162, 165–167, 176, 182, 185
Political parties, 114–139; evolution of, 115; in prefectural assemblies, 161; see also specific parties
Popular sovereignty, 56–60
Potsdam Declaration (or Proclamation), 25–26, 28, 30, 33, 36, 50, 175
Prefectures (ken), 14, 154, 160–166
Premier, see Prime Minister
Press, 113
Pressure groups, 139–152
Prime Minister, 62, 79–82; former, 78; office of, 84; list, 95–96; and local government, 160
Privy Council (Sūmitsuin), 15–17, 37, 60, 62
Privy Seal, Lord Keeper of (Naidaijin) 18, 62
Procurators (prosecutors), 169
Progressive Party (Kaishintō), 15, 39, 66, 116
Provinces, 4
Purge: of Japanese leaders, 31–33, 114; of Communists, 134; "Red Purge," 134
Pu-yi, Henry, 174

Rearmament, 179, 202–205
Recall, 159, 161–162
Referendum, 161
Reform Party (Kaishintō), see Progressive Party
Regencies, 8, 11, 60–63
Reparations, 179
Repatriation, of North Koreans, 199–200
Restoration of 1867–8, 13–14
"Reverse course": in local government, 162; in education, 163; in police system, 166–167
Rhee, Syngman, 199–200
Rightists, 110, 139
Riots, 89, 105, 110, 135, 140, 167, 179, 182
Roessler, Hermann, 15
Rosario Island, 178
Russo-Japanese War, 17, 19, 196
Ryukyu (Liuchiu) Islands, 120, 171, 178, 187–190

Saigō Takamori, 15, 141, 201
Saionji Kimmochi, Prince, 18, 78, 81, 89; Cabinet, 21

Saitō Makato, Admiral, 20, 82, 89
Sakhalin (Karafuto) Island, 26, 171, 178, 196
Sambetsu, 143
Samurai, 10, 13–15, 18
San Francisco treaty, see Japanese Peace Treaty
Sansom, George B., 4n, 24
Satō Eisaku, 99, 120–122; faction, 85, 122
Satō Isao, 38n.32, 40n
Satō Tatsuo, 38n, 41n
Satsuma, 14, 15, 18, 201
SCAP, 27; see also MacArthur, General Douglas
Schools, 162–165
Security Pact, United States-Japan (1951), 179–181, 203
Security Pact, United States-Japan (1960), 108–109, 127, 130, 144, 181–184; ratification of, 186–187
Seiyūkai Party, 19–21, 114, 146
Self-Defense Force, 142, 166, 203– 204, 207–208; Air, 204; Ground, 204
Senaga Kamejirō, 188
Senior statesmen (jūshin), 18, 52
Separation of powers, 68–70
"Seventeen-Article Constitution," of Prince Shōtoku, 2, 3
Shakai Taishūtō, see Socialist Mass Party
Shakaitō, see Socialist Party
Shamanism, 7
Shidehara Kijūrō, 20, 28, 30, 80, 81, 94, 116–118, 146; and new Constitution, 40–47; Cabinet, 36, 38, 80n, 116, 118
Shiga Kenjirō, 86
Shiga Yoshio, 132, 134
Shigemasa Seishi, 85
Shigemitsu Mamoru, 34, 118, 197, 206
Shikotan Island, 197
Shimizu Chō, 56
Shinobu Seisaburō, 67n, 101n, 103n
Shinoda Kosaku, 85
Shinto (Way of the Gods), 5–7, 11, 13, 22, 30–31, 50, 65, 67–68, 198; state (or shrine) Shinto, 31, 162; sect Shinto, 30; in education, 162
Shogun, 10–14
Shōtoku, Empress, 7, 60

Shōtoku, Regent Prince, 2–3
Sino-Japanese War: First, 17, 19, 171; Second, 174
Sino-Soviet alliance, 192, 195
Socialist International, 127–129
Socialist Mass Party (Shakai Taishūtō), 114, 123, 130; of Okinawa, 189
Socialist Party, 123–129; and constitutional amendment, 58, 66; and Throne, 65, Katayama Cabinet, 83; on responsible government, 87–89; and electoral system, 100–101, 103; and lower house Speaker, 103–105; and tyranny of the majority, 109–111; platform, 127; organization, 127–129; rightwing, 128; Nishio's criticism, 131; and Asanuma assassination, 141; and labor, 144–145; and Police Law, 166; and 1960 Security Pact, 181–182, 186; of Okinawa, 189; and Communist China, 195; and parliamentary democracy, 209
Sōdōmei (All-Japan Federation of Labor), 130, 143
Sofu Gan, 178
Sōhyō, 110, 111, 128, 141, 144, 181; and 1960 Security Pact, 183–186
Sone Eki, 130
South Sakhalin, 178
Southeast Asia, 2, 174–175, 188
Soviet Union, 25, 26, 28–29, 42, 53, 177, 178, 204; Japanese attitudes towards, 190; relations with, 196–198
Speaker, 104, 107, 112
Spratly Islands, 178
Standing committees, 104–105, 107
State-War-Navy Coordinating Committee (SWNCC), 39
States rights, 70, 109, 155
Stimson, 54
Stranger Clans, 2
Student movement, 113, 183, 185
Subversive Activities Prevention Bill, 109, 135
Succession, 8, 60–62
Sumitomo, 35
Sun Goddess (Amaterasu), 2, 5–8, 13, 60
Sunakawa case, 168

Supreme Commander for the Allied Powers, 27; *see also* MacArthur, General Douglas

Supreme Court (Court of Cassation, Taishin-in), 49, 62

Supreme Court, contemporary (Saikō Saibansho), 61–62, 74, 109, 168–169, 182

Suzuki Cabinet, 53–54

Suzuki Mosaburō, 34, 82, 89, 125

Suzuki Yoshio, 130

Taihō Code, 5

Taika ("Great Reform"), 4

Taira clan, 9–10

Taiwan (Formosa), 171, 175, 178–179, 188, 191, 195

Takagi Yasaka, 36n

Takayanagi Kenzō, 40n, 41n

Takeuchi Tatsuji, 16n.15, 24, 206

Tanaka Giichi, Baron, 20, 33, 81

Tanaka Kakuei, 85

T'ang dynasty of China, 3, 5–6, 8, 198

Taxes, 4, 8–9, 98, 162

Teachers Union (Nikkyōso), 141, 144, 163, 209

Terauchi, 81, 89

Terrorism, 89, 111, 140, 145

Textbooks, 163

Tōgō Shigenori, 34, 53, 54

Tōjō Hideki, 22, 34, 81, 118, 120, 164

Tokuda Kyūichi, 132, 134–135, 140

Tokugawa Shoguns, 12–13

Tokyo, 1, 12, 14, 158

Tokyo Imperial University, 90, 116, 118, 120, 127

Tomabeji Gizō, 118

Tosa clan, 14–15

Towns (chō), 158

Trade, 190

Trade Union Law, 143–144

Treaties: Harris, 13, 17; Portsmouth, 89; Diet approval of, 107–108; with Nationalist China, 191–192; *see also* Japanese Peace Treaty, Security Pact

Trotskyism, 165

Truman, Harry S., 25–26, 26n, 50, 177

Two-Chinas policy, 192, 195–196

Two-party system, 83, 100, 125, 209

Tyranny of the majority, 106, 109

Uesugi Shinkichi, 49

Ugaki Kazushige, General, 21

Uji, 3

Ukai Nobushige, 72

Ultranationalism, 30–31, 67

Unequal treaties, 17

United Kingdom, *see* Great Britain

United Nations: Security Council, 176; Command, 176; Strategic Trusteeship, 178; Charter, 187; Japanese membership in, 197

United States: and Allied control machinery, 26–29; 1960 election in, 100; and Korea, 171; *see also* Harris Treaty, Japanese Peace Treaty, Potsdam Declaration, Security Pact

Universities, 164

Vasilevski, 26

Villages (son), 158

Vining, Mrs. Elizabeth Gray, 64, 72

Volcano (Iwo) Islands, 178

Wa, 1, 3

Wakatsuki, 20, 81; Cabinet, 117

Wang Ch'ing-wei, 174

War Crimes Trial, 33–34, 120

Welfare state, 122, 209

Whitney, Courtney, 40n, 55n, 80n

World War I, 14, 19

World War II, 20, 22, 25

Yalta agreement, 196, 196n

Yamagata Aritomo, 18, 81, 90

Yamaguchi Otoya, 141

Yamamoto, 82

Yamato, 1–2, 6, 7

Yamazaki, Iwao, 141

Yamazaki Takeshi, 81

Yamazaki Tanshō, 49n

Yanaga, Chitoshi, 17n, 21n

Yoshida Cabinet, 28, 35, 83, 88–90, 118–120, 124, 132, 166

Yoshida Shigeru, 79, 80–81, 85, 88, 90, 93, 94, 121, 176, 180, 184; cited, 79n, 80n, 133n, 155, 166n; surprise dissolution, 86–87; resignation, 88; career, 116–117; on Article 9, 203

Yoshida Shōin, 141

Yugoslavia, 177

Zaibatsu, 35, 63, 120, 146

Zengakuren, 141, 165, 182, 184

Zenrō, 124, 130, 144–145